AF252146

Relationships 101

From Birth to Eternity

Kennedy D. Vanterpool

Book Design: Jim Bisakowski www.BookDesign.ca
ISBN-10: 0985542403
ISBN-13: 978-0-9855424-0-5

Published by Prosperity Publishing Press

PROSPERITYMINISTRY.COM

Acknowledgments

There are too many people to acknowledge, this end product needed many to complete it. You have been a source of inspiration and motivation. Your unselfish attitude, your obedience to the Spirit's prompting, your eagerness to share who you are and what He gave to you: Your patience in listening to me go on and on as I shared with you what He gave to me, is appreciated and duly noted in heaven.

Since I cannot name all, let me mention a few. When taking on a project like this, the family always has to bear the brunt of the adjustments to be made. So, I want to say thanks to my wife, Esther, our daughters Kenesha and Kenesma and son Kenesky, for running the business and doing such a fine job. This allowed me to finish this in four and a half months.

I am thankful to my parents Arthwyn and Marjorie Vanterpool who have sacrificed so much and still continue to do that for my family and I. Thanks to my outstanding editor, Desmond Vanterpool, my outspoken brother. Again you have done an excellent job despite your busy schedule.

To Ministers Dennis Barrow, Randolph Wallace, David Rougely, Van Runnels Kelly Marshal and Lionel Matthews some men I can always bounce off what seems to me like weird ideas that God gave, and helping to bring clarity. Thank you.

Thanks to the many Ministers who allowed me into your churches to teach the principles found herein: Especially Bethel Advent Church, Fondern Worship Center, New Life and Metropolitan Seventh-day Adventist Churches. To the church members for your feedback, I am eternally grateful.

Contents

Introduction

THE SPIRIT HAS BEEN IMPRESSING upon me lately that life is about relationships, and most important is the one with God. I was painting our house on May 24, 2007 when He impressed upon me to begin writing this book. Here I am being obedient to the Spirit. I must admit I had some reservations that there might be other books by this name already on the market and I was tempted to search the internet. I refrained myself and started writing. The suspense was killing me, so two days later I searched and sure enough there were several books with a similar title, nevertheless, this one deals with all relationships that will extend into eternity. It is not about marriage relationships. There are many books on the subject, even though the principles apply.

Enduring relationships is one of few subjects that ignite such pathos, passion, and push. Regardless of our culture, color, creed, cleverness, clout, or convictions we all want to love and be loved. We are relational beings. Yet the paradox of life is, we cannot live with people and we cannot live without them. It was God who said it is not good for man to be alone (Genesis 2:18). Still, we believe we can make it on our own. Too many people are alone, even if they have a family or attend church. We struggle and fight our battles alone and this is not what God wants. Other people help to make our lives what it is. The saying is true, "It is not what you know, it is who you know." The best person to know is God.

This is important because as Creator, He created us differently yet we want others to be just like us. We are into uniformity rather than unity. Sadly, our churches which are predominately women have turned the social and spiritual structure into a feminine atmosphere and rightly so because it is female dominated. This has kept many men away because they cannot be who God created them to be and worship and serve Him based on who they are as men. We are different.

It is ironic, because we can only know how to relate to God as we know how to relate to each other. The Apostle John made this point very clear, *"If a man say, I love God, and hateth his brother, he is a liar: for he that loveth not his brother whom he hath seen, how can he love God whom he hath not seen? (1 John 4:20).* God has given us one another to partner with before we can really learn to partner with Him. The key then to loving God is loving each other. If we have problems loving and relating to our fellowmen we will have problems loving and relating to God.

Unfortunately, we have limited relationships to marriage. So, we become serious about them when we are about to get married. Society and the church has subscribed to this concept. Some couples begin seeking counseling. Others do not, because they feel they are grown and they know how relationships work. Yet, when they encounter life's tests within their marriage, they flunk and some so badly they end up separating or divorcing. Many divorces are nasty and the children are the ones left to suffer the most.

Regrettably, this information has been and is being passed down generationally. This was true in my case, I did not get any counseling. After being married for a few years I started reading many books on the subject of marriage. I have made a great deal of mistakes. This cycle must stop or the divorce rate will continue to skyrocket. Life is not about marriage, it is about relationships. There are little or no special teachings or emphases on them unless it is in the context of marriage; that is why marriages are failing today.

Now if our children have to endure such pain and hurt from divorce, what effect do we think it will have upon them and their relationships? The fact is our children learn from us by watching

   You Were Made To Worship God 24/7

what we do, especially men, we were designed to follow other men. If we have difficulty with our relationships so will they. Many today are not getting married instead they are living together without the commitment of marriage. This brings with it, its own set of problems.

Some of us have not been teaching our children about developing and maintaining good relationships. That's because we are having problems with ours. Something must be done to stem the trend in our society. Here is where I believe the church has to play a major role, see chapter 20.

This predicament is compounded by us being such a mobile society. In America the average family moves every five years, for this reason we find it difficult to establish long lasting relationships. Thus, when it is time to move there is separation and this triggers the grieving process. This is extremely painful, especially, when you do not understand what is happening and refuse to get in touch with your emotions. We do not understand and are afraid of them. We find it easier not to get too close to our neighbors to avoid the pain when we are ready to move. The same thing happens in the work place. We do not allow ourselves to become too attached to our co-workers since we do not know how long we will be at that job. This has become more intense with larger corporations gobbling up smaller ones, downsizing. Jobs are now less secure. And so, we keep our distance and operate on a professional basis.

What we do not understand is we cannot practice this in a few areas of life, without it affecting all our lives. Eventually, it becomes a part of who we are. We are holistic beings; whatever happens in one area affects all. So, we do the same in other relationships; we do not get close to church members, family, children, spouses and whoever comes into our lives for the same fear. This makes life extremely difficult because we were made to be close and intimate, after all we are brothers and sisters because God is our Father. So, we have to live a guarded life and cannot experience the abundant life and freedom God has in store for us.

Even those of us who would not mind getting close have another big obstacle, time. We are so busy doing, that we do not have time to be who God designed us to be: Time to be still and reach out to God and others, including our family. We have become so self-centered and busy trying to get, that we do not have time to give of ourselves to anyone. It is "a dog-eat-dog world," rather than "brethren helping brethren."

In this book we will be dealing with developing relationships from birth and that will last throughout eternity. When we understand that relationships were meant to be eternal, we will be careful who we choose as friends, we do not want individuals who would influence us away from God's Kingdom. We will be looking at why we need, what is involved and how to go about developing eternal relationships. Thus, I will be speaking of relationships in general and not marriage. Let the journey begin.

Part I

THE WHY OF RELATIONSHIPS?

Chapter 1

God's Idea

WHEN GOD CREATED ADAM, He said it is not good for man to be alone (Genesis 2:18), this is not an option. God was not just talking about marriage. Since children cannot get married, He was talking about us not existing by ourselves. We need people in our lives at every age and stage. God designed us that way.

The Bible

When you read the Bible carefully you cannot come to any other conclusion than, every verse, chapter, and book is about how to relate to God and to each other. It is the best book written on relationships. For example, Jesus said, I am come that you may have life and to have it more abundantly (John 10:10). He has and is doing everything in His power for us to experience this. It can only be accomplished in the context of relationships. Many have interpreted this to mean we can only have this life in the context of marriage. That is why our marriages are failing; we are looking to our spouses for what they cannot give us. If we are not experiencing the abundant life in God, they cannot give it to us. God has never confined Himself to the marriage relationship.

The commandments of God echo relationships, the first four is how we relate to God and the last six is how we relate to our fellowmen.

In summarizing them, *"Jesus said unto him, Thou shalt love the Lord thy God with all thy heart, and with all thy soul, and with all thy mind. This is the first and great commandment. And the second is like unto it, Thou shalt love thy neighbour as thyself. On these two commandments hang all the law and the prophets"* (Matthew 22:37-40). This is a summary of what the Bible is all about; the rest of it tells us how to love God and each other.

Since God is love, it means He treasures relationships. He is relational by nature. He identifies Himself as a friend, Father, Son, and Spirit. The Trinity ascribes to the fact that God has a relationship with Himself. It is designed for us to copy, both with ourselves, our body, soul, spirit, others and God. God did not need us, He existed in a loving relationship with Himself. He desired us and therefore became pregnant with mankind and birthed us. That's why we are brothers and sisters and need to get along as such.

Furthermore, God measures our spiritual maturity by the quality of our relationships. In the final analysis He will not ask us about our earthly accomplishments, assets, or influences, it will be how did we treat people. Jesus will say,

> *Come, you who are blessed by my Father; take your inheritance, the kingdom prepared for you since the creation of the world. "Then the King will say to those on his right, For I was hungry and you gave me something to eat, I was thirsty and you gave me something to drink, I was a stranger and you invited me in, I needed clothes and you clothed me, I was sick and you looked after me, I was in prison and you came to visit me.' "The King will reply, 'I tell you the truth, whatever you did for one of the least of these brothers of mine, you did for me. (Matthew 25:34-36, 40 NIV).*

Life is related to people and how we treat them, what we do not realize it is ultimately how we are treating God.

There are more songs, books, magazines, seminars, CDs, DVDs, movies on relationships than any other subject. Yet, we are failing at them. This is evidenced by the divorces, wars, churches splitting, shacking up, fightings, and abuses.

Questioning

One of the best ways to develop relationships is by asking questions. We have been discouraged from doing this. Hence, we have difficulty with people who ask questions. They are ostracized and victimized. We are required to accept whatever is done or said without question. Thus, we live our lives and do not question anyone, not even God. He is not afraid of our questions. He said to question Him (Isaiah 1:18). The problem we have does not lie in our faith or religion it is what we do in the name of it. Faith is secure enough to handle questions and can never be threatened by them. Dogma or fanaticism is threatened by questions—because they are rigid and brittle, thus crumble under the spotlight of scrutiny through questions. That is why there is a difference between being a faithful member and being a dogmatic one. Fear has infiltrated our religions. What are we afraid of? Jesus did not have any problems with people asking questions. If you read the Bible carefully you will see that many of the prophets questioned Him. I had a professor in college who used to say no question is a silly one. We seem to be afraid of them. There are some questions we need to ask ourselves:

- How do I see, hear, or feel about myself?
- How do I relate to my Heavenly Father?
- How am I relating to the people I care about?
- How do I relate to people who do not care about me?
- How many genuine friends do I have?
- How many people am I a genuine friend of?
- Where am I learning about relationships?
- Where do I need to improve my relational skills?

Take a moment and think about these questions. Let down your defenses you have been using to block the pain that is associated with your past, that is affecting your present and future. Take a look into your relational world. My intention is not to be sadistic, spiteful, or superstitious. It's to think about your relationships. As you are going through life, how do you feel angry, frustrated, fearful, frantic, disappointed, or joyful, thankful, enjoying life and your relationships?

Are you one who has been wounded too deeply by God, family and friends? Is your pain so intense that it has left you paralyzed? Do not despair, you are not alone. I have counseled many and the truth is we are all in the same boat, just in different sections. We are longing to love and be loved, but, we are fearful of being hurt and rejected, because our emotional and relational world is a fresh gaping wound.

We all have a particular way we want to be loved. Thus, consciously or subconsciously we follow an unwritten script about how we should and are going to relate. These are based on assumptions and rules we have picked up along the way, which are embedded in our culture. We do not take time to question; we just follow them even though they are not leading to lasting relationships. Why? Have you wondered where you got your information about relationships?

How Do You Know?

Did your parents ever sat you down and instructed you on how to develop them? What about a mentor or your church? How many sermons have you heard on developing solid, eternal friendships? Where did we learn from then? We have come from broken, dysfunctional families who themselves did not know many good relationships.

     You Were Made To Worship God 24/7

The truth is, we get our understanding of relationships from the media. The Movies and Songwriters lead us to believe that if we just follow these three simple steps then we will be friends forever. If their formula is true, then why are there so many divorces, singing groups splitting up, and actors killing themselves? There is something wrong with their approach to relationships. In spite of our problems and baggage, there is still that need or longing to be in relationships. God does not want us to go and live in a cave alone.

God's Desire

It is one of God's greatest desires to have a relationship with us. He wants us to build up the Kingdom of God and to do it based on who we are. He is concerned and is interested in us personally. He always has our best interest at heart. His interest is personal, unique, and focused. So, we will relate differently based on how He designed us. As men and women God has made provision for us to relate to Him and each other differently—we cannot survive in this life or in eternity without one another. Our very design indicates we need to relate to each other and to God, and will do so differently.

One of the main reasons for eternity is relationships, since God is love and love shares. He wanted to share who He is and what He has with man. Thus, He created the human race like no other. He cannot have this kind of relationship with angels, since He made them differently.

God creates and has given us the ability to be creative. We become mesmerized when people accomplish great feats like going to the moon and phenomenal advancement in technology. We are fascinated by man's ability to clone and invent. That is because we are like God—notice I did not say we are God. But we are little gods

(Psalm 82:6, Isaiah 41:23, John 10:34-35). Remember the Tower of Babel in Genesis 11? They wanted to build a tower to reach into heaven. If God did not stop man, he would have found a way to reach heaven. That is the type of creative power God has given us. It was given, to bring honor and glory to Him. Sadly, we use it for selfish reasons.

God wants a relationship with us and for us to have a unique relationship with Him. He wants us to be just like Him, to duplicate Himself through us. He wants what is going on in His Kingdom to be going on here on earth. That's why in the Disciple's Prayer we find, *"Thy kingdom come thy will be done in earth as it is in heaven"* (*Matthew 6:10*). When Jesus was about to start His public ministry announced, *"Now after that John was put in prison, Jesus came into Galilee, preaching the gospel of the kingdom of God, "The time has come," he said, "The kingdom of God is near. Repent and believe the good news!"* (*Mark 1:14-15*). *"And he said unto them, I must preach the kingdom of God to other cities also: for therefore am I sent"* (*Luke 4:43*). *"But seek ye first the kingdom of God, and his righteousness; and all these things shall be added unto you"* (*Matthew 6:33*). *"And this gospel of the kingdom shall be preached in all the world for a witness unto all nations; and then shall the end come"* (*Matthew 24:14*). We can be a part of God's Earthly Kingdom by developing relationships with each other, God, and fulfill one of His greatest desires; live with Him and each other eternally.

Designed

We were made by God to relate to Him and one another. This is long before we ever think about getting married. Notice He created male and female so that we complement and not compete against each other. This is not just limited to marriage, because the family was designed so that there are males and females. That is why we have the admonition given in Genesis 1:28, *"Let them have dominion over the birds of the air, the fishes of the sea."* The "them" God was referring to were the male and female. They were to have dominion or rule over the earth together. Hence, no man can be successful in this life without the input of males and females in his life and vice versa. We cannot rule without relating and helping one another. I am not talking about marriage. Our relationships must be deep as we partner together if we are going to rule and be successful.

Notice first He made Adam then He taught him to be a son. God would come down in the Garden and talk to him. Afterward He taught Adam how to relate to the animals, by naming them, and then taught him how to take care of his environment. In the process He taught him about himself, when Adam looked he had no opposite. He recognized that the animals had males and females. It was only now that he was ready and able to handle his relationship with Eve.

We overlook these facts and make the mistake and run to the marriage relationship and forget our other relationships. We must learn to relate properly to others and our environment; we must develop a work ethic before we can talk about marriage. Adam realized this even though he was in a perfect environment with everything in abundance they were of no value to him without another human beings to share them with.

Another fact we overlook is that Adam and Eve were children before they got married, God's children. Adam was created first and he learned to relate to God, the world, the animals and other creatures before Eve came along. Adam was a son before he was a husband. He had to learn to relate to God as his Father, before he married Eve. (In the same manner we have to learn to relate to our parents, siblings, teachers, coworkers, employers, etcetera, by being taught by our earthly parents years before we can talk about relating to a spouse). After God married them establishing the family unit, He told them to be fruitful and multiply. I believe that they were husband and wife for some time before having children. They needed to learn to relate to each other.

Not just that, their children who came along had to learn from Adam and Eve how to relate to them as their parents, just as God taught them how to relate to Him as their Father. They were to teach their children how to relate to their brothers and sisters and afterwards how to relate to God. This was to be duplicated over the entire world. Parents are to teach their children how to relate to them as parents, then how to relate to their siblings, other people, and then how to relate to God. In that order, to some that may sound sacrilegious because God should come first. True. However, children have difficulty relating to the unseen. We have to lead them from the seen to the unseen. The Apostle John puts it in prospective for us, *"If a man say, I love God, and hateth his brother, he is a liar: for he that loveth not his brother whom he hath seen, how can he love God whom he hath not seen?* (1 John 4:20).

As parents we need to teach our children how they ought to relate to us, each other, and others before we can teach them about God. They are observing how we are relating to God so that when they have learned how to relate to us as parents and to their siblings then they will know how to relate to their heavenly Father. Often we bypass the human factor and go straight to God. Little children

          You Were Made To Worship God 24/7

have difficulty relating who they cannot see. They can see us and their concept of God is determined by us, especially the father, since God is seen as a male figure.

We know that sin came in and disrupted the plan. We have to get back to God's original plan. There are many who see the most important teaching they can give their children is how to relate to God. It becomes their focus and they forget to teach them how to relate to one another. This creates a problem because that was not God's intention. What we need to teach them is how to relate to the human race, because if we have difficulty relating to people we can see; we will have difficulty relating to God who we cannot see.

The Ideal

None had or will have the privilege of growing up in an ideal home because of sin. This reinforces the point that we need solid relationships to help us to come as close to the ideal as possible. Here is our dilemma, where are our role models? Who is going to parent me? I do not know how to because no one showed me. I do not have a role model. Here is where the church needs to step in and teach fathers and mothers how to be Biblical parents.

Many studies show fatherlessness is detrimental to children. They are more likely to run away from home, abuse drugs, go to jail, be homeless, commit suicide and many other antisocial behaviors. At first, we thought it was only affecting boys, we have found it is also injurious to girls.

Our churches today are full of spiritually immature men, because we are not fathering them. The Apostle Paul points this out in 1 Corinthians 4:14-15, *"I do not write this to shame you, but to warn and counsel you as my beloved children. After all, though you should have ten thousand teachers (guides to direct you) in Christ, yet you do not have many fathers. For I became your father in Christ Jesus through the glad tidings (the Gospel)" (Amplified Bible)*. He is here pointing out one of the problems in the Corinthian Church, which is still true, we have many teachers but few fathers. It takes a great deal of intestinal fortitude to get men to come alongside and guide males to maturity in Christ.

Jesus demonstrated this concept by first of all being under the authority and leadership of His Father (John 5:19). He then fathered His twelve disciples. Paul often referred to Timothy and Titus as his sons. We are admonished in the Scriptures to grow in grace and a knowledge of God, to move beyond the milk we used at first and begin to eat solid food or else we will be malnourished. How are our children going to grow up if they do not have a father? Research has proven the worth of a father. Still, in church we expect babes in Jesus to raise themselves. It is easier for men to follow men who know where they are going, and boys imitate their dads. There is not just the need to have fathers, but for fathers to father. When we bring someone to the Father and do not provide a father for them we produce illegitimate children.

I agree with David Murrow in his book, **"Why Men Hate Going to Church,"** "The strongest urge that God has placed within man is to reproduce. He wants to leave a linage and legacy. God's first command in the Garden was to be fruitful and multiply. Jesus last command in the Gospels was make disciples. A man will never be fulfilled unless he is reproducing spiritual sons." This I believe also applies to women, and they are doing a better job than we are because they more relational. We become great men and women through spiritual parenthood. It is how we build up the Kingdom of God. We have limited Christianity to reading the Bible, praying, and living to and for ourselves and immediate family. These are designed to make us better able to take care of all the people God has placed in our lives.

We Need Each Other

We cannot be successful without the opposite sex contributing to our lives. This begins before we are even conceived. For example, in order for us to be born there had to be a sperm from the man swimming in the woman's fallopian tube to meet the egg and create an embryo. Thus, we have something from the male and the female in us, it is logical to assume we need input from both to be successful. So, we cannot be complete in life without contributions coming from both sexes. God designed it that way because He wants us to relate to one another. This is how the Apostle Paul puts it, *"Nevertheless neither is the man without the woman, neither the woman without the man, in the Lord. For as the woman is of the man, even so is the man also by the woman; but all things of God"* (1 Corinthians 11:11-12).

Not wanting us to become self-centered, God commanded us to be fruitful and multiply. He wants to duplicate Himself through us. We have the same desire to duplicate ourselves in our children and others under our influence. Not for selfish reasons, it must be motivated by a godly love.

We Need God

We need more than earthly relationships because as good as they are, they are limited in their abilities to help us. Hence, we need a personal relationship with God. There will be times when we have to be alone. Like Jacob when he wrestled with God, Joseph down in Egypt, Jesus in the wilderness or in the Garden of Gethsemane when He begged His disciples to watch and pray with Him for just one hour, they fell asleep. The disciples were willing mentally and spiritually, but, they could not be there physically. We too will encounter our wilderness experiences and be alone.

The good news is we are never alone. Jesus promised in Matthew 28:20 *"I will be with you always even to the end of the world."* That is how strong our relationship with God should be, when our friends reached their limitations, we can still hold on to Him. Truthfully speaking, we can only handle being alone when we have seen or heard of others who handled it, so technically we are not alone, we have other people's experiences. Paul calls them a cloud of witnesses (Hebrews 12:1). Also, Jesus' experience is one we can always draw from, He was in all points tempted as we are yet without sin (Hebrews 4:15). Thus, we cannot survive this life without people. Paul was right when he wrote, *"No man liveth to himself"* (*Romans 14:7*).

Interestingly, it is when we begin to relate to each other and see the inability of humans to fulfill our lives; there is awakened within us a desire for Someone far greater than any human being. Here is where parents should come in and point their children to God. We are not ready for Him until we have learned to relate to our fellowmen and only God can help us to do that. There is a yearning within all of mankind to know God personally. When we are not experiencing an intimate relationship with Him we begin to substitute it with other things like sex, food, drugs, education, and other addictions. These are attempts to find Him. The wise man Solomon realized this and said,

> *"God is the source of all knowledge as well as all joy. He gives wisdom and happiness to those who please Him and takes it away from those who keep on sinning. Evil men work hard to store up riches which one day will be given to those who please God. All that man does to accomplish great things or to gain riches is useless. I concluded that life without God has no more purpose than chasing the wind"* (*Ecclesiastes 2:26 The Clear Word*).

How God Works

He chooses to work through relationships. His blessings and our salvation come through them. Others who know God told us about Him, whether through a dream, testimony, spoken, lived, or written. God chose to give us the Bible which came via His relationship with the writers.

When life seems to overwhelm us the only thing that will get us through the hard times is relationships. Look back in your life and you will realize that when you were in a crisis it was because of great friends you were able to survive: Whether it was terminal illness, death, or excruciating pains. It was not how much money we had, how powerful we were, or where we lived. When we are in one of life crises, it is all about who we know that counts. This souvenir scroll from Jamaica and the poem sums up beautifully what I am trying to say,

The Gift of Friendship

"Friendship is a priceless gift that cannot be bought or sold
But its value is far greater than a mountain of gold.
For the gold is cold and lifeless: it can neither see nor hear.
And in the time of trouble it is powerless to cheer.
It has no ears to listen, no heart to understand.
It cannot bring you comfort or reach out a helping hand.
So when you ask God for a gift, be thankful if, He sends
Not diamonds, pearls, or riches, but the love of real true friends.

Author Unknown

I could not have said it better. This is the essence of true relationships. Their worth cannot be measured physical resources. These are lifeless and cannot respond when we are in need. We fail to realize that these are limited in what they can do for us. When we are down and depressed all the resources we own can't bring comfort, they are unresponsive. Only our friends can listen, hear, and respond from their hearts. Do you have friends in your life you can count on when the chips are down? Have you developed eternal friendships so that when you need a friend, he/she is there? Can your friendship withstand the test of time and last throughout eternity?

Ruling

In addition, God wanted mankind to be like Him and rule over the earth—as He rules in Heaven. He gave this dominion to males and females. God has also like Himself placed the desire in us to want and to have relationships. We cannot rule without being able to relate to people. Ruling in God's economy is service.

If we try to rule people without fostering relationships they will rebel. Even if we are relating, it will be at a surface level. Our motive will be for selfish gain. We do not have the interest of those we are leading. Rulership without commitment leads to destruction. Life without relationships is miserable and we will soon find, is not worth living.

Relating

Men and women relate differently. We have to understand these differences, accept and then utilize them for maximum rulership together. If we don't, it will affect how we relate to other things, like money, work, time, marriage, stewardship, discipline, etcetera. When relationships do not become our priority we do not see people as important. We spend more time going after money, accumulating stuff and we see people as second class citizens. We become the center of our universe and people must bow down to us because of what we have. However, after we have accumulated all the wealth and have no one to share it with, we are most miserable.

If we have problems relating to people, there are only two reasons, we are not relating to God on an intimate level or we are concerned about money and material things. Remember these things only have value as you relate to people. For example, money has no value outside of your value for people. The same is true of our possessions, property, prestige, power, persuasion and anything else that we have. Here is how John summarizes it,

> *Because thou sayest, I am rich, and increased with goods, and have need of nothing; and knowest not that thou art wretched, and miserable, and poor, and blind, and naked: I counsel thee to buy of me gold tried in the fire, that thou mayest be rich; and white raiment, that thou mayest be clothed, and that the shame of thy nakedness do not appear; and anoint thine eyes with eyesalve, that thou mayest see (Revelation 3: 17-18).*

The sad thing is we are miserable, poor and blind and we do not even know it. Howard Hughes is a good example of this, even with his millions he starved to death. He had all the money in the world to buy all the food he wanted and more. Yet, he died of starvation. Here is a summary by the Wikipedia, The Free Encyclopedia, "Hughes died on April 5, 1976 while on an airplane….en route from his penthouse…to Methodist Hospital in Houston…His reclusive activities and drug use had made him practically unrecognizable; his hair, beard, fingernails, and toenails had grown grossly long, his once-strapping 6'4" frame now weighed barely 90 lbs, and the FBI had to resort to fingerprints to identify the body….Hughes was in extremely poor physical condition at the time of his death; X-rays revealed broken-off hypodermic needles still embedded in his arms and severe malnutrition."

I am not writing against riches. In contrast, we have from the same book, "John Davison Rockefeller, Sr. (July 8, 1839–May 23, 1937) was an American industrialist and philanthropist. Rockefeller revolutionized the oil industry and defined the structure of modern philanthropy. He always believed from a child that his purpose in life was to make as much money as possible, and then use it wisely to improve the lot of mankind." That is what He is still doing today even after He died. He understood the value of people and money.

Notice what was Rockefeller's purpose in life, it was not making money, but helping mankind with the money he made. His emphasis was on people not money. Money has no real value outside of its use for the good of mankind.

Fame

Man's greatness is not measured by how much he owns, it is by the number of people he has helped, influenced, or changed for the better. That person's name lives on in fame. That is why Jesus, who did not possess in His humanity any worldly possessions, no educational degrees, not a great family heritage. He is still one of the most talked about human beings. More books have been written about Him than anyone else. The reason for His success is He knew how to relate to people. He saw them as His brothers and sisters and treated them that way.

Other individuals who did not become obsessed with things whose names we will never forget are Mother Theressa, David Livingstone, Martin Luther King Jr., and Mahatma Ghandi to name a few. I heard someone say when the Pope visited Mother Theressa and left her his popemobile and limousine she sold them and used the money for her orphanage. Why are we still hearing so much about the legendary story of Robin Hood? It was because of how he related to people.

We know that money and resources are not what keep marriages and people together, there are many millionaires who have multiple divorces. Many family members are cruel and unkind to each other

     You Were Made To Worship God 24/7

when their parents die and they have to share the estate. This brings out the worst in a family. One of the reasons is because they learned that money was more important than family relationships.

Why Not More Emphasis

If earthly relationships are tied to heavenly ones then why is there not more emphasis on developing them? It is not taught or modeled in many homes, schools, churches or communities. We do not even know our next door neighbors. We are busy accumulating stuff and moving every five years. We have difficulty planting roots, because they will soon be pulled up. Unlike tree roots, when human roots are pulled up it causes great pain, anxiety, grief, and a flood of emotions.

One of the main reasons for moving is job related. Once upon a time you could easily begin your career with one company and retire. Not so anymore. With the advancement of technology, if we cannot keep up, others are brought in to take our places. Hence, there are some of us who have to change careers several times before we retire. This causes a disconnection between us and our coworkers, church members, neighbors and eventually our families. We have difficulty getting close to one another, we have to soon leave and go through the grieving process again, and again. To avoid this pain and unpleasant experiences we avoid getting close to others in the future.

We Need Relationships

Since relationships originated with God, it means they are very important. He is a God of purposes and does not do anything without purposes. His primary purpose is for us to have a relationship with Him. The reason why He created us is to share, commune, and enjoy life together. Since He is Spirit and we are flesh, He had to provide human relationships for us first to relate to and then take us from the earthly realm to the Heavenly.

Being like God, He made us to develop close eternal friendships with each other, sharing who we are and what He has given us. This is the only way to enjoy life. It is about sharing what we have and who we are. The former is easier. This is especially true of men. Since sharing involves our emotions and we have difficulty understanding and dealing with them. Sadly, we normally stay away from things we do not understand instead of trying to understand them. We put them in the bad box and try to move on without them. But, we still drag them along with us and eventually they become very heavy and they color our lives negatively.

Since relationships are God's idea, then He has in mind how they must be developed and maintained. So, we have to look to the Originator to know how. Thank God He has given us His manual, the Bible, on how to. To enjoy life we must know and understand the dynamics of friendships. Because I believe in addition to our characters, we should be building relationships that will last throughout eternity.

We have become lazy; and do not take time to read our manual. It is even worst now because everything comes with DVD instructions. All we have to do is insert it and listen to someone telling us what to do. We have become a very inactive people; we depend on others to tell us what to do, even in the spiritual realm. We no longer take time to think or listen to God speak to us through His Word. We pay our Pastors to do that for us.

We have become copycats. We do things because we see others doing them and the more people doing them the more correct we think they are. For example, many pray in Church, "Lord we invite your presence in this place." Why? This is God's house and we should be thanking Him for His presence, and the privilege He afforded us to be in His house? When I come to your house I do not invite you into your house, instead, I thank you for your invitation and the privilege. It is the same thing when we come to God's house. He is there to welcome us. Even if you have difficulty with that, if you are a child of God you brought Him with you because He lives in you (1 John 4:12-14).

God wants us to rely on the Spirit to lead our lives and not the church, school, society or anyone else. When we do, He will reveal to us what is truth for us. Understand who He uses most is people. He will give you affirmation and confirmation that He is speaking or working through them.

Chapter 2

God's Greatest Desire

GOD SENT JESUS TO DIE rather than give up His desire to have a relationship with us. He loves us and wants us to love Him back. Hence, our greatest desire should be learning how to love God with all our heart, mind and soul (Matthew 22:37). He wants to be our friend, just like He was with Adam and Eve. Jesus wants us to be His friends not servants (John 15:15). Friend here is deep. It is not just a casual relationship, but refers to a close trusted one. The same word is used to refer to the best-man in a wedding or the king's inner circle of friends. They do not need to go through the same method to get to the king like ordinary subjects.

The Scriptures

Everything in the Bible points towards God's desire to be our friend. He delights in and over us. This is clearest in Psalm 103:1-14. This passage screams relationship. God is bending backwards just to be our friend. Even though He is Spirit and we are made from dust. This passage points out what we need to do and what God is willing to do for us.

Our part is the Lord wants us to bless Him with everything we have within and without. For several reasons, because of what our God has done, and the Psalmist iterates them. We should not forget

His many benefits, forgiveness, healings, redemption, loving kindness, and tender mercies. He only gives us good things until we are full, our youth is renewed, He brings deliverance to the poor, and provides righteousness and judgment, He demonstrates His acts so that we can see how much He cares. He does not get angry with us very quickly like many of us do with each other. He is so gracious; He has not dealt with us according to our sins, and gives us what we desire. He is willing to remove our sins so far away from us, even though we are dust.

Wouldn't you like to have such a friend? This is how we should relate to each other. Wouldn't you like a friend who will easily forgive, redeem, satisfy you with good things, execute righteousness and judgment, One who is slow to get angry and will not deal with you as you deserve? If you do not know this God personally turn to the last page now.

Paul the apostle tells us,

> *Long before he laid down earth's foundations, he had us in mind, had settled on us as the focus of his love, to be made whole and holy by his love. Long, long ago he decided to adopt us into his family through Jesus Christ. (What pleasure he took in planning this!) He wanted us to enter into the celebration of his lavish gift-giving by the hand of his beloved Son (Ephesians 1:4-6 Msg).*

James puts it this way, "*God decided to give us life through the word of truth so we might be the most important of all the things he has made*" (*James 1:18 NCV*). He is pleased with and wants us. Hence, one of God's greatest desires is to have a relationship with us, to be our friend. Out of all creation He wants us and created everything on the earth for us. His interest is personal and unique. He made us for relationships. He has done everything in His power to connect with us and to maintain that connection.

      You Were Made To Worship God 24/7

Original Plan

God's original plan was to have a close and intimate relationship with us. It has not, nor will ever change (Malachi 3:6). We were made specifically for this purpose; that's why we are different to anyone or anything else in the universe. We are so unique that there is not anyone else on the face of the earth like you.

God came down and communicated face to face with Adam and Eve in the garden, before sin. Listen to the account:

> *Then the man and his wife heard the sound of the Lord God as he was walking in the garden in the cool of the day, and they hid from the Lord God among the trees of the garden. But the Lord God called to the man, 'Where are you?' He answered, 'I heard you in the garden, and I was afraid because I was naked; so I hid' (Genesis 3:8-10).*

How did they know it was the Lord? They heard Him walking in the garden. They were accustomed to that sound and knew it was God. That is not strange. There are some people whose walk you know because it is distinct. God was accustomed to coming down to walk and talk with them. They were connected. They would meet in their usual spot and it was strange not meeting them there. Not seeing them the Lord cried out, "Where are you?" In other words, how come you are not where we agreed to meet since our last visit? That sounds so far-fetched today. How did a holy God talk to human beings? Simple, they were both perfect.

Provision Made

The problem was, the moment our fore-parents sinned, there was an automatic separation between us and God. That was the first strike against us. We were born in sin and shaped in iniquity, our second strike. Yet, through relationships we have heard about Jesus and what He did for us. How He came and lived a sinless life, died on the cross, rose again and is sitting at the right hand of God making intercession for us. He provided a reconnection and if we refused His offer. That will be our third strike. However, we are not out of the game.

Because of Adam's sin, we were conceived, born in sin and fashioned in iniquity (Psalm 51:5): Automatically separating us from God. The prophet Isaiah tells us, *"Surely the arm of the LORD is not too short to save, nor his ear too dull to hear. But your iniquities have separated you from your God; your sins have hidden His face from you so that He will not hear"* (Isaiah 59:1-2). The sad thing is there is not anything we can do to bring about reconciliation because we are on two completely different levels. We live in this realm and the Lord lives in the heavens, one that is unattainable to us, thus complicating the disconnection. Isaiah says, *"For as the heavens are higher than the earth, so are my ways higher than your ways, and my thoughts than your thoughts"* (Isaiah 55:9). Paul further strengthens this point. *"O the depth of the riches both the wisdom and knowledge of God! How unsearchable are His judgments, and His ways past finding out!"* (Romans 11:33). Job puts it in the form of a question. *"Canst thou by searching find out God?"* (Job 11:7).

Sin has brought about a separation that has interrupted God's plan of developing and maintaining a relationship with us. Now there is a gulf that exists that is impossible to bridge. His thoughts and ways are so high we cannot even comprehend who He is. You see, God is holy. Sin in His presence is like a consuming fire (Deuteronomy 4:24; Isaiah 33:14; Hebrews 12:29). So, it is impossible, humanly speaking, to connect with God. We need help from the same realm that He is from. That's why God sent His Son, Jesus to bridge the gap and thus provide a reconnection. His Spirit then leads us into all truth as He reveals to us God's will.

This process will be completed in the earth made new. God Himself will be with us and be our God (Revelation 21). That is how bad His desire is to have a relationship with us.

Our Greatest Desire

Since we are made in the image of God, we have the same great desire, a relationship with God and our fellowmen. He is our Father and we are trying everything in our power to reconnect. Whether we are aware of it or not, all that we do is an attempt to bring about the reunion between ourselves, each other, and God. It is an innate desire, something we are born with. Thus, just like it is God's desire to have a friendship with us, it is our desire to have an eternal relationship with Him.

It is like someone who does not know his/her parents and has a strong desire to find them and is never comfortable until they do. The desire to know our Heavenly Father is stronger than that. Many are not aware of what is creating the void in our lives. The longing, aching, unfulfilled feelings within our hearts, it is a desire to know God. Not aware, we try to fill the void with many things which intensify the aches and pains.

The Big Problem

We want everybody to relate to God just like we do. We say men and women are different, yet, we want men to partner with God in the same manner women do. As men we like adventure, risk, achievement and challenge. We must be accepted for who we are, because this is the way God made us. Too many times because women are nurturers they want to change us into who they want us to be, even our mothers are guilty of this. If we let them we will become sissies. As men we believe in risk and reward, heroic acts, great accomplishments. Women on the other hand are into security and safety.

If as men we try to live out our God given values we find ourselves in trouble with females, in any setting.

As men, we have a desire to succeed and win in whatever we do. We are competitive and believe in competence that is why we have difficulty asking for directions, it means we are not very competent as a navigator. We feel we have failed if we do. We are not very expressive, verbal, and sensitive; we are not good at teaching, singing, and holding strangers hands. Women on the other hand are very comfortable with these and expect us men to be also. We have a need to be needed and so we have difficulty with church, because our women are better at doing church than us. Notice just about everything in most churches and ministries are designed for females and run by them. It has become a woman's world. Thus, most men are uncomfortable in church, since we do not feel needed, many men go where they feel needed and accepted for who they are: the golf course, bars, ball games etcetera. Many do not understand why most men are not in church, which is necessary for their partnership with God.

This was not always this way, because fishermen dropped their nets and followed Jesus, but, we cannot get men to drop their remote control and go to church for a few hours.

Greatest Dilemma

We produce our greatest dilemma by searching for our Heavenly Father using the same methods we use to find earthly parents, our senses. He is a spiritual being, thus needing other means of connection. The heavenly realm is absolutely opposed to the earthly. The spiritual realm operates in the sphere of faith. In the natural realm, it is impossible to understand the spiritual. Paul reminds us, *"The man without the Spirit does not accept the things that come from the*

Spirit of God, for they are foolishness to him, and he cannot understand them, because they are spiritually discerned" (1 Corinthians 2:14).

God is Spirit and we are flesh. These operate in completely different realms and are opposed to each other. *"Those who live according to the sinful nature (the body) have their minds set on what that nature desires; but those who live in accordance with the Spirit have their minds set on what the Spirit desires"* (Romans 8:5). There is no hope of them meeting down the road. They are like parallel lines, they will never meet. As humans, we want to do what comes naturally. This is contrary to the Spirit of God. The Psalmist tells us,

> *Wickedness is part of man's nature from the time he is born. His inclinations are toward self when he comes from his mother's womb. He can tell lies and do wrong from birth. Man has been bitten by the serpent and his body is full of the poison of sin. In turn he bites and poisons others; his instincts are as deaf to reason as snakes who cannot hear. A snake charmer can't reason with his cobra when it rears its head to strike; no magician can make it go contrary to its nature (Psalms 58:3-5 The Clear Word).*

We are wicked to the core the moment we are born. We do not have to be taught to lie, cheat, steal and be selfish, they come naturally. Jesus is the only exception, He lived a sinless life and hence the only one who can help us. Paul reminds us in Romans 3:23, *"We all have sinned and are coming short of the glory of God."* We do it on a consistent basis, saints and sinners alike. We are doomed coming out the gate with three strikes against us. We are destined to failure. We cannot help ourselves. *"The mind of sinful man is death, but the mind controlled by the Spirit is life and peace"* (Romans 8:6 NIV). It is only the Spirit of God that can arrest us.

Since we see, feel, and hear; we want the Spirit in the form of flesh and blood to relate to Him. But, He is Spirit, as is God and we have to allow the Spirit to place the spiritual desire for God in us. He is here to help. We have to choose.

It is our responsibility to get to know our Heavenly Father who created us. The best way is to experience Him personally, and then we will have a small idea as to who He really is. He is so incredible that we cannot find Him by searching, yet we can find Him if we search for Him with all our hearts. This can only happen when we accept Jesus as the Lord and Savior of our lives and this is what happens:

> *So from now on we regard no one from a worldly point of view. Though we once regarded Christ in this way, we do so no longer. Therefore, if anyone is in Christ, he is a new creation; the old has gone, the new has come! All this is from God, who reconciled us to himself through Christ and gave us the ministry of reconciliation: that God was reconciling the world to himself in Christ, not counting men's sins against them. And he has committed to us the message of reconciliation. We are therefore Christ's ambassadors, as though God were making his appeal through us. We implore you on Christ's behalf: Be reconciled to God. God made him who had no sin to be sin for us, so that in him we might become the righteousness of God (2 Corinthians 5:16-21 NIV).*

Before our reconciliation, we viewed Jesus from a worldly point of view. When we accept Him, we see Him for who He is—our Lord and Savior and the Savior of the world. There are too many of us who see Him as our Savior and not the Savior of those who wronged us. This is because when we come to Jesus, we are made over. There is a reconstruction or re-creation in our minds as we need to be reconciled to Him and thus remove the disconnection that sin has caused. We have the same body; but, we are no longer ruled by the body of flesh. We are ruled by the Spirit.

In addition, we no longer see God as our enemy. We become like Jesus and join Him in reconciling the world to Himself. Jesus, who knew no sin, was made sin for us so that we might become righteous like Him. God knew there was going to be a disconnection and so a plan was laid before the foundation of the world. And the moment separation took place, God initiated the plan to bridge the gap and again reconnect with man. And I say, "THANK YOU JESUS!!!" Are you connected to Jesus?

Obeying God

God wants obedience. We can only be His friends if we are. Jesus says, *"Ye are my friends, if ye do whatsoever I command you"* (John 15:14). The prerequisite for friendship with God is obedience. He is still God, the One who created us and knows what is best. Just like with our parents we did not always understand why they wanted us to do what they said; because of our relationship with them we normally did it. We loved them, and we knew they loved us. We must do the same with God. Not because we are afraid of the judgment or out of mere duty. We have to be like Jesus, *"As the Father hath loved me, so have I loved you: continue ye in my love. If ye keep my commandments, ye shall abide in my love; even as I have kept my Father's commandments, and abide in his love. These things have I spoken unto you, that my joy might remain in you, and that your joy might be full* (John 15:9-11). To maintain our relationship with God we must do the same.

The aim is to be like Him, letting our minds become like His. So that what is bound on earth is bound in heaven, His will be done on earth as it is done in heaven.

Great Lengths

God has gone through great lengths to fulfill His greatest desire, a relationship with us. He has made provision so that we can enjoy harmony within and without ourselves, with God, and others.

God in the Dirt

That is why He made us in His image and likeness. Not like angels or animals. Everything else God created He spoke it into existence. Not so with man. He got down in the dirt and formed man. Now you know how badly someone wants you when they get down on their knees.

First, it is a sign of love—the picture is that of a man proposing to his future wife. Second, it is a sign of humility—when men normally propose, they get down on their knees. God was willing to get His hands and knees dirty just for us. It is not that He was a little child who loved to play in dirt. This was God, the King of the universe getting down on His knees and getting dirty. He took the time to form man out of the dust of the ground and breathe into his nostrils and bring man to life (Genesis 2:7).

We normally have an aversion to dirt. We want to get rid of it. Yet, God stooped down and out of dirt formed and fashioned man like Himself. Also, it would have been easier for Him just to speak man into existence and save time. Instead, He took time out of His schedule, to get down in the dirt and formed you. You heard me right.

Jesus in the Dirt

Jesus while He was on earth demonstrated what happened at creation. One day He got down, spat in some dirt, mixed it together and rubbed it on a man's eyes and told him to go and wash in the Pool of Siloam. This fascinating story is found in John 9, one of the reasons is in the light of what took place before. In Chapter 8 early that morning Jesus went to the Mount of Olives to talk with His Father. Then He goes into the temple and people gathered and Jesus began to teach. While teaching the Scribes and Pharisees who could not get along, decided to get together to trap Him. They brought the woman caught in adultery. Jesus stoops down and begins to write in the dirt. He did not have to do that. This was an act of humility. She was embarrassed; I could imagine her head was downcast. Jesus decided to get down to her level, so that He could lift her up to His, demonstrating how much He wanted a relationship with this sinner. Even though we are buried in dirt He will come and get us out.

Jesus said to her *"Neither do I condemn thee go and sin no more."* He set her free. Then He told them He is the light of the world and was God, because before Abraham was "I am." They took stones to stone Him and He escaped. While passing He saw a man. This was no coincidence. This man who was born blind, had a divine appointment with Jesus. Be careful now, He had just left the temple or church for a divine appointment with a blind non-church member. He spent more time in the field with the people than He did in church. We have to get out of church and form relationships with people and the best way to establish them is by meeting people where they are and fulfilling their needs.

He was a beggar by profession. My God does not care what your vocation is. He wants you: Even if the world turns up its nose at you. He has a divine appointment with you today, even if the church has no use for you, your father and mother forsook you, your marriage is a failure and you are in the pits of hell, God wants you. You can never become insignificant to Him or sink too low, where He will not come down and seek you out. Jesus demonstrated this by His desire to bend down on more than one occasion to help mankind.

God is always doing that. When Adam sinned, He took the initiative and came down. He wants a relationship with us so badly that not even death could stop Him. Sin, the gates of hell, could not stop Jesus from desiring and doing everything in His power to have a relationship with us. While we were yet sinners He died for us. What is even more fascinating about this story is there is no indication that this man asked Jesus for healing. He had an appointment with a man whom He helped without the man even asking for help. He saw the need and fulfilled it.

God Takes Time for Us

When God created Man, He did not merely make Adam. Within Adam was the whole human race, including Mary, the body through whom Jesus came. God taking time out to create man shows how much He loves us. Someone has rightly said one of the best ways to spell love is TIME. God would take time out and come down from heaven and visit with Adam and Eve. It was like after a long day's work and you would just sit on your porch and one of the neighbors would come over to hang out. God would do that with them. This was the plan all along, God having someone like Himself that He could talk, laugh, and have fun with. He wants to do this with each of us. He has not changed. The Psalmist reminds us that in the presence of the Lord is fullness of joy. At His right hand there are pleasures for ever more (Psalm 16:11). One of the ways we demonstrate joy is by laughter. Since I am made like God I believe He laughs. Could you imagine what heaven would be like without laughter?

He continues to do the same thing today, even in our mother's womb. He takes His time and fashions us.

> *You shaped me before I was born; you put my bones together while I was in my mother's womb, I praise you, for this body is incredibly and wonderfully made. Your whole creation is*

       You Were Made To Worship God 24/7

amazing. When I was developing in my mother's womb, you knew everything that took place. To you nothing is hidden or mysterious. You saw my unformed body inside the womb. You knew how long I would live before I was born (Psalm 139:13-15 The Clear Word).

This gives us confidence because our God never changes. Just like He took time to make Adam, it is the same thing He did for us. He took His time and made us, knitting our bodies together, connecting bone to bone, sinew to sinew, and tendon to tendon. What a mighty God we serve.

He Comes Looking

Now even though Adam rebelled against God and messed up the relationship, He took the time and initiative to restore it. He came looking. That is the only way we could have a relationship with Him. And the beauty is He did it out of love, not out of what we can do or give to Him. That demonstrated love to its highest.

All that we have is dung compared to a holy and just God, yet, He went through great lengths to reconcile us unto Himself. He is still doing the same today and He comes and calls us like He called Adam, "Where are you?" He says through His prophet, *"Come now, and let us reason together, saith the LORD: though your sins be as scarlet, they shall be as white as snow; though they be red like crimson, they shall be as wool"* (Isaiah 1:18). *"Come unto me, all ye that labour and are heavy laden, and I will give you rest"* (Matthew 11:28). God has not stop coming and looking for His children who are lost, who are not where He intended for us to be.

Name Calling

There is something else I learned about God. What is the best word in any language? What word you love to hear more than any other.

For me it is Kennedy, I love to hear my name. What about you? I love the way my mother would call me especially when she is proud of me or wanted to show affection. She would call me Ken. It sounds like music in my ears. Our name gives us identity. It differentiates us from everybody else. Even if we have the same name, your name is unique to you.

God is into name calling. He understands how important our name is to us. When Adam sinned and God came looking for him, He called, Adam where are you? (Genesis 3:9). When He was pleased with Job and boasted about him. He said to Satan, *"Have you considered my servant Job?" (Job 1:8 & Job 2:3)*. God called Moses, Moses (twice) (Exodus 3:4). In Jeremiah 1:11, *"God said Jeremiah what seest thou?"* In Acts 9:11 God called Saul, Saul. When God describes Himself, He says, *"I am the God of Abraham, Isaac, and Jacob" (Exodus 3:6,15,16; 4:5)*.

God gave names to some of His children. In Genesis 17: 9 He told Abraham to name his son Isaac. We find in 2 Samuel 12:24, God told David to give Solomon his name. In Luke 1:13 He told Zachariah what to name his son, John.

God knows we love names. We love them so much that we are into name calling. We would call the name of the most famous person we know, to give people the illusion we are the best of friends. I remember the name I would drop was Dr. Benjamin Carson, whom I had the pleasure of meeting. In addition, my wife and I had the honor of taking her and their children around the island of Tortola when they visited. I just did it. This name calling is another indication that we long for relationships, especially with famous people. I want to let you know that Jesus is the most famous person who walked the face of the earth. The Spirit is the greatest person on the earth today and everyone who wants to know Him can. We do not have to make an appointment, go through body guards, red

          You Were Made To Worship God 24/7

tape, secretaries, or closed doors. He is easily accessible, *"And it shall come to pass, that before they call, I will answer; and while they are yet speaking, I will hear"* (Isaiah 65:24).

The Psalmist says, *"He shall call upon me, and I will answer him: I will be with him in trouble; I will deliver him, and honour him"* (Psalm 91:15). We can call at anytime even when we are in trouble and He wants to deliver and honor us in the process. Most people might help us out of trouble; however, they will not honor us. Instead, they want us to honor them for taking us out. God not only wants to take us out of our mess, He wants to honor and people admire us. Thus the best names to throw around are God, Jesus, and the Holy Spirit especially if we allow them to dwell in us.

He Changes Names

God is even into changing names. Abram to Abraham, Jacob to Israel, Sarai to Sarah, Do you know why? Because we are like God, He loves names, He has different names for Himself. His name describes who He is. I am that I am, Jehovah Jirah, Jehovah Shama, Jehovah Nise. Names are so important to God, John tells us in Revelation 2:17 He will give us new names. In the Bible the naming of anything indicates ownership. God wants to own us completely again.

He Knows Where We Live

In addition, God wants to have a relationship so badly He knows where we are living. How do I know? He sent Cornelius' men to meet Peter at Simon the Tanner in Acts 10. He sent Samuel to where David was living in order to anoint him as the next king of Israel. This is interesting because it shows real love and concern.

Dr. Luke reminds us that God is the One who determines where we live. *"From one man he made every nation of men, that they should inhabit the whole earth; and he determined the times set for them and the exact places where they should live*" (Acts 17:26). We are not living where we are living by accident; He designed it that way. He knows our address. Most leaders of our countries do not know where each citizen lives, however God does.

Speaking to God

He wants so much to be our friend He has made provision for us to speak to Him continually through prayer. We can tell Him all our sorrows, joys, including Him in every phase of our lives. Holding back nothing, our weakness, faults, emotions, good and bad. Not pretending who we are not, or trying to deny our feelings. Moses told God this is how I feel if you are going to destroy the children of Israel, blot my name out of your Book (Exodus 32:32), Job said to Him I wish I was not born (Job 3:3), Jeremiah gave God his resignation and took it back (Jeremiah 20:9), the Psalms are filled with honesty.

God did not see them as disrespectful; He saw them as being honest. We believe we can really hide our feelings from God. He sees this as hypocrisy. He wants us to tell Him what is on our minds. If you are angry with God for whatever reason, He can handle it. To be a friend you have to be genuine, faking destroys relationships. The book of Psalms teaches us how to be honest and frank with God. The Psalmists held back nothing, this is true worship. It is in this atmosphere that friendship thrives. We must have never ending conversation with God, talking with and to Him while we are doing everyday chores. As Paul says we are to pray without ceasing (1 Thessalonians 5:17)

Brother Lawrence in his classic book which he wrote in the seventeenth century has some relevant information for us today. Instead of praying long prayers, pray shorter conversational prayers throughout the day. Like, "You promised to be with me and I believe you are" "I love you therefore I am not afraid." "I call upon You now." "Your grace is sufficient for me." I trust you wholeheartedly." We have the mistaken concept that we must get away to worship, when we need to learn is to worship God in all that we do. Since He promised never to leave us or forsake us.

Another helpful hint from Brother Lawrence is "The key to friendship with God is not changing what you do, but changing your attitude toward what you do. What you do for yourself you begin doing it for God, whether it is eating, bathing, working, relaxing or taking out the trash." This is what Paul meant when He said whatever we do, do it all for the glory of God.

God Speaking To Us

He gave us His Word to know who He is, and what He requires of us. We must learn to meditate on it. That is, allowing God to speak to us. Many people have difficulty with this word. We believe it has come from other religions which are not Christian and we do not want anything to do with it. Some think we have to be super spiritual to meditate. It is merely concentrated thinking. I like the way Rick Warren, in his book, **"The Purpose Driven Life"** puts it, "When you think of a problem over and over in your mind that is called worry. When you think of God's Word over and over in your mind, that's meditation. If you know how to worry, you already know how to meditate!"

Just like we talk to Him all day we have to think about His Word all day. True we cannot be reading the Bible every minute, even though we need to know what He is saying to us. You can remember a Bible story and apply it to your own life. Remember a verse you have memorized or read.

Our Greatest Choice

We have to choose to want to be a friend of God more than the food we eat, or the desire for education, prestige, power or politics. We must have a passion that is greater than a desire for water when we are thirsty. This requires work like any other relationship, time, effort and energy. Understand that since we are different our friendship with God will be different. Be yourself. The relationship will be tested by periods when He will seem distant. We must cling to His promise, He will never leave or forsake us (Hebrews 13:5).

———•◆•———

Prepares Us for Life

WE CAN ONLY FULFILL OUR PURPOSES in life through relationships. We need God and others to grow, through testimonies and accountability. People help to keep us in line as we encourage each other. God wants us to experience and share our lives.

How to love is the greatest lesson God wants to teach us. Why? He is love. Everything about Him is; whatever He does is out of love. That is how He wants us to live. This is not easy; it goes contrary to our self absorbed nature. The greatest preparation we can make in this life is to learn to love in preparation to live and love eternally. And this is not in heaven either, but here on earth. Still, we cannot live and love eternally until we have learned to live and love in this world.

There is nothing we will take from this world into the next. Everything will be burned up, all the gold, silver, precious stones, beautiful houses, latest and oldest cars, everything physical will be destroyed. The only things we will be taking with us are our characters and the relationships we have formed. With that in mind should we not be developing more relationships of love? I think so!

The Home

Relationships prepare us to live in this life, and in the one to come. Why? This life is temporal, the other is eternal. That is why God made provision for us to be born within a family, so that we can be prepared to live eternally. This concept has not changed. True there are some of us who are doing a very poor job in our homes, and our world is messed up. Yet, even with the poor job being done, it prepares us. If you look at your family situation you will see that it has prepared you for every situation you encounter. Now I know many of us did not grow up under the ideal circumstances, the truth is who has? Do not make this an issue. I like the way Rick Warren puts it, "Longing for the ideal while criticizing the real is evidence of immaturity. On the other hand, settling for the real without striving for the ideal is complacency. Maturity is living with the tension."

Not even Jesus' home was ideal. Could you imagine being Jesus' brother or sister? He was always a tough act to follow. Everything you did, He could do better, He was perfect at it. You came home from school with an A, Jesus came home with 100%. You scored fifteen free throw shots in a row, Jesus did not missed one yet. Whenever you got up, it does not matter what hour in the morning, Jesus was already up.

We cannot pine over, be upset, or bitter about our past, regardless to how terrible our circumstances were. If we examine them carefully we will be aware that God orchestrated them to help prepare us to face whatever we are encountering right now. All our success is because of our past. Many of us would like to forget, but our past has made us into who we are today. But, do not become a product of your past; build your future on it. It is impossible to build on anything else. We cannot build it on someone else's. Too many of us want to be like celebrities. Even though we do not know what they had to go through to get where they are. We are just seeing the end product. The best gift you can give yourself is to be who God created you to be.

Home is the place where we should receive our first instructions in the area of relationships. Many parents do not have a clue about our relationship with each other, how can we be successful with our children? Also, there are so many single parents and children who have to bring up themselves. They have no one to teach them. They have children. How are they going to teach them about relationships?

Joseph's Home

Would you like to be Joseph? Could you imagine the family that he grew up in? (Genesis 37-50). His brothers despised Him. This was no ordinary hate, they wanted to kill him, but Reuben and Judah begged for his life. They threw him in a pit, against his repeated pleading. A caravan was passing and they sold him for thirty pieces of silver. I do not believe they were just passing. This was Joseph's appointed ride down into Egypt provided by God. I know you have difficulty with that since he was actually sold as a slave to the Egyptians who hated Joseph's and his people. His environment was a hostile one. God had a purpose for his life. He used his past, his home environment to prepare him for his purposes in life.

Our past cannot interfere with our purposes, only enhance them. Joseph's past made him content in this hostile environment. You see his past had prepared him for his future. I am not saying what his brothers or father did was right. But, God will use our past to prepare us for what lies ahead. He promised, *"Even though I walk though the valley of death I will fear no evil for thou are with me thy rod and thy staff the comfort me, thou preparest a table before me in the presence of my enemies"* (Psalm 23:4-5). It does not matter who is against you. God will prepare a table in their presence. He will invite all those who tried to keep you down, sell you into slavery, or make you a slave. This promise was literally fulfilled in Joseph's life. Remember when the brothers went down into Egypt they were invited to eat with Him, who up to this point were still Joseph's enemies. The Egyptians were also. God spread a table before them on behalf of Joseph. Even if your parents, brothers and sisters are against you when you are growing up, they could be your worst enemies, the Lord will one day lay a table before you in their presence.

Embrace Your Past

So, embrace your past and move into your prosperous future. That is God's promise to us (Jeremiah 29:11, Psalm 1:3, Psalm 139). We cannot allow our negatives experiences to keep us down. We have to be like Jesus when He faced death, looked beyond His present situation and see the joy that was set before Him and was able to endure the cross and the shame associated with it (Hebrews 12:2). Like Him, negative relationships may follow us and lead to our death. Nonetheless, because of our relationship with God, we will be prepared for whatever life throws at us. In this world we will continue to have tribulations and trials, however, Jesus said be of good cheer I have overcome the world. So can we!

I am saying it does not matter what our past was like. It may be awful, we have a glorious future. As I write I am thinking of Joni Erickson Tada who at the age of sixteen was a quadriplegic. Because of this rough childhood, more people in the world know Joni than she would ever be known without her unfortunate accident. She would not have been able to minister to and bless as many people as she has, had it not been for her past life, as serious as her accident was.

The Bible declares that all things work together for good to them that love the Lord (Romans 8:28). All things in our lives are not good, but the awesome God we serve will take our hurtful, heartless, and harsh past and turn it into a famous future. This is not the way God designed it. He has given us freedom of choice. We and our parents have made some terrible choices that are affecting us up to the third and fourth generations. When we admit and surrender our sins, God supernaturally turns these circumstances around in our favor as we develop a relationship with Him. We can have a wonderful relationship with the people who were mean to us.

Clarifies Our Purposes

While Joseph was down in Egypt he understood what his dreams meant. He understood his destiny. He knew why he had those dreams and why he was there, even as a slave. Do not allow your circumstances to distract you from your destiny. It was Thomas Edison who said, "I never did a day's work in my life, it was all fun." The reason why he could say that was because He knew his purposes and destiny. We can only have fun in our day's work when we know God's purposes and destiny for us.

There is no better feeling than when we know what our gifts and purposes, ministries, vocations and destiny are. And we use them to minister, meeting people's needs. We are internally motivated and not easily discouraged or distracted regardless to what is happening around us. We seldom succumb to external pressure. Relationships are easier to develop and maintain because we are comfortable with who we are, we know where we are going and how to get there. It is difficult for others to get us to do what they want. Hence, the relationships we will choose, will be those who are going in our direction. They will help to motivate us to fulfill our purposes and we will sever ties with those who are standing in the way of us accomplishing God's destiny for us.

Because Joseph knew his destiny he did not allow his brothers coming into town to distract him. He knew he needed all the energy to concentrate on it. He also knew that in order for him to continue being successful; he needed his family around him. After a while when you are alone fighting the enemy you get tired fast, so he needed his family to draw strength from in the years ahead. In addition, the dream was that he was going to rule over them, so it had to be fulfilled. Now based on the choices Joseph made he would decide if he was going to make it harder or easier for his family and thus harder or easier for himself. When we make relationships difficult for others we are making them much more difficult for ourselves. This is based on the Law of the Harvest Principle, what we sow we reap, and we reap more than we sow. And the Golden Rule, Joseph understood and practiced, "Do unto others as you would have them do unto you."

People do not always reciprocate in like manner. Sometimes it makes them real upset and they want to take your life because you are showing them up. They know this is how they should have acted towards you. Some do not take kindly to this behavior. They have problems running their own lives and are trying to run your life. When they cannot succeed they become very angry, to the point they may want to kill you like they did Jesus or Stephen, so be careful.

Life's Situations

Relationships prepare us to deal with all life's situations. He is a God of preparation. He never gives us an assignment that He has not prepared us to handle. Paul confirms this, *"There hath no temptation taken you but such as is common to man: but God is faithful, who will not suffer you to be tempted above that ye are able; but will with the temptation also make a way to escape, that ye may be able to bear it"* (1 Corinthians 10:13). He only shows up in the fullness of time, when everything is set and ready to go.

Therefore, do not be afraid when you pray and the Lord seems to be silent or He even says no. Remember the fullness of time for that situation you need so badly has not yet come. In other words it is not ripe, just hold on a little longer. He has given you the ability to hold on until the fullness of time.

Fighting

We were not designed by God to fight. He made us to relate and live together in harmony. He has promised that He will take care of our enemies (Exodus 32:32; Numbers 10:9; Deuteronomy 20:4; Joshua 10:25; 2 Samuel 3:18; Revelation 11:5). We normally see America as the savior of the world when there is conflict in other countries. However, America only intervenes when it is in her best interest. We have a God who will always act in our best interest.

It is impossible to begin or nourish relationships if we are in the fighting mode. It is still true, "You can catch more flies with honey than vinegar." But, to avoid fighting is not as easy as it sounds. We love and it is in our nature to take revenge. So, our natural response is to retaliate when we are hurt. Thus, to act differently can only be accomplished through a close relationship with God. (For more information on fighting see Chapter 13 in my book, *"Some Things We Do Not Have To Ask God for: Because He Is Our Father")*.

Do Not Worry

Another area we will never ever master is worrying. We were not created for it. God tells us over and over, "Don't worry." Once we learn to trust and develop an intimate relationship with Him, He promised to take care of our needs, wants and desires.

When we are worrying, we cannot enjoy life and develop lasting relationships. We become preoccupied and obsessed with things that we should not even worry about. Here is what happens when we worry, *"For though we walk in the flesh, we do not war after the flesh: (For the weapons of our warfare are not carnal, but mighty through God to the pulling down of strong holds;) Casting down imaginations, and every high thing that exalteth itself against the knowledge of God, and bringing into captivity every thought to the obedience of Christ"* (2 Corinthians 10:3-5). Our thoughts are the foundation and before we know it, we are building a wall that keeps even God out. Like the Israelites, we begin to see them as giants. This hinders the development of relationships. When we are worrying, our focus turns inwards. We become wrapped up in our world, and do not want to let anyone else in, not even God.

The Future

We have no control over it. We must learn to turn it over to God who knows our future before we were born or the world was formed. We have not yet learned like the apostle Paul to be content in whatever situation we find ourselves.

When we were young, we could not wait to be eighteen and start college, then could not wait to finish college and begin working; after that, to get married and have children. We wanted them to grow up so that we can begin to enjoy life. In order to do that, we cannot wait to retire. Now we are dying and realize we forgot to live. It does not matter what our situation is right now, God is always working it for our good. While we are in the now He is in the not yet. He has our future taken care of. Like a great and perfect parent our inheritance is secure for eternity.

The main reason why we cannot see into the future is so that we can develop a deeper abiding faith in God. If He had not designed it this way we would completely forget about Him and do things our way. Now we have to learn to trust and rely upon God and others. This is difficult and goes against our nature. If we look into our past we will see in many areas when God used those situations to teach us to rely on Him and at times the people He placed in our lives. For example, writing these books, I have to rely on others to do very serious editing for me, because I am lousy with the English language. I am very verbose, what I could say in a sentence I will take ten sentences to say. I write like I preach, so I need a great deal of human help to get the finished product. When it comes to publishing the books I have to rely on God to provide the resources. Every time I am about to publish, we have a financial crisis. However, the Lord always provides the resources.

For Becoming

God uses relationships to help us become who He created. Hence, we are born into a family where the growth and training begin to prepare us for accomplishing God's destiny.

He said in His Word, we are destroyed for a lack of knowledge, too many of us repeat this text out of context. It actually says because we have rejected knowledge (Hosea 4:6). It is not that we do not know, we disobedient. It is not human knowledge He is talking about. Just go to any Christian Bookstore and we will find material on any subject. But, one of the things I always try to warn any group that I speak to, please understand this is my experience, this is what God has shared with me. It is not yours and do not try to make it yours. Let the Spirit guide and reveal to you what He wants you to implement in your life and what He wants to teach you through me. The same goes for any book, sermon, seminar or speech you read or hear.

We get into trouble when we read a book or return from a seminar and are so excited and ready to implement all we have heard. A few hours or days later we are overwhelmed because the person we are trying to imitate has taken many years to arrive at that point. Yet, we think we can do it in five days. We are looking for a quick fix. When we do not get it, we become discouraged and end up further back in our experiences than before the seminar. The Bible says the Spirit will lead us into all truth. We are always trying to fix our lives. That is all good, because He will not do for us what we can do for ourselves. We need discernment to know when there is nothing we can do and turn it over to Jesus.

History

I am aware that this is an age old problem. When we look at even Bible characters they had difficulty with relationships. It started with Lucifer rebelling against God in heaven. Then it continued with our first parents, Adam and Eve also in a perfect setting, they severed their relationship they had with their perfect Heavenly Father. Then their son Cain did not have a good relationship with his brother and killed him. Neither did Isaac and Rebekah, it was so bad that the father loved Essau and the mother loved Jacob. They schemed against each other and the brothers almost killed one another.

Jacob because he was not taught and had not seen good relationships modeled did the same thing he saw his parents doing. Again, this shows the obvious is not always obvious to everybody. When we are not taught, what we see our parents doing, we think it is the normal and right. He did not learn from his own experience, Esau wanting to kill him, showed favoritism to one of his twelve sons, Joseph. This caused such rivalry that the brothers were ready to kill him and he was spared because of God's intervention (Genesis 37).

David did not want to discipline his sons because of the mistakes he made, especially with Bathsheba. It did not seem as though he was loved that much by his father and brothers. They did not even remember him when the prophet Samuel came looking for the next king of Israel. Listen to his brother's reaction when David asked a simple question about Goliath, the giant, *"And Eliab his eldest brother heard when he spake unto the men; and Eliab's anger was kindled against David, and he said, Why camest thou down hither? And with whom hast thou left those few sheep in the wilderness? I know thy pride, and the naughtiness of thine heart; for thou art come down that thou mightest see the battle"* (1 Samuel 17:28). They hated David. He was very good at friendships, not with fatherhood. One could say he was forced to develop friendships with Jonathan and his men because he was a fugitive. He became a great king because he worked at it. He could have done the same with fatherhood and being a great husband. He did not concentrate on these.

We cannot use history as an excuse, since if we do not learn from it, we will repeat the mistakes of our fore-parents.

No Excuses

We live in a society in which we are not encouraged to take responsibility for what we do. It is always someone else's fault or named a disease. This we know is not new, it was Adam and Eve's line. It does not matter what kind of home you grew up in, if you really want to learn about relationships and you depend upon the Lord, His Spirit will teach you. Actually God can use our negative situations and turn them inside out and be of benefit to us and others. The promise He made to us (Romans 8:28) there is a condition; we have to love the Lord with all our heart, mind, and soul. Our desire must be that we want to seek first His Kingdom and righteousness.

We cannot blame our lack of knowledge on our parents or whoever raised us. We have the Word and it is about relationships, that's why it was written, so that we could understand how to relate to God, ourselves, and each other. I really wanted to know and so He has given me an entire book on the subject. That is what God will do if we want anything that badly and it is in accordance with His will.

Our Parents

If we do not know how to relate to our parents, then we do not know and cannot teach our children how to relate to us. If we have problems relating to our parents, then our children will have problems relating to us. It is a cycle. We need to restore our relationships with our parents. For some of you this sounds impossible, they are dead. If you did not have closure with your parents or guardians, then write them a letter and close that chapter in your life. Then ask God for directions as to how to develop long lasting relationships and follow His leading. He will place people in your life to come alongside of you and help in developing solid relationships.

The Church

We live in a very fragmented society. As I pointed out earlier, we are a mobile society and I believe that the church has to step in to fill the void, by providing ministries that will meet the needs of families. Discipleship for children who do not have good parental role models, or parents who are in jail, in some cases adopt children. God has put within each of us all the resources to meet the needs of our communities.

Chapter 4

Prepares Us for Eternity

WE WERE PLANNED FOR ETERNITY and that has not change (Ecclesiastes 3:11 NIV). When we become a part of God's family we are eternally connected God and each other. We will be judged based on how we relate to people. *"Jesus said, I was hungry you fed me, thirsty you gave me drink, strange and you took me in, naked and you clothe me, sick and in prison and you visited me and then He added,* "Verily I say unto you, Inasmuch as ye did it not to one of the least of these, ye did it not to me" *(Matthew 25:34-45)*. He was not talking about Himself. He was talking about the people whose needs we met. Where we spend eternity will be determined by our relationships. Hence, we must see relationships in the context of eternity. This is important to God. We have limited life and it activities, including our relationships. We have not become Kingdom oriented and have restricted our lives only to the here and now; this is creating unending problems daily.

Eternity

We take our relationships lightly because we see them as merely earthly connections. We focus on what we can get out of them. With this attitude such relationships are short lived. Our focus has to be, what can I contribute to this relationship? Paul reminds us, *"Look not every man on his own things, but every man also on the things of others"* (Philippians 2:4). We must look out for the interest of others and their best interest is eternal life. What are we doing to foster that aspect of their lives? We fail to realize that relationships were created by God for eternity.

There is more to life than this. There is the life to come. But we are focusing so hard on the latter; we are of little help to our fellowmen. Church is contributing to this dilemma. We keep talking about going to heaven and we behave like that's where we will spend eternity. No, we will be spending it here on earth (Psalm 23:15; 37:9, 11, 22; Isaiah 45:18; Matthew 5:5). So, we must learn how to live on it now.

It has always been God's desire to live with us eternally. Since we will be living together, we must learn how to relate one to another, because eternity is a very long time. We must begin to look at life in the context of eternity and God's Kingdom. And the Kingdom is about relationships, God being the center of them all. We are like spokes in the wheel where He is the center, and are connected to Him and cannot just go in the direction we want, we must be in unity.

Thus, God wants our friendships not just for today but eternally. When we have come to the end of our journey, it does not matter how much we have accumulated or possessed, we cannot take it with us. In the Kingdom, it will only be other people who we knew on earth. That is another reason why we must be friendly, if we cannot get along now, we will not get into the Kingdom. If we have trouble in this life we will have trouble in the next. We have to learn to get along with each other now. John's summary is, *"By this shall all men know ye are my disciples if we have love one for another"* (John 13:35).

Always God's Plan

When God created Adam and Eve, the plan was for them and their descendants to live forever. Even though they messed up, Jesus came and restored us back to living eternally.

> *"And this is the record, that God hath given to us eternal life, and this life is in his Son. He that hath the Son hath life; and he that hath not the Son of God hath not life. These things have I written unto you that believe on the name of the Son of God; that ye may know that ye have eternal life, and that ye may believe on the name of the Son of God" (1 John 5;11-13).*

He has not changed His mind. He made provision so that the original plan will be accomplished, eternal life. Jesus makes it abundantly clear that we have already begun to experience eternal life here. It is all about Jesus wanting to come in and make His abode in us. *"My sheep hear my voice, and I know them, and they follow me: And I give unto them eternal life; and they shall never perish, neither shall any man pluck them out of my hand" (John 10:27-28).*

There are many who are still waiting for eternal life. Not understanding that it resides in a person. Jesus is eternal life and those who accept Him as their personal Lord and Savior has it. We do not have to wait for it, it is already ours. So, we have to start thinking, planning, living, in the context of eternity. We cannot live any other way. We do not have to worry or think about it if we accepted Jesus, just live it, and our entire prospective will change.

So, if you know you are stealing, gossiping, or cheating, these cannot be practiced throughout eternity. Your friends will be different, you will not want to invest so much time with people who are not going where you are going (make sure you have done all in your power with the help of the Spirit to lead them to Jesus, so you can be with them eternally).

Balance

If you have read any of my books you will find one of the key principles in life is balance. God is always concerned about this. In life everything has an opposite. Most times we are wise to find a happy medium. I am not talking about God's commands; there is no middle ground with these.

We always need to have a balance in our lives. Like balancing our past with our future and thus live in the present. We are in what theologians call the interregnum, between the already and the not yet. I call it the present. We cannot enjoy the past or the future without the present and we cannot have the present without the past and the future. It is the means that God uses to keep our lives balanced. For example, even though we are made to live eternally, we are living in this life and will die. However, we cannot live eternally until we have learned to live in this world. Therefore, our focus cannot be only on the life to come. We have to learn to live in this life in preparation for the one to come. Jesus being aware of this fact told us to occupy until He returns for us. This life then is preparation for next. Hence, we should be practicing in this life how we will be living in eternity.

Eternal Consequences

God wants us to understand that whatever we do or say has eternal consequences. If we understand that we already have eternal life, then we would learn to relate to each other now. I believe if we cannot get along here we will not get along there. That is why some of us who think we are heading there will not make it. Since the same trouble we are causing now we will want to cause there. For example, if we are stealing now we will want to do the same thing in heaven, dig up the streets paved with gold. If we are in the habit of gossiping then we will want to do it in the earth made new. Since it will not be happening, then we cannot get there.

We all will have to give an account to God. *"But I say unto you, that every idle word that men shall speak, they shall give account thereof in the day of judgment. For by thy words thou shalt be justified, and by thy words thou shalt be condemned"* (Matthew 12:36-37). If we are going to be judge for our words, imagine what will happen to our actions.

> *For none of us liveth to himself, and no man dieth to himself. For whether we live, we live unto the Lord; and whether we die, we die unto the Lord: whether we live therefore, or die, we are the Lord's. For to this end Christ both died, and rose, and revived, that he might be Lord both of the dead and living. But why dost thou judge thy brother? Or why dost thou set at nought thy brother? For we shall all stand before the judgment seat of Christ. For it is written, As I live, saith the Lord, every knee shall bow to me, and every tongue shall confess to God. So then every one of us shall give account of himself to God. Let us not therefore judge one another anymore: but judge this rather, that no man put a stumbling block or an occasion to fall in his brother's way* (Romans 14:7-13).

We see clearly in these two passages that life is about God and then our fellow men. It can be summed up in one word, relationship. We use words to communicate with God and each other. We will be judged based on what we and how we say. What kinds of words are we using to God and each other, condemning or loving? We will be judged by them.

Our life is centered around God whether we want it to or not. It does not matter if we live or die, it is unto Him. Since God is interested in all His children we have to be careful how we relate and treat each other. One of the things we have to avoid is judging one another (Matthew 7:1-2). It boils down to what type of relationships we have with each other. In the judgment we will be judged on how we treated God and each other. Our behavior has eternal consequences.

The Problem

Our biggest problem is that eternity is out of our sphere, our realm of understanding. It cannot be conceptualized. Eternity is another one of those spiritual concepts that we cannot understand being in the flesh, it is spiritual. And spiritual things need the Spirit to reveal them to us (Romans 8:16). It requires faith for us to accept the concept of eternity. Hence, one of the reasons why we do not think or act in the context of eternity. There is nothing in this life we can associate it with. Everything on earth eventually dies. Then, how could we fathom eternity? Since it is a spiritual concept, it is impossible to understand in the physical, thus we spend a great deal of time talking about heaven and not learning how to live on earth, where we will spend eternity. Isaiah clearly states, *"For thus saith the LORD that created the heavens; God himself that formed the earth and made it; he hath established it, he created it not in vain, he formed it to be inhabited: I am the LORD; and there is none else"* (Isaiah 45:18). The earth was made for mankind and that has not changed. God does not change (Malachi 3:6).

I believe that's why we focus on heaven so much rather than on eternity. Heaven is described in the Bible so it is easier to conceptualize, with its mansions and precious stones. We have taken this out of context most of these will be on earth.

Yes there are times He made adjustments to His plans because of His love for us, we continue to mess up. But, the original plan does not change. Psalm 37:9, 11, 22 says, *"For evildoers shall be cut off: but those that wait upon the LORD, they shall inherit the earth… But the meek shall inherit the earth; and shall delight themselves in the abundance of peace...For such as be blessed of him shall inherit the earth; and they that be cursed of him shall be cut off."*

Thus, we must learn to live on earth. Since all that is in the earth will be burned up according to 2 Peter 3 and Revelation 21. The only thing that will remain constant will be the people who are saved. So, we will be coming back to live on this earth eternally. It means that our focus must change and we must learn to live with each other now, if we want to live with each other in the New Earth. Before Jesus comes to take us out of this world, it is about relationships and these will continue after He brings us back to earth. Hence, we need to begin practicing now what we will be doing throughout eternity. Because here is what Paul says, *"Who [Jesus] died for us, that whether, we wake or sleep, we should live together with them. Wherefore comfort yourselves together, and edify one another, even as also ye do."* (1 Thessalonians 5:10-11). We will be living together eternally. Since God cannot die, we need to connect with Him who is eternal.

Earth

Even the heavens and earth will not last forever. Peter paints a gruesome picture of the past and future events in 2 Peter 3,

> *Knowing this first, that there shall come in the last days scoffers, walking after their own lusts, and saying, Where is the promise of his coming? For since the fathers fell asleep, all things continue as they were from the beginning of the creation. Whereby the world that then was, being overflowed with water, perished: But the heavens and the earth, which are now, by the same word are kept in store, reserved unto fire against the day of judgment and perdition of ungodly men...The Lord is not slack concerning his promise, as some men count slackness; but is longsuffering to usward, not willing that any should perish, but that all should come*

Peter is reminding us of the flood that destroyed the antediluvian world. And because of man's continued rebellion to God, the earth this time will be destroyed by fire. Everything will be burned up. The fires will be so intense that the very elements will melt. There are some who are saying Jesus is not coming; I was hearing that ever since I was a child. Be careful you are fulfilling prophecy. Peter makes it clear that our timing and God's are different. What is a thousand years for us, is one day for Him (2 Peter 3:8).

Before this destruction takes place God is giving us an opportunity to repent and accept Him, become His disciples and maintain a relationship with Him and each other. If you have not done so, just turn to the back of the book.

You will notice in verse 11, God is again referring to how we are to relate to each other with holy conversations and godliness. The emphasis again is on relationships. John describes the situation after the destruction takes place.

of God is with men, and he will dwell with them, and they shall be his people, and God himself shall be with them, and be their God. And God shall wipe away all tears from their eyes; and there shall be no more death, neither sorrow, nor crying, neither shall there be any more pain: for the former things are passed away. And he that sat upon the throne said, Behold, I make all things new. And he said unto me, Write: for these words are true and faithful….I am Alpha and Omega, the beginning and the end. I will give unto him that is athirst of the fountain of the water of life freely. He that overcometh shall inherit all things; and I will be his God, and he shall be my son. But the fearful, and unbelieving, and the abominable, and murderers, and whoremongers, and sorcerers, and idolaters, and all liars, shall have their part in the lake which burneth with fire and brimstone: which is the second death" (Revelations 21:1-8).

John is here referring to us and all the relationships we have developed over the years. God is about to accomplish what He had planned all along. Just like He did in the Garden, this time He will dwell with us, He will not just be coming down. Notice also that all the negative emotions associated with relationships are done away with, tears, sorrow, pain, and death. God will wipe away all tears from our eyes, no more separation, the old is passed away and everything is new. He will be with us just like He was with Adam and Eve. What God intended originally will come to pass.

Heaven

In additon, we associate eternity only with heaven. Christianity has centered the teachings of the church on it. It is not about the relating to God. Instead, it is about getting to heaven to spend the eternity. Like the Israelites we just want to get out of this world with the cesspool of crime, debauchery, lasciviousness, greed, killings, and robbery. We are tired of what is happening and want to get out. We are not concerned about helping people, befriending them, leading them to a saving knowledge of Jesus and developing a personal relationship with Him and with others.

We forget that we will not be spending eternity in heaven but on earth. Revelation tells us about a new heaven and a new earth. We will only be going to heaven for a vacation. It is like when your house gets damaged in a tornado, earthquake, fire, or hurricane and the damage and you cannot live in it. You decide to rebuild. If there are no relatives to stay with, we normally stay in a hotel until the house is repaired. Well that is exactly what will happen when this earth will be destroyed by fire. In other words, the earth will be renovated while we spend a thousand years in heaven. *"And they lived and reigned with Christ a thousand years"* (Revelation 20:4). This is fulfillment of what Jesus said in Matthew 14:1-3, *"Let not your heart be troubled: ye believe in God, believe also in me. In my Father's house are many mansions: if it were not so, I would have told you. I go to prepare a place for you. And if I go and prepare a place for you, I will come again, and receive you unto myself; that where I am, there ye may be also."* The word mansions really mean many rooms, like in a hotel.

Our Focus

As a result of this misunderstanding, we have focused so much on the past and the future we are living in them and cannot live in the present. God lives in the past, present, and the future at the same time; He wants us to do the same, He created us in His image. In order for us to live in the present, we must embrace the past and the future. The Spirit has to show us what to bring from the past and what is in our future in order to enjoy the present.

Living in the past or future is to our detriment. That is one of the reasons we cannot be content. As someone has said, "Today is the tomorrow you worried about yesterday." Thus we cannot enjoy life the way God meant for it to be enjoyed. Jesus tells us, *"The thief cometh not, but for to steal, and to kill, and to destroy: I am come that they might have life, and that they might have it more abundantly"* (John 10:10). The enemy steals our joy by getting us to focus on the past and we get stuck there or in the future where we long to be and cannot get there, hence, we can never enjoy life.

The past deals with what was, and the future has not yet arrived so one can never be satisfied. If we are always looking behind or into the future, then we cannot be who we were meant to be. Because we are always absent. We are here but not here. We are not living in the present and that is when God manifests and bless us, but we checked out. We become depressed when we live in the past. And there seems to be no glorious future. We are stuck in what was. When our future becomes our only focus, we are of no use to anyone. Our minds are beclouded and we cannot relate to what is going on around us. It is impossible to be rational.

Christians have taken it to another level. Our future extends to eternity this is not bad in itself. But, when we think of eternity we think of spending eternity in heaven. The enemy has kept us focused on heaven so much that we are of no earthly use. Our heads are always in the clouds.

I believe that's why some churches are closing down. We are not meeting people's needs, even though this is what God wants us to do. We focus so much on getting to heaven that we do not care how we treat our fellowmen. We are not using our gifts, purposes, vocations and destiny to minister and meet people's needs. We are using them for our own selfish gratification. We think heaven is like how we are living down here, selfishly and not caring for others. We are looking forward to our big mansion in the sky, especially those of us who live in shacks. We even resent those who now live in mansion, when we get to heaven we will show them.

The problem is the mansion we are looking for is a hotel with many rooms and it is not ours. Again our focus is on the physical, instead, we should be focusing on developing relationships. I would go so far to add that when we become Jesus' disciples, our gifts, purposes, ministries, vocations and destiny are to be used to develop relationships.

Afraid

We have not yet learned to marry the past with the present and thus look forward to a superb future. This is the only way to enjoy the present. We are taking the sum total of who we are into the future. So, if we do not know our past, we do not have a present or a future. We can only forget the past if we have not learned from it. That is why we keep making the same mistakes. Also, one of the reasons we have difficulty breaking bad habits or maintaining great relationships, we are afraid to let go of our past.

We have been praying, yet repeating the same sin. Why? We refuse to look into our past and find the cause. Is it generational, one beginning with you, your peers, society, or personal pressure? What is the precursor? What activates the sin? What is the trigger? When we look into our past, then the Spirit will show us a pattern. In seeing it and avoiding the stimuli we can begin to break the old pattern with a new and uplifting one. If there is a disconnection between our past, present, and future we have to go back. For many this is too painful and do not want to relive the experience.

By avoiding our past, we are doing things and not understanding why. We get angry over an issue that is not a big deal. Like your spouse dropped a plate accidentally and you knew it was, you saw it happen. Yet, you became unbelievably angry and you could not understand why you reacted that way. It may be that the breaking of the plate acted as a trigger for something in your past that has not been resolved. Perhaps you cannot remember your parent beating you unconscious for accidently breaking a plate. You have not forgiven him/her.

We cannot escape our past. We must deal with and confront the demons of our past or they will dictate our future, without our permission. They will destroy every relationship we try to foster.

Chapter 5

Why So Difficult?

ALL FAMILIES HAVE UNHEALTHY RELATIONSHIPS, so, we all need some relational skills to build authentic relationships. Paul adds, we have a major problem, *"For all seek their own, not the things which are Jesus Christ's" (Philippians 2:21)*. We are selfish. It is God's and our desire to have relationships with Him and each other and these prepare us for eternity. Why then is forming and maintaining them so difficult? There are many reasons and we will look at some in this chapter. This is not an exhaustive list, as you read I know you will think of others or even disagree with what I have. That is okay.

Have Not Been Told

Many take the concept of relationships too lightly. I was visiting a church and making the point about the lack of teaching in church on this subject. One member, who is a medical doctor, did not understand. He said we are always teaching our children about relationships by telling them right from wrong. That is one of our gravest dangers, we feel that it is obvious and should be natural. Regrettably it is not. God told us in Deuteronomy 6 &11 it must be deliberate. Even more so today because of our mobile society, the problems with divorce and jobs. Besides, just teaching children right from wrong will not teach them how to develop friendships.

Has anyone told or taught you the importance of relationships? I have not been taught at home, church, nor any schools up to the universities I have attended. This is not an indictment on my parents, they were not taught either. I have decided to break this cycle and I told my children that relationships are the most important aspect to life. And pass on to them the skills and knowledge that God has given me.

Many believe like that Doctor developing relationships should be obvious; it is mere common sense. As someone has pointed out, it is not so common any more. There are too many things we take for granted and we believe people should know what is obvious and learn. The Prophet Hosea said that we are destroyed for a lack of knowledge. Some things must be taught or caught.

How Do You Know?

How and where did you learn about developing relationships? Who taught you? Did anyone sat you down and instruct you on how to go about developing and maintaining relationships? I do not mean when you became a young adult and was about to get married. What about at church? How many sermons have you heard on developing solid, long lasting friendships? Where did you learn about them? If we be honest, most of us would admit, we get our instructions from our culture, television, and friends.

As we look at these models we realize that something is drastically wrong. Hollywood's approach is about me, myself, and I. Hence, their multiple divorces. It is about finding the right person. It does not matter how messed up you are, find the right person and everything will be fine. The one found only lasts for a few months to a few years, and then it is on to the next victim. We leave in our path victims who see themselves as failures. We can never find the right person, for when we do, we will mess them up, since we are not right. I must be the right person. And this starts with knowing God.

Not Always Obvious

There are times when what is obvious to you is not to me. That is why the Bible reminds us, that we are our brother's keeper (Genesis 4:9). That too is obvious. Many people are not aware of this and have to be taught this simple clear principle. We overlook the Bible saying, spiritual things are spiritually discerned. Even though some things are clear, if you are not spiritually minded you will miss them. You cannot make yourself spiritual, you must accept Jesus.

We have to stop assuming our children know because they are going to church and school, even if it is a church school. Sadly, too many schools and churches are about book knowledge, maintaining the status quo and preserving themselves as institutions. What proof do I have you ask, well how many churches and schools are teaching their students about friendships? How many Bible Studies are taught on the importance of relationships other than when people are about to get married? How many schools from Kindergarten to University have courses on this subject for all students?

We are holistic beings and what affects one area of our lives will affect all other areas. Life is always screaming for balance. We cannot tip the scale in any direction without it affecting our entire lives. All of us have encountered experiences where it was so clear that you were at a four way junction, you got there before all the other cars. But, there were two drivers who believed they got there first. And they would argue they were there before you too. You would argue the opposite and all three of you think you are right.

Or it is so plain that there was no need for your spouse or child to ask that question. If you are like me I used to get mad sometimes and would not answer because it is too obvious. I am learning it is not as clear to others as it is to me. I also found that I do the same thing and ask what seems like stupid questions to them. What I learned is that we are all different and will continue to see, hear, feel, and experience things differently. It is all a part of the plan God designed for us to get along by helping build each other up. Instead, we use these differences to tear each other down.

Revelation

I believe there are some things that seem obvious; but, they have to be revealed by the Spirit. I was always aware how extremely important relationships are. Like most, I believed they were important to marriage and that was my focus. There are many friendships suffering as a result of concentrating solely on marriage. What do we do with our other relationships our parents, siblings, co-workers, church members, classmates, etcetera? It is after living for fifty years that the Spirit revealed to me how crucial relationships are. Nobody told me, He revealed it to me. That is why I am on a quest to get the information out and make as many aware of the importance of relationships, beginning with my family.

If we have difficulties in other relationships they will affect our marriage negatively. We cannot help that because the negative influences we have in these relationships will take away the positives we have in our marriage. Furthermore, we will have difficulty in our relationship with God as well.

The Bible said of Jesus, He did not speak without speaking in parables so that in seeing they see not and hearing they hear not (Matthew 13:13-14). It was only for those who wanted to know. It was only for the spiritually minded.

Too Busy

Busyness, always doing, is a great enemy of relationships. We are busier than previous generations even though we have more conveniences. These were designed to give us more leisure time, yet we spend more time on them. The phone, the computer, and the TV take more time away from us than our job sometimes. Thus, when our schedules become crowded we begin to cheat on our relationships. We cut back on the time, energy, and attention needed for them to flourish and give them to church, acquisitions, achievements, meetings, and other things that rock our world.

What is important to God and should be to us is squeezed out. Other things are demanding our time and attention. Like, making a living, working, paying our bills or accomplishing goals we set for ourselves. These are not important in life. It is not about doing things. Life is about learning to love ourselves, others, and God. I have to remind myself of this so often because I can get caught up in my writing. I believe God wants me to finish ten books by the year 2010. Sometimes I have to remember my family and call some friends to get out of my own world.

What I have found is that people on their dying beds are not concerned about the office, how many points the Dow Jones Average increased or how much money they made today. It is always about relationships. We want to be surrounded by people. People whose lives we have impacted or impacted us.

It is not a Priority

We have not made relationships our priority. There are many other things striving for our attention and we cannot handle all of them in our life time, hence we must to learn to prioritize. We need wisdom to figure out what is most and least important. The most important thing in life is relationships but it is not high on our list of priorities. Many of us see our jobs, careers, or sports, as being more important than God, our spouses, children, and friends. Yet, we cannot accomplish or enjoy anything in life without close relationships with family, friends, and our God.

One of my biggest regrets in life is putting my job before my wife and children. I felt they had to suck it up because I was putting food on the table. I felt justified, because the Bible says, I am worst than an infidel if I do not provide for my family (1 Timothy 5:8).

What is ironic is even though we are having wars, shooting, and killing each other, the high divorce rate, children killing their parents and other children—we have not yet seen the need to teach this vital concept to all. All these problems stem from a lack of learning to relate to one another. We have been taught that the way to solve our problems is with the gun. Remember what Jesus said to Peter when he cut off Malchus' ear with his sword, he who lives by the sword will die by it (Matthew 26:52). To paraphrase today, "he who lives by the gun will die by the gun." It is based on the Law of the Harvest, if we sow strife we will reap strife, if we sow reconciliation that is what we will reap. If we sow love we will reap love. Do not misunderstand me, there are times when we need to use the gun, let the Lord tell us when.

I believe we must start at an early age, teaching our children the importance of developing and maintaining relationships for eternity, if we want to turn things around. The older ones have to continue to learn, practice, and teach others the importance of relating positively to one another. I do not know if you are like me, most times it is easier to teach than it is to live what I teach. The Apostle Paul found himself in a similar dilemma. He described it this way in Romans 7, the things he wanted to do he found himself not doing, the things he did not want to do he found himself doing.

     You Were Made To Worship God 24/7

We all find ourselves in this dilemma; that is why we have to consciously make relationships our priority.

What it Looks Like

The best way we learn as human beings is through modeling. Unfortunately, we do not have too many role models to learn from when it comes to good friendships. So, we do not know what it should look like. We have not seen many positive ones modeled. Where then do we get our information from when it comes to building and maintaining good relationships? Who is our source? It is not taught by many schools or churches therefore we have looked to the world and Hollywood more specifically for our standard on relationships. Their method has proven to be a failure on and off the screen. The main reason is their standard is manmade, and all man standards are self-centered. Many are not getting married and are shacking up, and those relationships fail.

Limitations

Since we do not understand the importance of relationships, we fail to understand their limitations. As human beings we have our limits. There is only so much we can do. For example, there are times when we fail or cannot keep our promises, not because we did not want to, but it was beyond our control. You promised to meet your child or a friend for lunch, you had enough time to reach there and get back to work on time. Nevertheless, you did not know there would have been a five car pileup and it would take two hours before the accident would be cleared. Or worse yet, you were in the accident. There was nothing you could have done.

When we disappoint people they become angry, some do not even want to hear what the problem was. I remembered I had to meet a classmate and there was a problem with the weather and I could not get there. He was angry, not just disappointed, even though it was beyond my control. When we do not understand the limitations of human relationships, we look to them for the wrong things—to complete who we are, for fulfillment, to bring us joy and happiness. That is why we need a relationship that is outside of us. One that is perfect, flawless, and can accomplish what human relationships cannot, a relationship with God.

Limit Our Relationships

Too many times we also limit our relationships to people who are just like us and Jesus shows us we can benefit from others who are different. Like the disciples, they were completely different to Jesus, they were sinners. They, including us today, were surprised when He called the tax collector. They were the scum of the earth, since they would tax the people above and beyond what the State required. We could then understand why the Scribes and the Pharisees were upset. I am sure we would have been upset too. Listen to the dialog,

> *And after these things he went forth, and saw a publican, named Levi, sitting at the receipt of custom: and he said unto him, Follow me. And he left all, rose up, and followed him. And Levi made him a great feast in his own house: and there was a great company of publicans and of others that sat down with them. But their Scribes and Pharisees murmured against his disciples, saying, Why do ye eat and drink with publicans and sinners? And Jesus answering said unto them, they that are whole need not a physician; but they that are sick. I came not to call the righteous, but sinners to repentance (Luke 5:27-32).*

Who else they expected Levi to invite? The only people He knew and hung out with were other tax collectors. Jesus wanted to change that, and so He called him to be a part of His group. That is what we have to do, help people change or add to their circle of friends by us becoming their friends. Like Jesus, when we become friends our lives should affect theirs positively, as we point them to Jesus. I have not read where Jesus told them about the gospel first then called them, He simply told them to follow Him. Too many times we want to make people like us before we allow them to become a part of our circle. When we allow ourselves to be lead by the Spirit, then He will direct us as to who we should make a part of our crowd. Do not be surprised if they do not look, talk, or view the world the same way you do.

If we should have to invite some friends for a last minute party, who would you invite? Those you hang out with. Most times it will be those in the same profession, because we have not widened our circle to include people outside of our profession. Oh do not pat yourself on the back yet? Would it only be church folks because they are the only ones you know and spend time with; no wonder the church is not growing. Some of us limit our friends to our family members. We are constantly putting up barriers as we decide who we will and not let in our circle. Let the Spirit guide you in this area. If God were like us, we would be out in the cold. If He decided to hang out with the holy, perfect, or and super spiritual we all would be in trouble. We can only relate to people as we include them in our circle and get to know them.

Be aware of those who as the old people say, "My spirit does not take." We do not know anything about them, but they trigger something in us about our past which we have not dealt with. It brings back negative feelings we thought were dead. It might be a legitimate feeling since the person is a pedophile, killer, or thief. I am not saying to ignore your feelings. Examine them to find out the reason why God placed that person in your life.

The Purpose

God allows relationships in our lives for purposes—different reasons and seasons. If we do not understand friendships then we cannot tell the difference. Thus, we have relationships for the wrong reasons. There are some that should have been severed a long time ago, including some family members. There are others to be operated from a distance. Make sure you have done everything in your power with the aid of the Spirit for reconciliation. The Bible says as far as possible live peaceable with all men (Romans 12:18). This means there are some people we cannot live with. We have Biblical evidence, for example: Jesus and Lucifer, Abraham and Lot, Jacob and Rebecca, Paul and Barnabas. There are times when God cannot bless us, until there are some people out of our lives. Like Abraham and Lot, it was only after their separation that Abraham began to experience God's manifold blessings.

Once the purpose for the relationship is accomplished then the relationship should be severed, not in anger or disrespect. Sometimes we think the more people we have in our lives the more successful we are. But, there are some periods in our lives when we have to get rid of some friends for a period of time or forever. Remember Gideon, at times we have to get rid of some people or we will be defeated. They have become baggage and are tiring us out. We are so desperate for human companionship; we take whoever comes along, once they are breathing. Our lives become overwhelming, miserable, and unbearable, because we are carrying some people who we should not be carrying.

Motives Impure

Often our motives for friendships are not right. Normally, it is about what we can get rather than contribute. So, we look for those who can give to us. This creates an imbalance. Also, we often seek people who have certain things in common, like our country, culture, creed, class, career, or church. We have difficulty relating to people who are different, it takes too much, and we are uncomfortable or afraid. This is one of the best ways to learn, expand our horizon and get to know others, who are really not much different to us.

Jesus would often seek out people who were different to Him. Like the party at Matthew's house, eating with publicans and sinners. The man at the pool at Bethesda, instead of going straight to church, Jesus went to look for this sick man. He searched out lepers, the deaf, dumb, and demon possessed. Not only to heal them, He wanted a relationship with them. He would not just heal the lepers; He would touch them, this was unheard of in Jesus' day. You stayed as far away as possible from them, they made you ceremonially unclean. He looked into people's eyes, He connected with them. His motives were pure. He did not help them for selfish reasons.

Hard Work

Relationships do not just happen—they require much work. Learning to be and accept ourselves as we are, is a task in and of itself. We have been taught we are not good enough as we are; there is always something we have to fix, add, or subtract. Also, trusting, learning, doing, courageous, being vigilant, and focusing on the other persons' needs, wants, and desires. Establishing and maintaining boundaries, knowing where our freedom ends and the other person's begin involves hard work. Work is not bad, even in the perfect Garden; God put Adam to hard. Hard work is a good thing.

That's why we have problems in relationships, we believe that there are just natural and they should just happen, especially for

Christians. No, they do not, they require solid work, being innovative, creative, and always listening.

Differences

It seems as if God has done a cruel thing by creating us different. That is not a fair statement, since He created us different to Himself. The greatest difference is between us and God. He is holy, we are unholy, He is perfect, we imperfect. He is just, we unjust. Yet, He wants to have a relationship with us, that is not just a desire. God has done everything possible to establish and maintain a relationship with us, while we were yet sinners, Christ died for us (Romans 5:8). All we like sheep have gone astray and the Lord has laid on Him the iniquity of us all (Isaiah 53:6).

God is the one who gave us different personalities, ethnic groups, preferences, to be valued and enjoyed, not merely to tolerate. We are looking for uniformity rather than what God wants, unity. That is why we must never allow differences to divide us. We have to stay focused on what is most important—learning to love each other as Jesus has loved us.

But, we have serious problems dealing with and accepting differences. We fail to see them as coming from God. We are so uniquely different that our very hearts have a distinctive heart beat, the only one of a kind finger prints, eye prints, voice print, out of all the billions of people who are living and have lived, all have their own unique prints. There is or never will be a duplication. When God made you He broke the mold. Hence, no one else born or unborn will be able to be like you and do what you were designed to. This also means we have our limitations that we have to learn to accept also.

God does not want us to minister using gifts He did not equip us with, this will create tension, discomfort, and will take a great deal of energy and effort and the results will be mediocre. So, trying to be like someone else does not work, the person is different. You won't experience fulfillment, satisfaction and fruitfulness. We need to accept graciously how God fashioned us and not try to have a makeover. Learn to celebrate who you are.

As God's children what we have in common is much greater than our differences. One Lord, one faith, one baptism, one body, one purpose, One Father, One Spirit, One Jesus, one hope, and one love. We share the same salvation, the same life, the same future. These are what we should be focusing on, rather than our individual differences. Conflict is usually a sign that our focus has shifted from what is important to what produces divisions. Like interpretations, styles, methods, preferences, and personalities.

One of the first things we have to teach our children is that differences are okay. The truth is children in the beginning do not see the differences, until we as parents point them out. And when we do, it is normally in a negative manner. We have to first learn, and then teach the positive aspects to our differences and what they are designed to accomplish. In the church we are encouraged to break off our relationships with our love ones if they are not of our faith. And the reason is because they are different from us.

When God created the universe it was perfect. No disconnections existed. There were differences which are not bad, contrary to what we learned. In God's realm, in order for anything to work, there must be differences. This is just for functional purposes; still, harmony and unity existed. Even though God was God, He would literally come down in the Garden and walk and talk with Adam and Eve. Nothing separated them. You could not want anything more different. God who was in existence throughout eternity came down and hung out with mankind who was created. Adam messed up. The moment He sinned, a disconnection immediately took place. Man, who was created to be holy and live forever, became unholy and began to die. God had a plan to bring about a reconnection. He wanted to maintain a relationship with man even though the differences were even more pronounced: Sinful human beings and a Holy God.

Differences were God's idea and we have to learn to embrace them. He is so much into differences that every blade of grass, snowflake, leaf, stone, fingerprint, retina of our eyes, and more are different. God delights in differences. We are afraid of them. We see them as inferior or superior, as better or worse, so much so that we resent them. The majority of the problems of the world stems from differences. We believe we have to rectify what God has messed up, in that we believe that everybody should be just like us.

Our Image

We are always creating images. We are so good at it that we have created God in our own image. Because He is different from us we want to make Him just like us. We have a picture of who He is and we want others to see and experience Him the same way we do. If we examine that picture we will discover it is the spitting image of us. We want to make God into our image. If people do not believe or see Him the way we do, we believe they are not saved and know Him personally. In fact, they will be going to hell. It is impossible to confine God to our image and our likeness. We need to let others experience Him the way He wants them to.

There are those of us who do not like our own image and want to change it. We are too short or too tall, too thin or too fat, hair is too long or too short, too grey or too black, too light or too dark. We are not satisfied with our own image and so we want to make it over. An extreme example of this is Michael Jackson, his sister, many other celebrities who are not satisfied with who they are and have gone through drastic changes to recreate their image physically. Many of us do not accept the differences and want to change them even though some of them cannot be changed.

God has made each of us unique and special. Yet, we resent it and want to make everybody into our own image. And if we dwell on this concept too long we would soon become like Hitler, we will try to get rid of all who are different. We cannot stop there, because we will have to kill everyone else on the planet, since it cannot stop with people of our own race. Then, we will have to get rid of all those of the opposite sex. After that, those who do not see things the way we see them. Next, those who do not hear things the way we hear them or do not like the same things we like. We will never stop until we have killed everyone else on the earth. Then we have to take our own life, because we do not have anybody who is opposite to us. It will be too late to realize that we need the differences in order to survive in life.

We have to be careful in our relationships not trying to make others over into our own image. We only do this because we are insecure, uncomfortable with who we are and we think everybody else has the same problem we have. We must accept ourselves completely first, before we can accept others. We must learn to let others be themselves and find a way to relate to them. Do not try to change them into our image, we cannot. That is why a pure relationship with God is so vital, because only He can do the changing. He will not change them into our image but into His (2 Corinth 3:18).

Relating

Men and women relate differently. Men do not use or think in terms of relationship, even though we want and need them. Most men have had bad experiences with relationships, when we think of them they bring back memories of hurt, pain, and misunderstandings. We see relationships as between a man and a woman not a man and another man. We call that gay. To have a relationship with another man means we have to deal first with an enormous amount of fear and suspicion.

We see relationships differently, as men we see them in the context of activity. Thus as men, we have our school buddies, sports buddies, work buddies etcetera. We express relationships in these terms. So, a man will not go to another man and say let us have a relationship. This would arouse suspicion, since it was not expressed in terms of an activity. Instead, we would say let us go hunting, fishing or to the ball game. We could do this for a hundred years and never describe what we have as a relationship.

We form relationships differently. Women form their relationships face-to-face, as men we relate to each other side-by-side. Men bond with each other by doing stuff together, going to a game, to eat, to war, work on something together. That is why most men are intimidated with forming circles in church. That is a face to face relationship.

The thing that draws men closest together is going through adversity together, like war. Women can sit together and in a few minutes are best of friends. Men take their time and will draw back if he feels he is being pushed into a relationship. That is why, for men, serving God is about doing, being active, doing things together, not just sitting in the pew and being lectured to. Men are task and goal oriented. We do not mind working together as a team to accomplish a task or goal. But, there must be a beginning and an end in sight or we will feel unproductive. Once that is accomplished then we move on to the next and the next. That is the environment we strive in. Women on the other hand are about relating face to face. It does not matter if we have or have not grown or moved on spiritually, once they are relating, they are fine.

     You Were Made To Worship God 24/7

We have to understand these differences so we can know how to relate to males and females. It is not that they are bad, just different: Differences that were designed by God Himself.

Part II

THE WHAT OF RELATIONSHIPS?

Chapter 6

A Basic Ingredient

BEFORE WE CAN THINK of getting into any relationship, we must know who we are first. To know that, we must know who God is. We cannot know who we are if we do not know our Creator. There must be a reconnection between God and us, to answer three of life's basic questions. If we cannot answer these positively, we will be frustrated, furious, and fuming all the time. We will be unable to handle any relationships because we will take our frustrations and anger out on ourselves and everybody else.

The first question is, who am I?
The second is, why am I here?
The third is, where am I going?

If we cannot answer these positively and unequivocally, we cannot help ourselves and others. When we are disconnected, disjointed and detached from ourselves, it is impossible to experience the joy that is unspeakable and full of glory that God has for us. If we do not know our gifts, purposes, ministries, vocations, and destiny in life, then we cannot understand or accept who we are in other areas of our lives. Thus, there are some things we like about ourselves and others we hate. That is why we cannot be who we are. We are one person in church and someone else during the week. We have perfected the art of pretending and have grown comfortable wearing these masks. We have difficulty connecting with who we really are because we are not sure after pretending for so long.

If we cannot answer these three basic questions, it is impossible to relate to ourselves, others, and God, because a rift exists between all three. Furthermore, we cannot handle the many problems of life. We do not possess the confidence needed, because our feet are not planted on solid ground.

Easily Influenced

When we do not know who we are, we are easily discouraged, diverted, distracted, and dissuaded. People who know who they are, what they are doing, and where they are going will take us along with them, even if we do not plan to go. This does not make for a good relationship. Remember Jim Jones who took almost one thousand people to Guyana and got many to commit suicide. It is a terrible and dangerous thing when we do not know who we are. People will influence us to do what we never thought of ever doing.

Not knowing ourselves and what we are capable of, we cannot trust ourselves, since the core of our being is corrupt. The prophet asked, *"The heart is deceitful above all things, and desperately wicked: who can know it?"* (Jeremiah 17:9). We are incapable of changing ourselves, *"Can the Ethiopian change his skin or the leopard his spots? Then may ye also do good that are accustomed to do evil"* (Jeremiah 13:23). We are unpredictable and in dire need of help. There is only One person who can help us answer these questions.

To find out how to get the maximum use out of any product, we ask the manufacturer. That is why they provide a manual. Others can give us a fairly good idea what it is about. Still, if we want the real deal, we go to the inventor, the source. God made us and He is the best person to tell us about ourselves.

Bondage

If we do not know who we are in Christ, then we are in bondage and cannot experience freedom. Freedom can only be ascertained on the basis of truth. Jesus said, ""*If you hold to my teaching, you are really my disciples. Then you will know the truth, and the truth will set you free*" (John 8:32 NIV). There is no freedom without knowledge, which must be truth. Freedom can only exist where truth (Jesus) is present. If we are not truthful with ourselves, pretending to be someone else, or afraid to get in touch with ourselves, we cannot experience freedom. If we are not free, then whoever we have a relationship with our main objective will be to imprison them. We want people to be where we are.

The Scribes and Pharisees responded in the following verse, "*They answered him, "We are Abraham's descendants and have never been slaves of anyone. How can you say that we shall be set free?*" (John 8:33). The worst kind of bondage is to be in it and not know. Ignorance is the worst form of bondage. They did not know who Jesus was so they were not free. Also, when we are in bondage, we will abuse ourselves and others. If you continue to read, they eventually killed Jesus (verse 37). This happens when we do not know who or whose we are and who others are. It creates a disconnection within and without and we cannot have peace of mind. And since we cannot enjoy peace, neither will anyone around us, like the old saying, "Misery loves company." We will try to make everyone around us miserable since we love to project onto others what is in us. We become our own hostage. We become a slave to sin and entangled with the yoke of bondage (Galatians 5:1). What are we in bondage to?

Our Past

There is no connection between our past, present, and future. We are living a disconnected life. It is only when we know what is true, in our body, soul and spirit that we can be free. It is knowing the truth—the truth about God, ourselves, families, church, environment, and our entire sphere. It is then we will be made free to operate how God wants us to and not be intimidated by those who will seek to imprison us.

We forget very quickly, that's why God reminds us often, do not forget what I have done for you. Most people are terrified of their past and are still in bondage to it. The pain is too intense and do not want to relive the hurt. God gave us the defense mechanism of denial when the news we receive is unbearable. But, we abuse it by trying to forget the incidents ever happened. When we refuse to deal with our past, we become prisoners to and of it.

There are skeletons in our closets that we prefer to ignore; by keeping the door closed. Even though the stench is killing us, we prefer to live with it, rather than open the door and confront our skeletons and then bury them. At times the pain is excruciating and we do not want to experience it again. The smell is easier to live with, we are accustomed to it. In addition, we are afraid of the conflict or the rift that it will bring in the family or relationship. We do not want to be the one who is responsible for splitting up our great, loving, and caring family. But, we hate and cannot stand the relative who caused the pain. They pretend like nothing happened. We think we are handling it by not remembering it consciously. Yet, it is affecting us from the subconscious level, in ways we do not understand.

Since we are made in God's image, we were made never to forget. We remember, whether we want to or not, and it is so devastating when it is remembered at the subconscious level. It affects our relationships and we are not even aware. That is why the person who was abused, and tries to forget it ever happened, becomes an abuser. The woman whose mother married an alcoholic and does not come to terms with the effect it has on her life, will normally marry one.

When we refuse to deal with our past, we begin to do the same things that our family did to us. We do not want to be like them. Yet, that is our focus and we become who we focus on. Also, that is the only way we know. The Bible says by beholding we become changed into the image of who we are beholding (2 Corinthians 3:18). It is ironic that we are trying so hard not to become like our abuser. But they become our focus and we become obsessed with them and they guide our lives because we are in bondage to our past.

Who We Are Not

God designed us in such a way that we copy Him in all areas of our lives. Many of us are copying other peoples' lifestyles, pretending to be who we are not. In other words, we are frauds. It is because we do not know who we are; we want to be like others. One reason why so many people do not know who they are, they want to be like the stars. They see them as their role models. They dress, talk, and try to do all that they do. They have their voices on their cell phones. Relationships are difficult to develop when we are imitators of others.

Our Work

We are so attached to our jobs and careers, they have become our identity. Not knowing who we are, we hide behind what we do. Do you know the real you apart from your roles and responsibilities? What would happen if you lost your job and were unable to work because of an injury? Does your job define who you are? This is prevalent in our society, including the church. This is also a means of bondage.

When you ask people to tell you a little about themselves, almost without failure, after saying their names, they tell what they do. I am a lawyer, doctor, teacher, student, mother, father, wife, or husband. We believe we are defined by what we do. And so we feel, hear, or see ourselves as being important based on our profession. What happens when we lose our job and cannot work? Some commit or attempt suicide. Take for example the late, great Christopher Reeve who played Superman. After his accident and being a quadriplegic, he thought about committing suicide and his wife had to talk him out of it.

I remembered, after resigning from the First Missouri City Seventh-day Adventist Church, I had lost my identity. Some people no longer saw me as a pastor since I was not in charge of a church. I found myself having to remind them I am still one, because that gave me my identity. In many circles, it was one of prestige, importance and I did not want to give that up. I am a child of God. The title is not important–I am. I was a person before I became a pastor and continue to be.

Because we define ourselves by what we do, many individuals are in professions that they loathe. They are doing it because society says it is prestigious or it brings a great deal of money. So they enter what society calls the "top fields"—a doctor, lawyer, scientist, computer programmer, or an engineer. Thus, they are disconnecting with themselves, since that is not who God designed them to be. It is not that they enjoy doing what they have chosen; they cannot, since they are outside the will of God. Some children are not sure what they want to do; their parents influence them to get into one of the prestigious professions, even though that is not the endowment or giftedness that God has given to the children.

The child may be good at painting or mechanics. But, these are not prestigious enough and one does not make as much money from these, (not true). Yet, the child is miserable, he is in bondage, this is not his calling. As a result, he hates going to work, to the point where it is making him sick. That's because he is not where God wants him to be. He is living a disconnected, disjointed, dejected, downcast, and depressed life. You cannot develop long lasting friendships in this manner, since you are not true to yourself.

I remember reading of a doctor who had a very successful practice and received many accolades. But, he could not take it anymore. In a speech at one of his award ceremonies, he told his parents this is for them; I did not want to do this, I wanted to be a musician, but I became a doctor for you. I cannot do this any longer. I am going to fulfill my life-long dream, and he quit. That sounds extreme; but, we have to follow God's directions and fulfill His purposes and destiny, not ours or our parents.

Our Purposes

If we do not know who we are, then we cannot accept who we are, or anyone else. Besides, we cannot know what our purposes are. They are tied to who we are; our uniqueness, gifts, idiosyncrasies, abilities, talents, etcetera. Nobody else can fulfill our purposes. Since God is a God of purpose, He has specific reasons for making us the way He did, why we were placed on this earth, and living where we are.

We have to be comfortable and accept who we are because if we do not, we will want to fulfill other people's purposes. We will be jealous or sabotage other people's missions or ministries. When we do not know what our purposes are, we become very frustrated and we pass on our frustrations to those closest to us. We tend to forget the opposite is also true. Happiness, joy, and confidence also love company. When we are happy and confident and all the other positive attributes, we want to share it with others.

A person who is confused will have difficulty enjoying life and will be unable to make sound decisions. You will be blown here and there by different voices. I remember in February 2003 when the Lord was calling me to a different purpose for my life—the area of writing—I gave the church my resignation. Sister Allen, a loving and sweet member, came to our home and pleaded with me to re-consider because the church needed me. I listened and withdrew my resignation because it made me feel good to know I was need-ed. My spirit was not at peace, God had already spoken. There was a disconnection, I was not where He wanted me. It was about a month later, full of embarrassment, I had to resign again and do what God called me to do. This is my fourth book since then and He has already planted in my spirit six more.

This is what happens when we do not know what our purposes are in life. Others who have good intentions can influence us to do or be where God does not want us to be. It was a learning experi-ence. I have been asked since to Pastor Churches and I know that this is not where God wants me right now. With my years of experi-ence as a member, a Pastor and now a member, He has qualified me to write on the subjects He has given. When we do not under-stand our purposes, we will be easily led. And on our way, we are frustrated and realize this is not where we wanted or needed to be. Relationships cannot grow in this type of environment.

Experiencing Freedom

While I was visiting my brother, Frankie in St. Martin, he made a statement that I have not forgotten. "There are many Christians who are delivered but have not yet been made free." We believe we are free in theory because that is what the Bible says. This is mere-ly intellectual. Here is where many of us remain and thus cannot experience real freedom. We believe that God is a wonderful, powerful and awesome King and He can meet our needs, wants, and desires. How do we know? He did it miraculously for us; we have read and heard about Him doing it for others. We believe God can get us out of financial bondage and keep the weight off. At this point we are no different to the devils, *"Thou believest that there is one God; thou doest well: the devils also believe, and* **tremble** *(James 2:19 KJV).* They go a step further and tremble.

We have to go a step further and put our faith into action by allowing the Spirit to connect with our spirit to tell us it is true and together can make it happen (Romans 8:16). Our minds have to become like His mind. When the Bible says, "Know the truth," it is an experiential knowledge of God. When we can experience God's freedom in us then we will believe He can free others. Here is a perfect example,

> *Peter…was kept in prison: but prayer was made without ceasing of the church unto God for him. And when he had considered the thing, he came to the house of Mary….where many were gathered together praying. And as Peter knocked at the door of the gate, a damsel came to hearken, named Rhoda. And when she knew Peter's voice, she opened not the gate for gladness, but ran in, and told how Peter stood before the gate. And they said unto her, Thou art mad. But she constantly affirmed that it was even so. Then said they, It is his angel. But Peter continued knocking: and when they had opened the door, and saw him, they were astonished. But he, beckoning unto them with the hand to hold their peace, declared unto them how the Lord had brought him out of the prison (Acts 12:5,12-14).*

Rhoda was excited, but, the others did not believe even though they were praying for Peter's release, they did not believe that God could or would do it for them. So, they did not believe He would do it for Peter. First, we must apply the Word to ourselves, then we will be able to apply it to others.

Balance

One of the keys to life is balance. It is impossible to accomplish anything without knowing who we are and why we are here. Here is the apostle Peter's command, *"Be well balanced (temperate, sober of mind), be vigilant and cautious at all times; for that enemy of yours, the devil, roams around like a lion roaring [in fierce hunger], seeking someone to seize upon and devour"* (1 Peter 5:8, Amplified Bible).

This causes serious relational issues within us and with our love ones. This is so easy because we spend a lot of time doing what we enjoy doing. What happens in the process, the other areas of our lives are seriously affected? For example, right now I have to live what I am telling you, because I feel like continuing to write and write because God has placed so much in me. Nevertheless, I know who I am and what He wants from me. It is easy to hear the Spirit saying, "You have other responsibilities you have to attend to." I must listen or else I would suffer the consequences. I have a family, friends, and workers who need me.

Life is about balance. If we fail to live as such, we will be forced to do so. God has programmed us for it. The lack of balance produces stress and when we are stressed our relationships suffer. We become more concerned about meeting our needs not the needs of others. We begin to reason, it's because of our family and friends why we are stressed out. Stress when prolonged produces physical and psychological illness. This affects our relationships and the vicious cycle continues.

How Can We Know Who We Are?

Honesty

Can the real you stand up under all circumstances? Are you happy with the person in the mirror? What about the relationships you have formed? What are your motives for them? Many of us are afraid to examine who we really are and why we do what we do? Afraid of what we will find. One way to know is if you always need noise around you and do not spend time at Jesus feet like Mary. Not listening to a preacher or music, just you and the Lord. I mean time in prayer and listening to God. Do you just pray or do you take the time to listen.

The first step in getting to know who we really are—we must be honest with ourselves. If we cannot, neither can we be honest with anyone else, including God. We have to be willing to examine ourselves, even when we are afraid and tempted to bury issues. We should be like the Psalmist who when he was fearful or might cover up anything, he asked, *"Search me, O God, and know my heart: try me, and know my thoughts: And see if there be any wicked way in me, and lead me in the way everlasting (Psalms 139:23-24)*. David was not merely asking for a surface search, realizing he could not do it himself. He asked the only One who could do the best heart searching and cleansing because He made the heart.

The reason why we must ask God to do this for us, our heart is deceitfully wicked and can fool us (Jeremiah 17:9). So, we have to accept Jesus as Lord and Savior of our lives. If you have not, then do so now by turning to the back of the book.

Accepting Who We Are

Once we are honest with our soul searching and God reveals who we are, He will help us to accept ourselves and others as they are. We will not only see ourselves as unique, one of a kind, there is no one else in the universe like us. We will also accept this same fact about others. Also, God will help us make the necessary changes. Paul points out, *"Therefore, if anyone is in Christ, he is a new creation; the old has gone, the new has come!"* (2 Corinthians 5:17 NIV). There is an exchange of the old for the new and better qualities. These changes are internal; they have to do with our minds and spirits. They have to be renewed daily.

> *Therefore, I urge you, brothers, in view of God's mercy, to offer your bodies as living sacrifices, holy and pleasing to God—this is your spiritual act of worship. Do not conform any longer to the pattern of this world, but be transformed by the renewing of your mind. Then you will be able to test and approve what God's will is—his good, pleasing and perfect will (Romans 12:1-2 NIV).*

When we think of change, it is normally external. We have been led to believe that if we look good it means that we are good. Jesus told the most beautiful of all creatures, Lucifer, that he was a devil on the inside. God wants to begin on the inside. Once we allow Him to change our mind-set and our attitude, our outside will be transformed and we will be able to accept ourselves. Besides, we will be able to accept others as they are. In other words, our obsession with the outward would change to inward, in ourselves and with others.

Spirit Lead

We have to learn to operate at a different level, not with our senses; in the physical, social, psychological or even mental realm: But in the Spirit. If not we will loathe ourselves and others. The good news is that the Spirit is ready and willing to lead, *"Howbeit when he, the Spirit of truth, is come, he will guide you into all truth"* (John 16:13). This is the most difficult aspect of a disciple's life, because the flesh is warring with the spirit and wants to take over. When we allow the Lord to be in charge, we begin to understand freedom.

When we totally and wholeheartedly surrender to the Spirit, He tells us who we are and we can accept everything true about ourselves, our past, and all our flaws. We can accept everything about others and still love them in the Spirit. This will bring about rest in us. He will reveal to us our gifts, purposes, ministries, vocations, destiny, and God's will for us and how to accomplish it, providing the balance we need to enjoy life. He will bring the relationships that will help us. This will be accomplished as He sets us free and unleashes His resurrection power in us, to help our fellowmen.

Rejection

We have been taught since creation that if people really know who we are, they will reject us. Like Adam and Eve, they hid from God, not wanting Him to reject them. Nobody wants to be rejected. We are social beings and just like God, we love and want relationships. Thus, we spend our entire lives hiding, trying to be who we are not so that people will not reject us. The sad thing is we end up rejecting ourselves and feel rejected by others and some commit suicide.

Why? We turn our focus outward, on our jobs, earning a living, working in the church, playing golf and other games to escape from the real person inside. We all have done some things in our lives that we would like to forget. We were not designed to forget. We try to run faster and faster from ourselves by doing, rather than being. The problem is we cannot run or hide from ourselves because everywhere we go we are there. The best thing to do is to get to know you, by getting in touch with God. Then work with Him helping others do the same and begin to enjoy life to its fullest.

Time to be Alone

There are some people who are so disconnected with themselves they cannot spend time alone. They cannot be quiet for a moment. Noise must be around them. The radio, the TV, a movie must be playing, or they must be reading something. If they cannot be doing any of the above, then they are on the telephone. They have to be in constant activity or have noise around them so that they do not have to think or focus on themselves. Why? Because they do not like who they were, are, or who they are becoming.

Jesus, our supreme example, took time to be alone in a quiet place away from the crowd. No noise, distractions, nobody but Him and God. To know you, you must able to spend time with yourself, getting to know the real you. We have to connect with ourselves in order to truly connect with our Father and know His will for our lives. Then God will reveal to us, who we need to take time out and connect with on that day. We can only be helpful when we are happy with ourselves. Then we will be happy with and for others and be willing to help them.

Accepting Our Uniqueness

God made us unique individuals. We are not like any other on this earth, with our flaws or anything else. If we cannot accept our uniqueness, we are disconnected from ourselves. Also, no one will accept us, and want to be our friend. If we do not like who we are, then no one else can like us either. Because we are not sure who we are and want to be like someone else, there will be two of the same person alive. That means, there is no need for us because the person we are trying to be like already exists. People will not be able to love us since they have to love the person we are trying to be like. We are actors.

We cannot be anyone else. Our past, families, country of origin, environment, gifts and abilities help to shape us into the unique individuals we are. We have to accept this and our reasons for living. We cannot go back and ask for smaller ears, a longer chin, to be taller or shorter. We have to accept who we are or we cannot accept others and have a rich relationship with them.

Reconnecting With Our Past

This means understanding and accepting our past. It helps us to reconnect with ourselves. Without personal acceptance, life becomes a living hell. It can be a wonderful, eye-opening experience and it can also be a scary, painful, and frightening one. Still, it is liberating. I know I mentioned the visit to my parents before. But, it was an eye-opener. I understand why I get so upset with my wife when it appears as though she wanted to tell me what to do. I understand better why I am so angry, because I was able to look into my past with my parents. Some of it was painful to relive. They are and were great parents; still, like all parents, they made some mistakes and will continue to make them until they die, and so will I.

Since I understand my past, I am enjoying the present and looking forward to a glorious future. Also, it is helping me to avoid some future mistakes. As someone has said, and I paraphrase, if we do not learn from our past mistakes we are bound to repeat them in the future. Without our history, it is impossible to know our destiny. If we do not know where we came from, we cannot know where we are going. In life there are several paths, and not knowing which one to take, we will take the one with the least conflict. That does not make it the right path.

But, if we know where we came from and understand our previous experiences, we will know that we still need to be in our wildernesses, pits, prisons, or that it is time to enter our palaces or be heading to the promise land. We will know and can accept the season we are in right now. Thus, we will be better able to relate to those around us and will learn to be content wherever we are.

Oh sure, we all love and want to be in the palace. Yet, nobody goes there immediately. Even if we were born in one, we still have to go through our pits, prisons and wilderness experiences. For example, Moses was in the palace and he had to end up in his pits, the wilderness of Median, tending sheep for forty years. Jesus, who was in the palace of palaces, had to come down to earth and go through His pits, prisons, and wildernesses, But, right now He is in His palace. We can now understand that He understands what we are going through. So, we can have confidence and faith in Him knowing He understands and believes that He can and will help us.

We have to be honest with ourselves and have a desire to want to know the truth at all cost—why we behave the way we do, breaking our generational curses. And the only way is by reconnecting with our past. Even if your parents are dead, then find individuals who knew them and learn about them. Be aware of those who glorify the dead. You want to talk to people who are honest and will tell you the truth about your dead parents.

In conclusion, when we know who we are and how unique: We will want to be a disciple of Jesus. There is a desire to know our gifts, purposes, ministries, vocations, and destiny and there is a passion from within to live life to its fullest. We realize we do not have to prove anything to anybody. There is harmony within and without. We become focused and not easily sidetracked. Like Jesus we will not give in when Satan tests us in our wilderness experiences (Matthew 4). Hence, we are better equipped to develop long lasting relationships.

———•◆•———

Chapter 7

The Key Ingredient

AT SOME POINT IN LIFE we will come to the same conclusion King Solomon came to, if God is not number one in our lives, *"Therefore I hated life; because the work that is wrought under the sun is grievous unto me: for all is vanity and vexation of spirit. Yea, I hated all my labour which I had taken under the sun: because I should leave it unto the man that shall be after me"* (Ecclesiastes 2:17-18). Solomon had worked himself to the bones and looking back was disappointed. He was busy and had not accomplished anything worthwhile. He was concerned about work and not relationships. When your life is out of balance, you cannot experience contentment and peace. We were not made just to work: We were made to share not just what we have, but who we are. The best way to do this is through relationships.

Challenges of Life

I am not surprised that Duke University and the University of Phoenix in their study last year on friendship found that Americans have fewer friends than they had twenty years ago. It shows that those who reported having no one to discuss matters with almost doubled to 25%. We are so busy and mobile, we are insulating ourselves from each other. We do not know our next door neighbors. That's no way to live. Alas, this carries over into our families; we do not know our spouse or children either. We have become so wrapped up into our own little world.

Even the Bible admonishes us,

> *Let nothing be done through strife or vainglory; but in lowliness of mind let each esteem other better than themselves. Look not every man on his own things, but every man also on the things of others. Let this mind be in you, which was also in Christ Jesus: Who, being in the form of God, thought it not robbery to be equal with God: But made himself of no reputation, and took upon him the form of a servant, and was made in the likeness of men: And being found in fashion as a man, he humbled himself, and became obedient unto death, even the death of the cross (Philippians 2:3-8).*

This is a great challenge especially in this age. We are too concerned about ourselves, but, we have to humble ourselves like Jesus did. If we don't then with such an attitude friendships are hard to come by and we need them. We take relationships for granted. They provide a shoulder to lean or cry on when life throws us curve balls or bouncers. They help us emotionally, few are aware of the health benefits. Studies have shown that female friendships help to stave off diseases by lowering blood pressure, heart rate and cholesterol. Positive relationships enhance and lengthen our lives.

We are busy, at times our responsibilities seem overwhelming and so we focus on living by bread alone. The last thing on our mind is sharing our lives with others. We do not have the time to form long and lasting friendships. Hence, our friendship circle keeps shrinking. Thus, the older we get the fewer friends we have. We become so busy with the pressures of parenting, work, spouses, and taking care of our aging parents, we have little left. We fail to see that positive relationships don't hinder, instead they enhance our families.

A Great Obstacle

One of the greatest obstacles to any relationship is time. It is the single most important ingredient of any relationship. God understanding this would come down in the Garden of Eden and spend time with Adam and Eve (Genesis 3:8). He was showing us from way back then that spending time is an important aspect of relationships. Without it growth or survival is impossible. To the point where many spell the word love, TIME. That is how crucial it is. It is more so for the person whose love language is time *(See Gary Chapman book, The Five Love Languages)*. It is important that we understand these and love people the way they want to be loved and not love them how we want to be loved. This is easier because it comes naturally. To love others how they want to be loved takes time, effort and creativity, this does not come naturally. However, the harvest is bountiful.

Do Not Have the Time

We have heard this line often. God made sure we would not have any excuses. He gave us the same amount daily, 24 hours, 1,440 minutes, and 86,400 seconds. So, none of us have more time than the other. This forces us to decide what is important and give time to it. The amount we give to anything tells its value to us. Hence, we make time for what is important to us. We decide this based on our training and find time for those things, which are based on self-ishness. We are told to look out for ourselves. This is contrary to the Bible, Paul the Apostle tells us in *Romans 14: 7 "No man liveth to himself."* He further states, *"As we have therefore opportunity, let us do good unto all men, especially unto them who are of the household of faith"* (Galatians 6:10). The story of the Good Samaritan in Luke 10:30-37 reminds us that we are never to become too busy for our fellowmen. He was on a journey, but stopped and helped a bruised and broken man. He did not make excuses saying, "It's none of my business." "I am too busy" or "I have an appointment." This was a golden moment, and he took it. All around us are people who need the compassion of Christ. They need us to see their pain as a golden opportunity to serve them in Jesus' name.

So, when people tell us they did not have time, normally it is because we were not important to them at that moment. There was someone or something else more important. Or they forgot, or got caught up in something that was beyond their control. Be careful, do not judge without the truth. This can destroy relationships. The chief enemy to kindness is busyness. We have our priorities, jobs, duties, responsibilities, and we're too busy. But if we're too busy to be kind, that's too busy. Normally, we are busy about the wrong things. We need wisdom and guidance to know what is important, not according to us, but in advancing God's Kingdom. We need the Spirit to show us what is priority.

Life is measured by time. As a result, it is the most precious gift we can give anyone. We all are allotted a certain amount. We can make more clothes, money, etcetera, but we cannot make more time. Consequently, when we give time to someone or something we are giving a part of who we are, a portion of our lives. Once given we can never get it back. Relationships are measured by how much of ourselves we are willing to give. Sorry to say this generation, like most generations before is more into possessions than people. We put them before people, more often than we care to admit. You say you do not, let me ask you, how many genuine friends do you have and when was the last time you took time off from work to help them? Or worst yet, when last did you do this for a family member? I rest my case. I was proud of my daughter, Kenesha who on August 20, 2007, took time off to help a friend finalize her wedding plans.

Balancing Act

We have to work, carryout our duties at home, school, church, community and everywhere else we go. Life then becomes a balancing act. Yet, we are like Martha; we want to be doing rather than listening; to people's pain and anguish, or to Jesus speaking to us however He chooses. Remember what happened when Jesus visited Mary and Martha's home?

> *As Jesus and his disciples were on their way, he came to a village where a woman named Martha opened her home to him. She had a sister called Mary, who sat at the Lord's feet listening to what he said. But Martha was distracted by all the preparations that had to be made. She came to him and asked, "Lord, don't you care that my sister has left me to do the work by myself? Tell her to help me!" "Martha, Martha," the Lord answered, "you are worried and upset about many things, but only one thing is needed. Mary has chosen what is better, and it will not be taken away from her (Luke 10:38-42).*

Martha did not understand the concept of balance. I believe she was a workaholic, easily distracted by doing. There are times when we have to leave the work alone and listen to people. It was time to sit at the feet of Jesus, not prepare a meal. He had the ability to prepare meals. After all, He fed the multitudes miraculously with Manna from heaven and with a little boy's lunch. When we know Jesus, there are some things we do not have to worry about because He will take care of them. We have to know when to do what, and the Spirit will tell us when to listen.

We often major in minors. Because we do not take the time to listen, we do not know what people need. Mary understood what Jesus needed, to be listened too. Martha thought He wanted a meal. We have to learn to listen and tune in to people and find out what is their present need.

Investing Our Time

Regrettably, we were taught to spend most of our adult life investing our time in making money, acquiring assets and bigger and better "toys." The truth is we should be spending more time investing in eternal relationships: Investing more time, getting to know each other. What are his strengths and weaknesses? How does she want to be loved? What does he want out of life? Is it according to what God wants for her? When we can honestly answer these questions then we can begin to think about marriage. I did not know this and so I brought a great deal of baggage to our marriage. I was hoping that I can further hide from myself by focusing on my new wife. Once we can answer the previous questions then the husband and wife will spend a great deal of time getting to know and understand one another. Besides, it will be easier to open up to each other and be honest because we are comfortable and content with who we are.

When the children come along we are better able to handle them, since we are both on the same page, in total agreement, in our understanding, teachings, disciplining, loving, listening and training them to fulfill their God given purposes in life. The children would feel good about themselves because they are learning from us, we are taking time out for them. This will boost their confidence and contentment since the message they get is, they are loved and are very important. Everybody loves to be loved and feel important. When we take time out for people and be present for them mentally, physically, socially, psychologically and even financially, it conveys that they are singular, special, and significant to us.

Many of us think we need more possessions, power, prestige, when what we need is more and deeper relationships. These are what the Kingdom is about. It is expanded and maintained through relationships. If we are going to spend eternity together, it means, we have to invest more time getting to know each other.

Examination Time

How are you investing your time? Most of us grownups devote our time to our jobs, when we get home more work or we take our work home with us. We were taught if we sit around and talk and have fun we are wasting time. We believe we must be working every waking moment or else we are lazy. You cannot even take time for yourself. I remembered when I was pastoring churches I was afraid to let people know I slept in the day, because I felt they would think I was lazy, even though I would do a great deal of my studying, reading, and sermon preparation until two or three a.m. I am a night person.

The bottom line is, it is about making money. Even the youth when they start working that is their motive. I know when I started it was mine. What are we working for? If the truth be told we are working for three basic ingredients necessary for life, they are food, clothing, and shelter. Most of the time that is it! There are those of us working for an inheritance for our grandchildren as the Bible admonishes us to do (Proverbs 13:22). Jesus knowing this, told us do not worry about these things in Matthew 6. I will provide them daily. This is what I want you to concentrate all your energies upon, the Kingdom of God. This does not mean we have to stop working, work is a part of the Kingdom. Jesus and God continue to work (John 5:17). What we have to do is change our motive for working. We should be working to advance His Kingdom. It should not be to make more money, buy bigger or faster cars, or be the envy of our neighbors.

When the Kingdom of God becomes our focus, this will help us get our priorities straight. Whatever we do, will be done to the honor and glory of God (1 Corinthians 10:31). Hence, we are no longer working for our employer but for God. It is only then we will truly find time for God, family, friends, and fellowmen. These are the ones who will be in the Kingdom in the final analysis. Thus, we will not be working ridiculous hours. That is not about advancing the Kingdom, but our or our boss's kingdom. We will find time for God and others because attending church once a week is not enough to deepen or enhance the desire for intimate relationships.

People Oriented

That is why Paul admonished us not to forsake the assembling of ourselves together. We have to take time for fellowship. This helps to enhance relationships. Spending time together, for men it is doing things together, getting to know one another and in the process getting to know God better. I know we all have to work; however, I am a firm believer that if God gave us a ministry to run, the Lord will work it out so that we can. I have heard of too many stories where not only were they able to attend the church services or ministry; they even got a raise in the process. I am not saying that you will. However, God will bless you.

Jesus was not concerned about the things of this world; He could have gotten them whenever He needed them. Like when His taxes were due, He told His disciples to go in the mouth of a fish to get the money. He had access to all that He needed, desired and wanted, because He created everything. His priority was us. We do not understand when we become Jesus' disciple we have access to these resources because we are heirs and joint heirs of Him. In order to access our needs, wants, and desires our emphasis must be the wellbeing of our fellowmen and an intimate relationship or partnership with God. So that our wants, needs, or desires will be in accordance with what He wants for us. Our interest cannot be God and people with the motive to get from them. He promised to supply and He owns everything.

    You Were Made To Worship God 24/7

Needed In All Areas

Just about everything we do in life requires time. There are so many things clamoring for our attention. Hence, the need to know what is important and should take priority.

Learning to Listen

We are normally very good talkers, but poor listeners. One reason, listening involves a great deal of work and time. We are so much in a hurry we don't take time to listen. At times, that is all people want. Most of us are smart enough to figure out our own problems; however, they are not clear to us, since the facts are jumbled up in our minds, we need help. When we get someone to listen, things become clearer. That's because we can dissect the problem into smaller pieces.

You ever had that experience when you talked to someone who really listened and suddenly, it is like a bulb went off in your head and the answer was clear as crystal. You say to yourself, why did not I see this before? This reinforces the fact of how important listening is to relationships and how important relationships are to us. Even though we are aware of this; still, we have not yet learned to listen to one another when we are experiencing difficulty in our lives.

Knowing

We fail to be a student of each other. We want to be teachers and do not understand that before we can teach, we must be students first. This is not just limited to school. Learning never stops, neither in this life nor the one to come. Thus, we have to start learning to be a student of life and people, taking time to know one another. God designed us all differently, we know that intellectually. Yet, we haven't learned to appreciate those differences. We use them to attack each other rather than to unite us together as God intended.

Our differences were intended to complement each other, instead we use them to compete and fight one another. If we learn this simple principle, it will save us a great deal of depression, distress, and despondency. As the saying goes, there is more than one way to skin a cat. We believe that we have the patent on how to do certain things and will not even entertain the idea of doing it another way. With this mind set, we need to understand that our intention is to be in control. We want to be in charge.

One of God's reasons for inventing different ways to do the same thing is to help us to learn from each other. He does not give us a monopoly on anything. Have you ever come up with an idea and you shared it with someone and they added something that you never thought about and made it better? Women are very good at this. When we share with them they incubate it, like they do our sperm and when they give it back to us they turn the idea into something far better than what we gave them. Just like we give them a sperm and they produce an entire baby.

I would get upset with my wife about that, I felt I was stupid. How come I did not think of that? I mean it is so obvious and simple. Now I understand, I am a male, my thinking is focused, we think in a straight line. While women think in a grid. That is why most women can multi task and most men cannot. This is God's way of getting us to depend on one another to be successful in life. That is why we are different. We are not inferior to each other. We were designed to complement. We have so much to learn, therefore, we have to become students of life, and more specifically of people.

What is Important?

We find time for what is important. To know what is, look where you are spending the most of your time. Or better yet look in your checkbook. Where are you spending most of your money you took the time to work so hard for? Do not tell me you do not have control, you made the decisions what you will spend money and time on. You can change those decisions whenever you want.

In Conclusion, we waste a lot of time chasing rainbows. One of the major reasons why we have difficulty with relationships is because we do not know who we are. We are not aware of the gifts God has given us, which are unique and are designed so that we can carry out His purposes. To accomplish these, relationships must be our priority as we minister to the needs of people using the unique gifts God made us with. Let the Spirit guide you.

Chapter 8

An Inevitable Ingredient

CONFLICT BECAME A PART OF OUR EXISTENCE ever since sin entered our world. God knowing this has deposited within us the abilities and capabilities to deal with it. The greatest conflict in the world is the one between God and the Devil and we are caught right in the middle. Consequently, whenever there is more than one person conflict will exist. We are all different, we see, taste, hear, and feel differently. Yet, we have not learned to accept each other's uniqueness. We need to learn to resolve conflicts to have on-going relationships.

Definition

Conflict is a difference of opinion between two or more people. Thing are seen in a different light by others. Competition produces conflict, this occurs naturally between living organisms which co-exist in an environment with limited resources. Like animals compete over water, food, and mates. People compete for education, recognition, and possessions.

In the course of a week, we are all involved in numerous conflicts that need to be dealt with through resolution; these can occur any-where. A conflict or reconciliation situation is one in which there is a conflict of interests, what one wants is not necessarily what the other wants and where both sides prefer to search for solutions, rather than giving in or breaking off contact.

History of Conflict

Heaven

According to the Bible conflict started in heaven (Revelation 12:7-11; Isaiah 14:12-15). Satan wanted to be God. In Isaiah he had an "I disease." Most conflicts arise from the same "I disease." We want to exalt ourselves above others and God. We have within us the innate desire to want to lead. As a result of sin, it has been warped. Yes, it was given by God to be used in dominating the earth (Genesis 1:26-28). Instead, we are using it to dominate each other, this produces conflict. We do not understand the other person's inalienable right given by God, freedom. When anyone tries to take this away from us, there will automatically be conflict.

Earth

The originator of conflict was cast in the earth and ever since that has been his mode of operation, divide and conquer. He started his conflict with God then between Adam and Eve and God. The devil has plunged the entire human race into conflict with God. *"Wherefore, as by one man sin entered into the world, and death by sin; and so death passed upon all men, for that all have sinned" (Romans 5:12).* It continues to mushroom and the conflict between Cain and Abel led to Cain killing his brother. Then, we had the tower of Babel where there was rebellion against God and He had to confound their languages. We have conflicts in families, the nation, and the entire world. We cannot escape them. They teach us about life and how to handle it. We are told how to overcome conflicts; we do so by the blood of the lamb and our testimony (Revelation 12:11). We must be willing to give up our lives for those who are different to us. Just like Jesus did while we were yet sinners He died for us (Romans 8:5).

Today

Peace on earth may not be attainable, but peace within our hearts is a must, if we want to enjoy this life. Few of us enjoy dealing with conflicts. This is particularly true when the conflict becomes hostile and strong feelings are involved. Resolving conflict can be mentally exhausting and emotionally draining. But it is important to realize conflict that requires resolution is neither good nor bad. There can be positive and negative outcomes. It can be destructive or beneficial to our relationship. The important point is to manage the conflict, not suppress it or let it escalate out of control. Many of us seek to avoid conflict when it arises, but we should use it for creativity and motivation.

We will be constantly negotiating and resolving conflict all through life. With organizations becoming less hierarchical, less based on positional authority, clear boundaries of responsibility and authority: It is likely that conflict will be an even greater component of organizations in the future. Studies have shown that negotiation or resolution skills are among the most significant determinants of career success. The Bible has the information on conflict resolution. Even though resolution is an art form to some degree, there are specific techniques in the Bible that anyone can learn with the aid of the Spirit. Grasping these techniques and developing our skills will be a critical component of our career and personal success.

Reasons for Conflict

Selfishness

Most of what we do is out of selfishness, we think of ourselves more than we think about God or others. Paul tells us, *"For all seek their own, not the things which are Jesus Christ's"* (Philippians 2:21). The Psalmist puts it this way,

> *Wickedness is part of man's nature from the time he is born. His inclinations are toward self when he comes from his mother's womb. He can tell lies and do wrong from birth. Man has been bitten by the serpent, and his body is full of the poison of sin. In turn, he bites and poisons others; his instincts are as deaf to reason as snakes who cannot hear. A snake charmer can't reason with his cobra when it rears its head to strike; no magician can make it go contrary to its nature (Psalm 58:3-5 TCW).*

Lack of Respect

This is tied in to selfishness, a lack of respect for each other. We see ourselves as superior to others, we can do things better, accomplish more. We have a superiority complex. We are taught this by our parents, teachers, pastors, politicians, community, and church leaders. Be all that you can be is good. But, what about the other person being all he can be? How much am I willing to help my neighbor to become all she can be? If it interferes with my becoming all I can be then there is conflict. We live in conflict daily. We need to learn how to handle it, if we want to enjoy our friendships and be our brother's keeper.

Previous Decisions

Life really boils down to making the right decisions. In order to do that, we need the wisdom of God. A knowledge of God that ties our past with our present and future (2 Peter 1:9). Our decision making sometimes creates conflict. Can you think of any decisions you have made that are still creating conflict today?

As a result of the decision I made in 1992 to Pastor Sheffield Congregational Advent Church, I am not accepted as a legitimate Pastor of the Seventh-day Adventist Church. But, I cherish those years; I learned so much from that experience and have made lasting friends as a result. I would not trade them for anything.

The Bible is filled with decisions that are even having serious repercussions today and the one that comes to mind first is Abraham, Sarah, and Hagar. That fight is still being carried out in the Middle East today. Other examples of bad decisions some that almost and others that led to death:

Jacob and Rachael
Jacob and Joseph
David and Bathsheba
Paul and Stephen
Paul and Barnabas
Paul and Peter
Peter and Jesus
The religious leaders and Jesus

We have to be careful with the decisions we make daily because they are impacting people's lives for good or for evil.

Different Conflicts

All of us engage in many conflict resolutions during a week but that does not mean we become better at it. To become better, we need to be aware of the structure and dynamics of negotiation and to think systematically, objectively, and critically about our own method of bringing about reconciliation. When we are engaged in resolutions, we need to reflect on what happened and figure out what we did effectively and improve. In what area of conflict do we

need more help? Because conflicts can exist at a variety of levels
and areas of our lives:

intrapersonal conflict
interpersonal conflict
emotional conflict
group conflict
organizational conflict
community conflict
international conflict
environmental resources conflict
inter-societal conflict
intra-societal conflict
ideological conflict
diplomatic conflict
economic conflict
military conflict
religious-based conflict

To be effective in handling conflict, we need to know its source.
The more difficult type of conflict is when values are the root cause.
A conflict over facts, or assumptions, will be resolved quicker than
one over values. It is extremely difficult to "prove" that a value is
"right" or "correct".

Handling Conflict

God knowing that we will have to deal with conflict has not left us
in the dark. Jesus gave us the model. What I find is that companies
are taking the same concepts and utilizing them and they work,
because they are given by God.

> *"Moreover if thy brother shall trespass against thee, go and tell
> him his fault between thee and him alone: if he shall hear thee,
> thou hast gained thy brother. But if he will not hear thee, then*

     You Were Made To Worship God 24/7

This, to me, is one of the most challenging areas of a disciple's life. It is so tough that many of us are afraid to follow God's method. What makes it even more taxing is that conflicts are emotionally defined and driven. We are afraid of anything that is emotionally charged and do everything to get around it. This is even further complicated because it says we should approach the person who has wronged us. Many of us wait for the person to come to us, since they are the ones at fault. No, God is saying go to the person and that is contrary to our nature. It is easier to deal with people in a group than one on one. It takes more guts to tell off a person in private than it is to do in public, especially if the person is repentant.

To add to the challenge, conflict is an ongoing process that occurs against a backdrop of continuing relationships and events; we have to do it often and at times with the same people. So if we are going to resolve conflicts, hard work is involved. It requires the thoughts, perceptions, memories, and emotions of us and the persons involved. We have to consider the other person. That in itself is too much for us because we do not think for ourselves. That too is hard work.

Furthermore, perceptions are more powerful than reality and we have to take that into consideration. Some memories are negative and we do not want to revisit them. Our emotions get out of control sometimes. Yet, all these need to be addressed within ourselves and with those we have conflict.

It is impossible to avoid conflicts, thus we need to learn how to handle them and bring about reconciliation. It is always good to have a plan in place to help prevent conflicts and to deal with them when they do come up. Let's look at some steps to take in handling conflicts before, during and after.

BEFORE

STOP—Learn how to control your emotions, so that during a conflict you can stop before you lose control of them and make the conflict worse. Ask yourself some tough questions:

- How comfortable am I about the conflict?
- How do I see the other person who wronged me?
- What assumptions have I made about the person?
- How much do I trust them?
- How important is it for me to avoid conflict?
- How much do I like or dislike the other person?
- How important is it not to look stupid?
- How important winning is for me?

These will help to clarify the direction you should go if you answer them truthfully. This is sometimes difficult because you are emotionally charged and are only seeing it from a substantive or rational prospective and not an emotional or psychological one. But, to be successful you need to combine both. Since the psychological is more challenging, asking yourself these questions will help.

START to deal with it immediately, the longer you stay and dwell on it the angrier you become over the conflict. Then you will find more reasons why the person is wrong and the need for them to come to you rather than you going to them. Communication breaks down when we do not take action. Often we just hope things will just go away. But waiting only intensifies problems. By taking effective action quickly, you can ensure that the situation does not get worse. This keeps the line of communication open and miscommunication is reduced. When conflict arises as the Bible points out, go to the person first, so that you will not be tempted to share it with others to get them siding with you. This gives you more ammunition to prove you are right and you begin to dig your heals in. You see the other person as wrong and he/she has to come to you for forgiveness because it is his/her fault.

SOLUTIONS—Begin to think of solutions that will satisfy both of you. There is no one "best" style; we need to find a style that is comfortable for us. Yet, we can negotiate successfully; everyone can reach agreements where all sides feel that some of their needs have been satisfied. This involves a lot of alertness, active listening, good communication skills, great flexibility, good preparation, and above all, a sharing of responsibility for solving the problem, not a view that this is "their" problem.

STANDARD—You must have an objective standard and the best one is the Bible. Make your negotiated decisions based on it, not your emotions; try to find objective criteria that both parties can use to evaluate alternatives; do not succumb to emotional pleasing, assertiveness, or stubbornness.

Based on the thoughts and emotions that arise in the process of conflict resolution, formulate specific intentions about the strategies we will use in the negotiation. These may be quite general. For example, the Bible tells us how to handle it on the personal level

(Matthew 18) and this same principle can be taken in dealing with conflict anywhere.

SOLUTION—Before the negotiations, it is helpful to plan. We need to be aware if we are in a win-win or win-lose situation. The key to successful reconciliation is to shift it to a "win-win" even if it looks like a "win-lose" one. Almost all negotiations have at least some elements of win-win. Successful discussions often depend on finding the win-win in any situation. Only shift to a win-lose mode if all else fails.

We need to be sure of our goals, positions, underlying interests and communicate why they are important. Try to figure out the best resolution we can expect, what is a fair, reasonable and is a minimally acceptable deal. What information do we have and need. We must give some thought to our strategy. It is very important to be clear on what are our real goals and issues and what's important to us. Try to figure out these for the other person as well. Many negotiations fail because we are so worried about being taken advantage of that we forget our needs. When we lose track of our own goals we will break off negotiations even if our needs were met, since we become more concerned with whether the other side "won."

To be successful in reconciliation it is important that everybody wins. The objective is agreement not victory. We have to know how we stand on these two issues. How important or unimportant is it to satisfy our needs? And how important or unimportant is it to satisfy other's needs?

You must figure out what is the best alternative if you do not get what you want in the reconciliation. We have to remember that the other party involved sees, hears, feels, and experiences things differently. We are used to identifying our own interests, but a critical element in negotiation is to understand the other person's underlying interests and needs.

     You Were Made To Worship God 24/7

A key part in finding common interests is problem identification. It must be defined in a way that is mutually acceptable to both sides. How? Depersonalizing it reduces the other person's defensiveness. Thus, the student negotiating a problem with a professor will be more effective by defining the problem as "I need to understand this material better" or "I do not understand this" rather than "You're not teaching the material very well."

SITUATION—There is a tendency to think about conflict or the negotiating situation as an isolated incident. It is more useful to think about it as a process, or a complex series of events over time involving both external and internal psychological and social factors. Conflicts typically are affected by preceding incidents and in turn produce results and outcomes that affect the conflict dynamics.

Next, once aware of the conflict, both parties experience emotional reactions to it and think about it differently. These emotions and thoughts are crucial to the course of the developing conflict. For example, a negotiation can be greatly affected if people react in anger because of past conflict.

DURING

START with a positive approach: Try to establish rapport and mutual trust before starting; go for a small concession early. Do not place too much emphasis on initial offers. These are normally points of departure; they tend to be extreme and idealistic. Focus on the other person's interests and your own goals and principles, while you think of other possibilities or those you may have already thought about.

SEPARATE—Learn to separate people from problems. Notice what the Bible says, *"Go and tell him his fault,"* it did not say to tell him what a bad person he is, but talk about the fault. That is another reason why the Bible tells us, confess our faults one to another (James 5:16). It is about the problem not the person. We all have faults. It is critical to address problems, not personalities and avoid the tendency to attack our opponent personally. Here is why, when we feel threatened, we defend ourselves. We are backing the person in a corner; anytime we feel trapped we come out swinging. We will defend ourselves at any cost. So, we cannot get to the problem since we have created another problem. Thus, even though they allowed us into their house, they will not let us in their hearts.

However, if your opponent attacks you personally, try to maintain a rational, goal oriented frame of mind: do not let him hook you into an emotional reaction. Let the other blow off steam without taking it personally; try to understand the problem behind the aggression. Make sure you send signals that you know what the conflict and issues are about and not make it personal. This helps prevent the other person from getting defensive.

SKILLS—Use Active Listening Skills; rephrase, ask questions, let them see, hear, and understand that you accept the other as an equal. Show respect and their right to differ from you. Be receptive. Spend more time listening and make direct eye contact.

SIGNIFY—that the conflict does exist.

SUBTLE NO—Many studies support the view that how we approach a negotiation will play a key role in how it proceeds. We have a much better chance of coming to an outcome involving mutual gains if we approach the negotiation wanting to reach this kind of outcome. It is critical to constantly reinforce our interest in the other side's concerns and our determination to find a mutually satisfactory resolution. We all have sinned and are coming short of God's glory (Romans 3:23).

SAY—What you feel is the problem. What is causing the disagreement? What do you want? Do this face to face. Avoid as much as possible using the phone, e-mail, and other non-visual communication vehicles. A lack of facial expressions, vocal intonation, and other cues can result in a negotiation breakdown. Constantly reiterate your interest in the concerns of the other side and your determination to find a mutually satisfactory resolution.

STAY TUNED—Listen to the other person's ideas and feelings. Do unto others as you would have them do unto you. Remember we all have a story, the person listened to yours out of respect, now listen to theirs.

SITUATIONS—Sometimes conflicts escalate, the atmosphere becomes charged with anger, frustration, resentment, mistrust, hostility, and a sense of futility. Communication channels close down and we begin to criticize and blame the other person. We focus on our next assault. The original issues become blurred and ill-defined and new issues are added as the conflict becomes personalized. Even if we are willing to make concessions often hostility prevents agreements. In such a conflict, our perceived differences become magnified, we get locked into our initial positions and we resort to lies, threats, distortions, and other attempts to force the other person to comply with our demands. It's not easy to shift this situation to a win-win. Nevertheless here are some suggestions:

- Try some humor in context to reduce the tension.
- Let them "vent," admit their views, agree where you can.
- Listen actively, rephrase, and mirror the one speaking, use eye contact, lean forward.
- Control issues by searching for ways to slice the large issue into smaller pieces.
- Depersonalize it—separate the issues from the person.

- Seek for common ground and enemies: conflict magnifies perceived differences.
- Focus more on a clear understanding of the other's needs and less on your position and figure out ways to move toward them.
- Emphasize the positives.
- Find a legitimate or objective criterion to evaluate the solution (e.g. the Bible).
- Have a strategy; anticipate how the other will respond; how strong is your position, and situation; how important is the issue; how important will it be to stick to a hardened position? You may be right but unhappy.

AFTER

In most conflict resolution or negotiation situations you will have a continuing relationship with the other person so it is important to leave the situation with both sides feeling they have "won." It is very important that the other person does not feel that he or she "lost." When the other person loses, the results are often lack of commitment to the agreement or even worse, retaliation.

SOMEONE—If we still cannot agree, we need to ask someone else to help us work it out. It must be someone both parties trust and respect. Or else that will develop another conflict and take away from the original one. The place and time must be agreed upon and clearly communicated. The one chosen for the resolution of the conflict must:

- Avoid taking sides and shun the appearance of favoritism.
- Instead admit the conflict and have both parties come up with joint solutions.
- If one has threatened another physically, immediate action should be taken. There are some conflicts where the only

    You Were Made To Worship God 24/7

resolution is removing the person out of your life, church, or place of employment. Report treats to the authorities.

The Advantages of Conflicts

Conflicts help to enhance our fellowship, and it restores harmony. However, our fellowship is taken to another level. We become more intimate or closer to one another. Because healing has taken place we begin to experience growth and maturity in our walk with God and our fellowmen. Those of us who have experienced genuine reconciliation can confirm this. It is one of those things in life that one has to experience in order to understand and enjoy the full impact. It is a joy that is unspeakable and full of glory.

The Originator of Conflict has designed our conflicts for evil, like John 10:10 says he comes to steal, kill, and destroy. His intentions are to obliterate, annihilate, and devastate us in the process. However, God takes all his evil intentions and works them out, turn them around for our good (Romans 8:28). This helps us to trust and depend even more upon the Lord.

In some cases He produces multiplication out of the Enemy's conflict. For example Paul and Barnabas could not agree on whether they should take John Mark on their second missionary journey. In their first journey John Mark turned back and went home, it was a little too rough for him. Well Paul thought they should not take him again. Barnabas thought they should. Unable to resolve the conflict, Paul went with Silas and Barnabas with John Mark. They were able to cover twice as much ground as a result (Act 15:36-40). Later they reconciled and became the best of friends.

Since our lives consist of conflicts at every level and every day it behooves us to learn how to handle them: If we want to have friends and develop everlasting friendships.

Chapter 9

A Powerful Ingredient

One of the single most effective ways to develop or improve rela-tionships is by listening. I believe that is the reason why God gave us two ears and one mouth. Listening is one of the most powerful forces in the universe. People are drawn to those who listen. That is why the Bible admonishes us, "My *dear brothers, take note of this: Everyone should be quick to listen, slow to speak and slow to become angry" (James 1:19)*. Notice, there are no exceptions to this rule. If we want to develop relationships we must do it God's way and learn to listen more than we speak.

Burning Desire

There is within each of us a desire to want to be heard. When a group of people get together, everyone is trying to tell their story. Each wants to be heard and awaiting their opportunity to speak. Hence, they are not listening to the person that is speaking. The desire to be heard is an intense yearning. It is a part of who we are. Stop and think for a moment, this can be a fantastic thing if every-one got their chance to speak. So, we have to take turns listening to each other. In order for this to happen we must make a con-scious effort to listen. At times we have to literally tell ourselves, "I will listen to my spouse, child, or friend for the next x number of minutes." Give them your undivided attention, determined not just to hear what they say, but listen intensely.

Our nature is we want to talk rather than listen. So when we get together, everybody is trying to speak at the same time. Even if we have to interrupt, make fun of or change the subject of the one speaking. We will do everything in our power to get others to listen. People want to tell us what is wrong in their lives if they believe we will listen to what they have to say and not judge them.

Great Hindrance

One of our greatest hindrances to relationships is the inability to listen. We normally hear but we do not understand because we are not listening. We all have a story and we want someone to listen to us, but, we are not willing to listen to others. However, nobody is listening to anybody, and we are reaping what we have sown. We are not listening to others, and others are not listening to us. We are competing to get our stories heard. That's one reason why I am writing, I want others to hear what I have to say.

Our nature does not help either. We are a very self-centered, self-seeking, and selfish and so preoccupied with ourselves that we cannot see other's needs. That's why God told us, *"Look not every man on his own things, but every man also on the things of others" (Philippians 2:4)*. **W**e have become so focused on our own story we fail to realize that those we are talking to, have their story and want to be heard. But we are so much into ourselves we do not notice. In Philippians 2, Paul says, forget yourself and your needs and meet the needs of others around you. If we follow this principle, in the process, our needs are miraculously met.

We are too anxious to give advice, rather than listen to people who will normally come up with their own solutions to their problems. What happens to us is that there is too much going on in our heads at the same time. All we need is someone we can tell our story to. One who will listen intensely and we know they are listening. This loosens the grip our problems have on us because we are now dealing with it. Furthermore, we are dealing with it in pieces, not the whole, and so we are not overwhelmed. Also, we can think more clearly and it is easier to come up with our own solutions with a clearer mind.

It's Importance

Next to breathing, listening is one of the most prominent activities in our lives. One would think we would be better at it. This is not surprising because the activity of breathing that we do more than anything else, we do not do well either. The things that should be simple we do not do well: Like forgiveness, listening, relating to one another, loving one another. So, most of us choose to be poor listeners. Research indicates the average person forgets 50 percent of what they hear within seconds of a conversation. In two days, we lose 75 percent and a week after we forget over 90 percent of what was discussed. This occurs because we allow many barriers to be erected that interfere with our listening on a regular basis. Here are some:

- We want others to listen to our story.
- Our perception of the speaker or his topic, if we do not like either we will have difficulty listening.
- Being able to think five times faster than the person speaking—leads to impatience.
- Distracted by noises—internal, like thinking on something else, rushing; External, other conversations going on close to us, the TV; Emotional, such as some words used arouse strong feelings within us.

These and other barriers affect our ability to hear the other person clearly. So, we have to make a conscious effort to listen. We must avoid emotional involvement while we are listening. This causes us to hear what we want to hear—not what the person is actually saying. We have to try and remain objective and open-minded. We must learn to avoid distractions to be good listeners. Unfortunately, our world is full of them. We must learn to be present mentally, emotionally, and physically. We cannot allow our minds to be distracted. This must be done consciously and requires a great deal of work, but, the benefits are enormous.

The Quickest Way

Since listening is so important, one of the quickest and best ways to develop relationships is by listening. The best way to love and be loved is through the inspired process of listening, one of the most powerful forces in the universe. People are gripped by people who listen. Not just pretending they are, but can enter into the process with you.

Because we all have our stories to tell no one wants to listen, all we need to do is start listening to others. Give them as much time as they need, because eventually their story will come to an end. The person will now have no other choice than to listen to your story.

Difficulties

Sometimes you will find that some people have difficulty telling their story. Some repeat themselves often. Others are slow of speech, be patient. The reward is they will eventually listen to you. We have to take turns listening to each other, if we want others to hear our story. It is only when we have listened that people are ready to tell us what their needs are.

   You Were Made To Worship God 24/7

Another difficulty, the story is not always the real story at first. People test us with information. They will give a little of the story to see our reaction. Depending upon how we react will determine if they continue. We cannot be thinking this will take too much time, or I am not qualified to handle this situation. Sure there will be some you cannot handle. These however are few and far between, the Spirit of God will reveal to us when we encounter them. He will also tell us who to refer them to.

Learn to Listen

I am convinced that one of the most profound ways of showing love is lovingly listening. We can only help people after we have listened. Unless we listen, we cannot know anybody, including our children. True we know facts and statistics about them. We do not spend time listening to our children, spouses, friends, co-workers and last, but most important those who hate us. We should give a listening ear to all. We take a lot of things for granted and do not challenge ourselves, the status quo, the accepted norms of society.

It is one of the most powerful forces in the universe, a magnetic and dynamic force. Without listening we are unable to know people. This can be first hand information from the person, listening to someone telling us or we read about them, even then we have to listen to what we are reading.

It is Simple

The good news is that listening is not as difficult as we make. I did not say it is easy, it is simple. Unfortunately, the simplicity gets obscured by the stressors of life which continues to pile up and are not resolved. When we are having difficulty in life, it seems impossible to take time to listen to others who are experiencing difficulties.

However, we need to learn to leave our world and enter the world of others.

Always remember that effective listening is a two way street. The first is, listening involves understanding the message being sent by the one speaking as they want us to hear it. The second, and the one most neglected, is that effective listening involves feedback from the listener to demonstrate that he heard the message as it was intended by the speaker. This requires a four letter word that many of us have come to despise, work. If it is within our power, make sure the environment is conducive for communicating, that is to say no one is in a hurry, if so wait, if possible. Develop the ability to have tunnel vision; mentally put on blinders like they physically put on horses, in other words, let the speaker be your focus. Look at the nonverbal queues, like clenched fists, facial expressions, raised eyebrows, these speak louder than what you are hearing. Be an active listener; give feedback to make sure you understand what the speaker is saying.

Our Example

Be patient and allow them to tell their story. Be like Jesus, remember the woman with the issue of blood. He was on His way to Jarius' house to heal his daughter when this woman touched Jesus garment. Before this took place He gave Jarius His undivided attention and was on His way to his house. But, He was interrupted by one of His daughters and He gave her His complete attention, this is how the Bible puts it, *"But the woman fearing and trembling, knowing what was done in her, came and fell down before him, and told him all the truth."* What was the truth? *"And a certain woman, which had an issue of blood twelve years, And had suffered many things and saw several different physicians, and had spent all that she had, and was nothing bettered, but rather grew worse"* (Mark 5:33, 25-26).

The truth was she told Jesus twelve years of history. It took so long that while she was speaking one of Jarius' servants came and told him not to bother Jesus because his daughter was dead. Jesus gave him comfort and told him do not worry, his daughter is fine. He had not forgotten Jarius. He gave her His full attention and she told Him everything. She wanted someone to listen to her story and Jesus did: Even after she was healed. Do not miss that. After our miracles, we still need someone to relate to.

Listen to God

You know it hit me one day, suppose God would do to us what we do to Him and others. He wants to tell us His story and we would not listen. We are not just quick to speak to others; we do the same to God. How many times have we before, while or after praying take some time to listen to Him speak to us? In our prayers we are asking God to respond to our cries, pleas, and biddings. How much time do we spend listening? The Israelites did the same thing and this is what He did to them, *"Therefore thus saith the LORD God of hosts, the God of Israel; Behold, I will bring upon Judah and upon all the inhabitants of Jerusalem all the evil that I have pronounced against them: because I have spoken unto them, but they have not heard; and I have called unto them, but they have not answered"* (Jeremiah 35:17).

God does not ask us to do something that He does not practice. He listens very well, here is a promise, *"And it shall come to pass, that before they call, I will answer; and while they are yet speaking, I will hear"* (Isaiah 65:24). Now you know someone is listening if they answer correctly before we call all the time. We have no doubt they will hear what we have to say. You know the Spirit can give us this same ability, that before people call us we can answer them and listen to what they have to say.

Qualities Needed

We all are experiencing troubles, torments, tribulations, trials and other negative contradictions in our lives. Once we are aware and accept this, we can help one another. How? By utilizing certain qualities when we listen. These will be challenging at first because they are unfamiliar, but they can transform our lives and those around us if we utilize them. The good news is that these qualities are already in us, we just have to utilize them. Peter the outspoken one said in 2 Peter 1:3, 8, *"According as his divine power hath given unto us **all things** that pertain unto life and godliness, through the knowledge of him that hath called us to glory and virtue: For if these things be **in you**, and abound, they make you that ye shall neither be barren nor unfruitful in the knowledge of our Lord Jesus Christ"* [Emphasis supplied]. God has already deposited in us all that we need to be effective listeners.

Love

The first quality in listening is love. If we have agape love for the person we are listening to they will tell us their real story. Jesus, *"By this shall all men know that you are my disciples, if you have love one to another"* (John 13:35). When we love the person we are listening to, they will experience it. Then that person will open up like they never did before, the real person will come through and you will find yourself falling in love with them. This is very good. Do not panic! Just be careful, do not be afraid to fall in love. I am not talking about romance or marriage. Love the way Jesus loves them, with our mind, body, and soul, willing to lay down our life for them. We have a great deal of pent up love within us, let it out and a good way to is listening to others

Acceptance

This quality contradicts what the person is experiencing at the moment. They have difficulty accepting themselves because of what is occurring within. They need acceptance now more than any other time, especially if they are hurt and are looked down upon or they are blamed for what is happening. We can convey to them that we accept them even in their distress. Yes it is hard, however, it is made easier if we put ourselves in their shoes and respond to them as we would want others to respond to us. Remember how it felt when someone accepted you when you were down and depressed. You snapped out of your depression.

That is the way Jesus looks at us when we sin. He does not condemn us, remember the woman caught in adultery in John 8. He said to her, neither do I condemn you, go and sin no more. Jesus had all the rights in the world to look down upon her because she was a sinner an adulterer. He was holy and sinless, yet, he accepted her as she was. Sometimes this is all it takes to turn people's lives around, acceptance.

Respect

Lack of respect is the number one problem in our society and a great barrier to listening. This quality has been lost. Disrespect lies at the root of the many societal ills. It is at the heart of all oppression. Slavery is as a result of the lack of respect for another ethnic group. Women abuse comes from disrespect for women. Racism is a lack of respect for people of a different ethnic background. Religious hatred is a lack of respect of another person's belief. Regrettably, we do not respect and many do not know how to respect others. How can we even have respect for others when we do not have respect for ourselves?

How do we show respect to people? By hanging on to every word the person is saying. Demonstrating that what the person is experiencing or experienced is worthy of our full attention. We normally listen to people we respect and even more so to people who respect us. Could you imagine what would happen if we would only show respect to others, they would listen to us.

It is impossible to truly listen to someone if we do not respect them. God respects us so much that He listens. Also, He has given us freedom of choice. We can choose to do what we want and when He wants. Of course, there are consequences; however, we choose and He respects our choice.

Humility

Humility is not a natural part of our nature. Our desire is to rule over our fellowmen. It is innate, given to us at creation (Genesis 1:26-28). Jesus has demonstrated to us the more He has entrusted us with the greater should be our humility. He who was in the form of God gave it all up. He came to minister rather than to be ministered unto (Matthew 20:28).

Genuine Concern

We are more concerned about policies than people. We are quick to condemn those who are not following the law. Yes we all should be obedient to the laws; however, everybody who breaks the law is not doing so deliberately. We need to listen before we can condemn them. We have some classic examples in the Bible. In Luke 6:1-2 we read, *"And it came to pass on the second Sabbath after the first, that he went through the corn fields; and his disciples plucked the ears of corn, and did eat, rubbing them in their hands. And certain of the Pharisees said unto them, Why do ye that which is not lawful to do on the Sabbath days?*

They were hungry, ministering with Jesus all week and did not have time to prepare their Sabbath meal. They ate on the run. Instead of finding out the reason and seeing what they could do to help the disciples they condemned them. They were not concerned about them; they were concerned about the law.

Again in verses 6-7, *"And it came to pass also on another Sabbath, that he entered into the synagogue and taught: and there was a man whose right hand was withered. And the Scribes and Pharisees watched him, whether he would heal on the Sabbath day; that they might find an accusation against him."* Their concern was not the sick man being healed, they were not happy to know that they had Jesus in their midst who could take care of their sick. No, their biggest problem was that it was the Sabbath. They did not understand they were speaking to the One created the Sabbath thus He needed to show them how to keep it. He was doing that by healing the sick man. Instead, they planned how they would kill Jesus for what He had done.

Tranquility

In order to listen, learn tranquility, live in the present a part of the time every day. Sometimes ask yourself: "What is happening now? This friend is talking. I am quiet. There is endless time. I hear every word." Then suddenly you begin to hear not only what they are saying, also what they are trying to say, and you sense the whole truth. You acknowledge the person's existence, not just their story, but you see the person as a transparent whole.

Then watch your self-assertiveness. And give it up. Remember, it is not enough just to will to listen to people. One must really listen. Only then does the magic begin.

These may be hard to adopt at first. As you examine them carefully, is this not the way you wish people would treat you? If we can just practice, doing unto others as we would have them do unto us. You will find that people will begin doing to us the same things. The saying is true, we reap what we sow. If we implement these qualities found within, it will help bring us out of the depressions we find ourselves in. We will become more attractive to people and they will seek out our presence. These qualities for helping to heal relationships are universal. We are all human beings. The cultural differences are interesting and rich, but any *divisions* between us on the basis of culture are unjustified.

Why Listen

Listening is an art that when done well, delivers tremendous benefits. The goal of listening well is to achieve win-win communication. This not only fosters understanding, validation, affirmation, and appreciation, but it also creates an atmosphere of trust, honor and respect. When someone truly listens to you, do not you feel special? Someone who listens well easily establishes rapport. Good listeners attract others because they focus on the speaker completely. Their positive energy makes you want to be around them. They are effective in their jobs because, by listening and asking the appropriate questions, they know exactly what needs to be done and how to do it.

Brings Clarity

Under normal circumstances we have the ability that God has put within us to come up with answers to our problems. But, we encounter stressors, some of which are emotionally or physically painful. Like the death of a love one, loss of a job, divorce, sudden deadly illness etcetera. This interrupts our ability to sort out the information coming in and solve our dilemmas. We become confused, we are not able to compare and contrast it with previous experiences. Thus it is not stored in its proper place in our minds.

It is like a footnote there. However, we want to know more than just the foot note, we want to read the entire reference real badly.

The unknown becomes our focus and it is impossible to get it out of our minds. We cannot think clearly, we begin to act out, since we are obsessed with wanting to know more. In the process more footnotes are added and they begin to pile up one upon the other. When people listen it brings about clarity, not just to the listener, but also to the speaker.

A Creative Force

When we are listened to, it recreates us, makes us unfold and expand. Ideas actually begin to grow within us and come to life. I can testify of that when people really listen to me, I say some things I never said or wrote before. It is powerful. That is why whatever I am writing on I talk to anyone who is willing to listen. It is like when people laugh at your jokes you become funnier, and if they do not, every tiny little joke in you begins to dry up. When people listen it makes us happy and free. And if you are a listener, it is the secret of having a good time in society (because everybody around you becomes lively and interesting), of comforting people, of doing them good. When we listen to people there is an alternating current that recharges us so we never get tired of each other. We are constantly being re-created.

Listening draws people to us. Who are the people, for example, to whom you go for advice? Not to the hard, practical ones who can tell you exactly what to do, but to the listeners; that is, the kindest, least censorious, least bossy people you know. It is because by pouring out your problem to them; you then know what to do about it yourself.

Now, there are brilliant people who cannot listen much. They have no ingoing wires on their apparatus. They are entertaining, but exhausting too. I think it is because these lecturers, these brilliant performers, by not giving us a chance to talk, do not let this little creative fountain inside us begin to spring, cast up new thoughts, unexpected laughter and wisdom. That is why, when someone has listened to you, you go home rested and lighthearted.

Flowing of Creative Force

Now this little creative ability is in us all. If we are very tired, strained, have no solitude, run too many errands, talk to too many people, eat or drink too much, this ability is clouded. The result is we stop living from within and we begin living from without. That is, we go along on mere willpower without imagination.

When people listen to us, with quiet, fascinated attention the creative ability begins to work again, to accelerate in the most surprising way. I notice people are attracted to me not when I want to be the center of attention. People seek me out when I decide to deliberately listen. They are drawn like a magnet. This is not that easy for me, because I always have an opinion and something to say. But it is not about me.

CONCLUSION: Listening is harder than you think. Creative listeners are those who want you to be recklessly yourself, even at your very worst, even insulting, bad-tempered. They are laughing and just delighted with any manifestation of yourself bad or good. For true listeners know that if you are bad-tempered it does not mean that you are always so. They do not love you just when you are nice; they love all of you all the time.

We should all know this: that listening, not talking, is the gifted, great and the imaginative role. And the true listener is much more beloved, magnetic than the talker, and he is more effective, learns more and does more good. So try listening. Listen to the people God placed and is placing in your life, those who love you, who do not, who bore you, and your enemies. It will work a small or even a great miracle.

Chapter 10

An Unavoidable Ingredient

WHEN WE HAVE LISTENED this unavoidable ingredient kicks in. God created us with the ability to connect with people at a deep, intimate level as we develop relationships that will last through out eternity. It is called Bonding. This is a basic human need. We were made by God for relationships and we are by nature relational beings. Without solid bonding with God and others we encounter many and varied physical, psychological, and emotional problems. We cannot prosper without these deep connections.

Too often we limit our needs to just spiritual, financial, and physical. We leave out the emotional and psychological. We need others in our lives in these times. Do you have anyone you can be your real self with?

What is Bonding?

It is the ability to connect emotionally to another person. This attachment is so strong that we can relate to each other at the deepest level possible. I am not talking about marriage even though it is included. When two people have a bond, they share who they are with the other person, their deepest thoughts, hopes, dreams, feelings, fears, with no dread of being rejected. This type of bond existed between Jonathan and David (1 Samuel 18:3). Our greatest fear and why we have difficulty bonding is the fear of rejection.

The Bible and Bonding

The Psalmist and Jeremiah tell us that we are like a tree planted by rivers of water (Jeremiah 17:8, Psalm 1:3). Trees like all living organisms are interdependent. Notice how plants grow. They are connected to things outside of themselves. They need the soil, sun, rain, air, and other ingredients to grow and be healthy. The leaves are connected to the stem and the stem is connected to the trunk which is connected to the roots, which are buried in the ground from which water and nutrients are extracted for growth. The leaves trap the sunlight and turn the radiant energy into chemical energy which helps in the growth and the production of fruits. The most powerful passage on bonding is a tree analogy,

> *I am the true vine, and my Father is the gardener. He cuts off every branch in me that bears no fruit, while every branch that does bear fruit he prunes so that it will be even more fruitful… Remain in me, and I will remain in you. No branch can bear fruit by itself; it must remain in the vine. Neither can you bear fruit unless you remain in me. "I am the vine; you are the branches. If a man remains in me and I in him, he will bear much fruit; apart from me you can do nothing. If anyone does not remain in me, he is like a branch that is thrown away and withers; such branches are picked up, thrown into the fire and burned. If you remain in me and my words remain in you, ask whatever you wish, and it will be given you. This is to my Father's glory, that you bear much fruit, showing yourselves to be my disciples (John 15:1-8 NIV).*

We are the branches and we cannot survive alone. Life is about interconnections, there is a connection that exists between God and all of creation. Being a relational being, He created a relational universe, that is to say everything relates to everything else. We are no exceptions. Notice one of the ways we glorify God and show we are disciples like the branches, we are fruitful. We are interconnected. It does not matter how great our accomplishments, wealth, or popularity unless we are bonded to God and each other, we will suffer physically, psychologically, socially, financially mentally, and every other ally. Many times we are misdiagnosed because the cause of our illnesses, addictions, depressions and other ailments are as a direct result of not being able to bond.

Another analogy is the body, 1 Corinthians 12. Even though there are several different parts they cannot operate independently. The body is one, and operates as such. It needs resources from the outside and inside to function and stay alive. Similarly, we cannot be our true selves without being connected and bonded to others and everything else.

It's Importance

Since relationships or bonding is the foundation of God's nature and we are created like Him, then bonding is one of our most fundamental needs. The essence of who we are. Without relationships, that is bonding to God and our fellowmen we cannot be who we really are. We cease to be human beings. As John says in chapter 15, if we are cut off from the vine, if there is no sunlight, water, or oxygen the branches will die. Similarly, we begin to die when we are not connected to God and other human beings. If we want to live to our fullest potential, we must be rooted and grounded in love. We must draw from God and each other, just like the vine, we being the branches we have to share and be intimate with each other. The bond has to be similar to the branches of the vine. Like the tree we have to learn to give and receive. If we want to bear fruits in our lives, like Jesus commands we cannot do it by ourselves, it must be with God, others, and ourselves. We cannot grow in isolation.

When we are bonded to God and our fellowmen we have compassion one for another. Stress is easier to handle, suicide is not an option. Our accomplishments have greater meaning and a different focus. Our accomplishments are seen as greater responsibilities to minister with God and each other. That is, our motive is helping others. It is not with the objective to hoard or try to hide who we really are.

Reconciliation

God saw this as being so important that when Adam and Eve severed the bond that existed between them, they were thrust into isolation. They began to die like a branch detached from the tree. They were alienated from God and each other. From then until now, this has been our greatest predicament. It was and is so bad we had to be reconciled to God and each other. Listen to Paul,

> *For God was pleased to have all his fullness dwell in him, and through him to* **reconcile** *to himself all things, whether things on earth or things in heaven, by making peace through his blood, shed on the cross. Once you were alienated from God and were enemies in your minds because of your evil behavior. But now he has* **reconciled** *you by Christ's physical body through death to present you holy in his sight, without blemish and free from accusation (Colossians 1:19-22 NIV).*

The good news of the gospel is reconciliation. That is, restoring the relationship that existed between God and man, man and man, man and the universe, before the fall. God wants the bonding that existed in the Garden of Eden to be restored. This is a very difficult task because we are born in sin and shaped in iniquity, disconnected. It is an extremely difficult and complicated task because we are going against our human nature. Yet, it must be done or else we are doomed to a life of isolation and alienation where we begin to deteriorate and will eventually die.

God decided to help us in this process, by giving us all the same ministry, *"Therefore, if anyone is in Christ, he is a new creation; the old has gone, the new has come! All this is from God, who reconciled us to himself through Christ and gave us the ministry of reconciliation: that God was reconciling the world to himself in Christ, not counting men's sins against them. And he has committed to us the message of reconciliation"* (2 Corinthians 5:17-19 NIV). This is the same responsibility God gave Jesus, the ministry of reconciliation. We have to be reconciled to God and each other. That is, bonded or connected together, just like God was with Adam and Eve and they with each other. This desire is so strong that He wants us to be one, just like the Father, Son and Spirit are one (John 17).

Failure to Bond

The evidence from the latest research overwhelmingly shows, the person who does not have strong bonds with others, affect their ability to recover from many physical diseases, like cancer, heart attacks, and strokes. Researchers have found that if you give patients pets to care for after a heart attack, they recover much faster than those who do not have one. Research has found it depends upon our emotional ties whether we will get a heart attack or not. Do you know that the very chemistry of our blood changes when we have a bitter thought? The medical profession is now seeing man as a holistic being and is adding to their training, how to become more loving and trusting to their patients.

The research shows that when we bond with God and others we are alive, growing, and can survive almost any difficulty we encounter.

When we are not, we are literally dying through physical, psychological and psychosomatic diseases. The Wise Man Solomon shows how drastically the condition of our heart affects the rest of our lives:

"Keep thy heart with all diligence; for out of it are the issues of life" (Proverbs 4:23).

"A heart at peace gives life to the body, but envy rots the bones" (Proverbs 14:30 NIV).

"A merry heart maketh a cheerful countenance: but by sorrow of the heart the spirit is broken. The heart of him that hath understanding seeketh knowledge: but the mouth of fools feedeth on foolishness. All the days of the afflicted are evil: but he that is of a merry heart hath a continual feast" (Proverbs 15:13-15).

"A merry heart doeth good like a medicine: but a broken spirit drieth the bones" (Proverbs 17:22).

"The spirit of a man will sustain his infirmity; but a wounded spirit who can bear? (Proverbs 18:14).

Science is now catching up with what God knew and said long ago. Our physical, emotional, and psychological well being depends on the condition of our heart and spirit. Our heart is dependent upon how deep the bonds exist between us, God and each other. If we know how to bond with the Godhead and others we will follow His plans and begin to develop in all areas. We will start to experience the abundant life now and eternal life in the hereafter. If we do not know how to bond, we are in for some serious, emotional, physical, and psychological sicknesses. And it does not matter how much we read our Bibles and pray, that alone will not solve our problems. We have to learn how to bond and it is never too late. However, like everything else, the older we get the more challenging it becomes.

The Church

Unfortunately, many in the church, including the pastor, make it more difficult for us to bond by saying from the pulpit, things like, "I do not need anyone but Jesus." "Jesus alone is the answer to your problems." Yet, we have to answer: What happens to those we have hurt or wronged? Even Jesus says, if we have aught against our brothers we must first make it right with them before coming to worship Him (Matthew 5:24). What about those who God gave the gift of counseling to? When these statements are made from the pulpit, it makes those who go and seek help from outside the church (counseling) feel guilty because Jesus did not take away their problems. What we fail to understand is that the Bible says we are to bear one another's burdens. God has given gifts to His Children to help us deal with our problems. Some see counseling as humanistic, however all are not, there are some genuine Christian Counselors who can help us with our bonding and other issues. The Apostle Paul affirms that God operates through people,

> *For, when we were come into Macedonia, our flesh had no rest, but we were troubled on every side; without were fightings, within were fears. Nevertheless God, that comforteth those that are cast down, comforted us by the coming of Titus; And not by his coming only, but by the consolation wherewith he was comforted in you, when he told us your earnest desire, your mourning, your fervent mind toward me; so that I rejoiced the more (2 Corinthians 7:5-7).*

Here Paul shows the practical and human way God loves and helps us. He was depressed and fearful. God met those needs by sending Titus who had a relationship with God and Paul. Also, he adds because he knew they cared and were concerned caused him to rejoice and come out his depression. This is the way God works with us. So, we can never say we do not need any one other than Jesus. He uses people to fulfill our needs.

It is important that we bond with the Spirit, so that He is the One directing us or else others will direct our lives for us. Let us not allow people to do to us what the Pharisees did, *"For they bind heavy burdens and grievous to be borne, and lay them on men's shoulders; but they themselves will not move them with one of their fingers"* (Matthew 23:4).

Sanctification

We tend to forget the relational aspect of sanctification, becoming like Jesus. It is dependent on us working out our relationships with God, others, and ourselves. If there is a problem in any one of these, we are in serious trouble. Any teaching against relationships is of the Devil. John reminds us, *"We know that we have passed from death unto life, because we love the brethren. He that loveth not his brother abideth in death"* (1 John 3:14). Too often we are more concerned about being right doctrinally and are not concerned about people hurting. We cannot love God without loving each other, (1 John 4:20). One of the ways we show love is through compassion, just like Jesus, *"If you had known what these words mean, 'I desire mercy, not sacrifice,' you would not have condemned the innocent"* (Matthew 12:7). This help us not to allow people to suffer in isolation, instead we try bonding with them.

When We Do Not Bond

When we do not bond, the desire to do so is intensified. If it is not met, the desire becomes so intense that we withdraw from people. We are aware that we do not have relationships and so we rebel. We try to understand how is it that everyone we know has such wonderful relationships and we cannot get along with our family.

When we see others getting along, we become angry and upset wishing we had such relationships. If our wish is not fulfilled then we become depressed. This is because we want relationships so badly but seem impossible to attain. It is like the Wise Man said, *"Hope deferred makes the heart sick" (Proverbs 13:12)*.

If no one enters our life by this time, we isolate ourselves, not just physically. We withdraw psychological, mentally, socially, and in every way, not just from others but also from ourselves. Then we become suicidal and we have to see if we are still alive. Some people feel so dead internally, they cut themselves to see if they are still alive and can feel.

There are some who chose the more acceptable way in our society by driving themselves to achieve. They receive many accolades, enormous salaries. However, they and their families are hurting because they are just present physically, not in any other manner. Inside they are dead.

Signs of a Lack of Bonding

Many times we are so caught up in the symptoms, we fail to see the real cause. Lack of bonding is often misdiagnosed. If you have more than one of these signs get psychological help from a Christian Counselor, since the only way out is through relationships. Anything else would be treating the symptoms.

Depression is not normally seen as a result of this lack in our lives. The depressed is tired of being with people and not being able to be emotionally attached. This intensifies it. When we cannot attach emotionally to people we attach to things. We must by our nature be emotionally connected to people and things in our universe. When we cannot bond to people, we become addicted to things like, drugs, food, sex, achievements, work, religion, money, material things etcetera. The Apostle Paul captures it very well when he wrote,

> *They are darkened in their understanding and separated from the life of God because of the ignorance that is in them due to the hardening of their hearts. Having lost all sensitivity, they have given themselves over to sensuality so as to indulge in every kind of impurity, with a continual lust for more. You, however, did not come to know Christ that way. Surely you heard of him and were taught in him in accordance with the truth that is in Jesus. You were taught, with regard to your former way of life, to put off your old self, which is being corrupted by its deceitful desires (Ephesians 4:18-24 NIV).*

Notice there is a rift between us and God, described as darkness and hardness of our hearts. We are no longer sensitive to Him and people, we become obsessed with gaining it back. But, we go about it the wrong way. We become sensual and our lust cannot be satisfied. We must be attached to something or someone. Thus, we will bond even if it means bonding with the fridge, the bottle, a prostitute, another man's wife or husband. The problem with addictions is that they are not real desires: They are a part of the false self. We need to find the true self and what it needs, and that is solid, intimate relationships.

Since life only has meaning in the context of relationships, when we do not have them, we feel useless and empty on the inside. This is the worst feeling in the world. We do not feel our need for love, and we cannot accept or feel others love for us. So, when we do not have relationships we surmise it is because we are un-loveable and the reason is we are bad. Thus, no one is going to ever love us. We see the value of ourselves from what others think of us. We feel we are responsible and guilty; hence, try to become good by doing good deeds to get rid of the guilt. Things like reading the

Bible, praying, asking for forgiveness over and over, volunteering, and being in church always. This makes it impossible to experience forgiveness because our guilt is not based on sin. It is a lack of bonding, isolation, and loneliness.

When we remain shut off from people emotionally we begin to die and the first sign is our thinking becomes warped. We begin to believe that people are always talking about us and it gets even worse, we think they are about to harm us. We believe all that these people need to do is change their thinking. This is impossible because they have to make sense of their world even if their thinking is paranoid. This is their reality. They need outside help, Christian counseling.

Emptiness

Once we remain turned off from God and people emotionally, we feel empty inside. This is one of the most difficult feelings to deal with. We become so disconnected with ourselves, we cannot feel our own need for love, and we cannot experience others love for us. This creates a problem because even though we need love and others try to love us, we are not feeling this need and cannot receive their love. Hence, growth cannot take place, until we feel the need for love and begin accepting this love. Paul tells us, *"That Christ may dwell in your hearts by faith; that ye, being rooted and grounded in love, May be able to comprehend with all saints what is the breadth, and length, and depth, and height" (Ephesians 3:17-18).* There needs to be a bonding with Jesus, but that is not enough. We need each other to understand God's love, because He demonstrates His love through others. Our pure love for each other shows the love of God.

He puts His love within us and as we work along with the Spirit that love fills us up and it is shared with others. When we are disconnected from God and our fellowmen, there is a feeling of sadness that is felt in our bowels. The lack of joy is so intense, the only thing that can bring it out is love.

Fears of Bonding

When we are not taught how to bond with others it creates a fear within us, because we do not know how to do it. Becoming intimate is extremely difficult, if not impossible. Our ability to bond is determined by the environment that we grew up in. Our caretakers determine how we bond by the way they bonded with us. If they mistreated, abandoned, abused, constantly threatened, and resented then we will not be able to trust others and hence will disconnect from people. Developing and maintaining relationships will be a huge challenge. Since bonding is about trusting others and becoming vulnerable, the more vulnerable we become, the more we are rewarded with love.

However, if we cannot trust God and others, we develop the attitude, we do not need anybody and our problems are many. This is because we remember the hurt we experienced when we tried to get close to people. We get stuck in this area of our lives at the age it happened. As we get older we fail to upgrade our reality.

How We View Ourselves

We are bad, that is why we are alone. Thus, nobody loves us, since we are unlovable. So we scare people away. This brings back memories of being rejected earlier in life. We begin to spiral downward. Because we are alone our distorted thinking gets even worse and we begin to believe our sins are worse than anyone else. That's because we are alone and not hearing what others are experiencing. This increases our isolation from others. Without interaction we turn on ourselves and begin to believe we do not deserve to be loved since we think we need to earn people's love. This is impossible. Our isolation intensifies because we begin to think that our needs are too much for anyone to handle. We do not understand, in order for people to love us, they must see our needs. Even though there is the conviction that we need the help of others because of how we have been taught, we deny these feelings. We do not understand that this need is Biblical, therefore legitimate. The feelings we have bottled up, fear, anger, and sadness we think will overwhelm anyone we come in contact with. Hence, we keep to ourselves.

How We View Others

Everyone is seen in the light of those who hurt us in the past. We cannot trust anyone, as we have been hurt when we did in the past. This is further complicated if we were abandoned when we were younger. We feel that no one will remain with us. Hence, our conclusion of people is that they are mean and judgmental. They will not listen and we cannot be their friend. So, we cannot tell them our real needs: They will reject us like others did. Or they will use it to control us. We believe we can only experience freedom when we are alone. So that even if people show that they care, it is not true. They are trying to control us.

How We View God

Our view of God is determined by our view of people, *"If a man say, I love God, and hateth his brother, he is a liar: for he that loveth not his brother whom he hath seen, how can he love God whom he hath not seen?"* (1 John 4:20). If we have not learned how to love our fellowmen, it is impossible to love God. Also, God's love is demonstrated through His people. *"By this shall all men know that ye are my disciples, if ye have love one to another."* (John 13:35).

Unfortunately, we think that in order for others to love us we must do good works, to be good. We translate this same concept to God, in order for Him to love us, we must be good. Since we are bad then He does not want anything to do with us. Because others do not understand us and become very angry, so does God. People will not listen to what we have to say, they pretend to do so at times. God will do the same to us. Since He will not listen then He will not answer our prayers. He will be controlling and keep us in bondage. We see ourselves as too bad so God will not forgive us. The truth is we cannot earn love. We can win others approval but love is just given. Love just needs someone to love.

How Do We Bond

It is a slow tedious process. First, we have to overcome our negative experiences to bonding. Second, we have to upgrade our old maps of relationships. Third, it must be done in the context of relationships which we were not successful at.

Recognize Our Need

We are not taught the importance of bonding: Many who were, got hurt in the process. The Bible shows the importance of bonding. The most vivid is Paul description of the Church as a body. We need each other and should suffer together. If we are suffering from addictions do not just see it as a physical problem. Look into your life and see if you have difficulty bonding that is, sharing who you are, your inner thoughts and feelings with people. If you do look back in your life and try to remember your childhood and see if there was a closeness that existed in your family. If not, seek help through counseling to learn how.

Depend on the Spirit

We have not been taught to ask people when we have a need, even though it is clearly seen in the Bible. Instead, we focus on not letting our right hand know what our left hand is doing. So we seldom ask for help. If we need help, we need to ask for it. The challenge comes, ask who? We have been hurt by others therefore we have difficulty trusting people. Here is where the Spirit comes in, ask Him who you should ask for help. We have to listen. It is okay to pray the actual prayer of David in Psalm 139:23-24, *"Search me, O God, and know my heart: try me, and know my thoughts: And see if there be any wicked way in me, and lead me in the way everlasting."* He will reveal to us what they are, and bring the people in our lives that will help us.

Be Vulnerable

In order to bond one must become vulnerable. We cannot reach out to others by sharing our inner thoughts and feelings and still remain in isolation. We must open up. This will be difficult and challenging to start. In order for love to grow vulnerability is a necessity. We have to be willing to take risks. Risk of getting hurt again, I know this is easier said than done. We must allow ourselves to value others emotionally. There are people who want to help, so we have to listen with our ears, feelings, and eyes as the Spirit directs us to them. Having an accountability partner will be most helpful, see chapter 13 on this subject.

Thought Process

Our old way of thinking will try to dominate our thought pattern. These must be challenged or we will quickly find ourselves retreating into isolation. We have to avoid making our past, our future. Since our distorted thinking was learned in the context of relationships they can only be unlearned in them.

We have to be in tune with who we are and be aware of when the old patterns begin to surface. Accept those feelings and begin to change them by talking to yourself. I am still alive because God has purposes for me. Jesus died for me this gives me value. I will let these persons into my world to love me and I will love them.

Dependence

We have been made to dominate (Genesis 1:26-28) not depend on others. What we do not understand about this domination, it is not over people but the universe. The only way we can dominate is by depending on each other. Paul reminds us, *"Submit one to another" (Ephesians 4:21)*. God has made us with needs that can only be fulfilled by others. Instead, we try to be hard and suppress those feelings. Learn to feel your feelings and they will lead to intimacy. Let this be done in the right context, because if you are not married then do not fulfill your feelings and have sex or kill.

Deal with Our Anger

In isolation we become angry, and upset with ourselves and so as not to project it on to others who are trying to love us, we withdraw further. The intention is not to hurt them. We fail to realize, it is natural to be angry toward the people we need and love. Too many see anger as an unlovable part of who we are. We need to become comfortable with our anger. It is as natural as breathing and it is an integral part of relationships. Anger is an emotion given by God to warn us when things are not right.

Show Compassion

We need to look for those who need our help. Allow ourselves to enter into their feelings, thoughts, and emotions. Experience their hurt and this will soften our hearts. Make sure you have already begun to experience your own feelings before you can identify with other's feelings. Paul's admonition helps, *"Praise be to the God and Father of our Lord Jesus Christ, the Father of compassion and the God of all comfort, who comforts us in all our troubles, so that we can comfort those in any trouble with the comfort we ourselves have received from God. For just as the sufferings of Christ flow over into our lives, so also through Christ our comfort overflows"* (2 Corinthians 1:3-5). God demonstrates compassion towards us and many times we do not see it, since we fail to see He works through people. Like I showed you when Paul needed comfort the Lord sent Titus to him (2 Corinthians 7:5-7). Being into relationships, the Gospels are filled with examples of Jesus having compassion on people.

In conclusion, God wants us to enjoy this life (John 10:10), it is a practice run for eternity. It is His desire to do exceedingly abundantly above all we can ask or think (Ephesians 3:20). These cannot be accomplished outside of bonding, being able to share our inner being with God and others. We cannot enjoy life without being our true selves. We cannot hide behind defense mechanisms, independence, anger, or anything else. We must be real, true to God, ourselves, and others to enjoy life to its fullest.

The key then to bonding is to be yourself, who God created you to be and not who you or others want you to be. Do not be afraid to ask for help. Jesus was not, He asked His disciples to help Him feed the multitude and to stay awake with Him in the Garden of Gethsemane. He was His true self crying over Jerusalem, and at Lazarus funeral. This is the only way to be intimate with our fellowmen and bond like the Godhead. If you need more help in this area, read Dr. Henry Cloud's book **"Changes That Heal,"** or see a Christian Counselor who understands bonding.

———•◦•———

Chapter 11

An Elusive Ingredient

I WAS TALKING TO MY FRIEND and colleague Pastor Dennis Barrow on July 27, 2007 and he brought up this subject that I found was very deep and powerful. I first decided to practice it in my own life, because God knows I have confused these two: In my relationship with God, my family, and others. I asked, "Can I use this concept?" He said. "Yes."

God was so gracious that in our Family Worship the same night, we were reading Luke 8 and there He revealed to me more about this subject. Before, I thought that time was our biggest enemy. Now, I believe that this is the biggest enemy to any relationship; we turn distractions into issues and waste a great deal of time on the non-essentials of life. Issues that should be dealt with are ignored and they cause a great deal of heartache and stress which could have been avoided. The challenge is being able to distinguish between them. Often we turn distractions into issues and issues into distractions, this destroys our relationships.

What is a Distraction?

It is anything that will take you away from your intended purpose or destination. It is designed to keep you from reaching your intended goal. Like, if you are on your way to the airport and you just finished eating. You have your ticket, passport, luggage, and gas in the car, you see a Burger King sign and you exit. That is a distraction, it takes you away from your intended destination. There was no need to exit, you already ate. This can turn into a major issue if you miss your flight. Another example, Jesus told His disciples that He must die, Peter said no way, Jesus said get thee behind me Satan (Matthew 16:23). Peter was being a distraction.

What is an Issue?

Anything designed to hinder you from accomplishing your intended purpose or destination which you should deal with. If not, it will be to your detriment. The major difference is issues have to do with morality, legality or ethics. Thus, they have to be dealt with promptly. You have to confront the person because if you do not then death normally follows. It is usually something you cannot walk away from. For example, your friend is trying to force you to have sex, take drugs or to do something you do not want to do, that is an issue, not just a distraction. The individuals who create issues for you and are aware of it, are not really your friends.

Jesus was a perfect example of this, Peter in the Garden of Gethsemane cut off Malchus' ear. Jesus saw that as an issue, someone's ear was destroyed and it needed to be restored. He dealt with it and moved on, so must we.

Avoiding Distractions

The best way to avoid distractions is to know who you are, where you are going, how you are going to get there and making adequate preparation for the trip. In other words, you must be a disciple of Jesus, know your God given gifts, purposes, ministries, vocations and destiny.

David is a good example, remember his encounter with Goliath in 1 Samuel 17. Jesse, his father asked him to take some food to his brothers in the army. He was obedient and carried out his father request. When he got there, there was an issue; Goliath was defiling the Lord God of Israel. He was not a mere distraction, morality was involved He was disrespecting the Creator. Someone had to confront Goliath and God had a man.

Now what is amazing to me is instead of David's brothers becoming upset with Goliath who was the issue, they were distracted by David. Even though he was about to deal with the issue. Look at their response,

> *And Eliab his eldest brother heard when he spake unto the men; and Eliab's anger was kindled against David, and he said, Why camest thou down hither? And with whom hast thou left those few sheep in the wilderness? I know thy pride, and the naughtiness of thine heart; for thou art come down that thou mightest see the battle. And David said, What have I now done? Is there not a cause? And he turned from him toward another, and spake after the same manner: and the people answered him again after the former manner (1 Sam 17:28-30).*

If the issue is not taken care of, we are easily distracted and these distractions become serious issues since we must blame someone for our failure. Look at what his brothers did. Goliath was the issue. They did not know how to deal with him so they made David their issue. He was easier to deal with than Goliath. When we fail to make the necessary preparations, we have to find a scapegoat to blame for our short comings.

David simply asked his brothers, "What have I done?" In other words, why are you treating me so, I was obedient to my father and I brought food for you. I am not the issue Goliath is, let us concentrate on him. David did the right thing, he walked away from his brothers or it could have easily turned into a major issue. You know how brothers can be sometimes, especially the younger ones who are growing into manhood. David saw them as a distraction.

Handling Issues

David's concern was Goliath, his purpose was to kill the giant. He did not lose sight of that fact and he said it publicly. Words of David response got to the ears of King Saul and he asked for him. *"And David said to Saul, Let no man's heart fail because of him; thy servant will go and fight with this Philistine. And Saul said to David, Thou art not able to go against this Philistine to fight with him: for thou art but a youth, and he a man of war from his youth,"* verses 32-33.

Saul had some issues with David, first he could not fight, he is too small, he is a boy, he had no training in combat. Whereas his opponent was fighting since he was a boy. David on the other hand saw these as mere distractions. Saul saw them as major issues. If you do not know the difference people will try to make you believe distractions are issues. If you do not know the difference you will be distracted from your purposes. If David had used up his energy on the distractions, his brothers and the King, Goliath would have won. Also, David would have destroyed his relationship with his brothers and King Saul, who he needed later.

Knowing the Difference

What is it that made David able to differentiate between distractions and issues? The answer is found in 1 Samuel 16:13 *"Then Samuel took the horn of oil, and anointed him in the midst of his brethren: and the Spirit of the LORD came upon David from that day forward. So Samuel rose up, and went to Ramah."* He was anointed by God and the Spirit was upon him. That is the only way you can differentiate between them. David could have turned his brothers accusations into a big issue, the king's concerns about his youth and inexperience into issues and not accomplish what God anointed him for.

Keep your eyes upon the Lord, because your anointing is not enough. Saul too was anointed 1 Samuel 15:1 just like David. But, Saul tried to govern and live his life outside of the will of God. David chose instead to depend upon the Lord in all that He did. He knew God's purposes for his life. He knew this was the reason why the Lord wanted him to come and visit his brothers. Goliath became his focus and no one was going to stop him from accomplishing God's purpose for his life.

God Prepares Us

David knew that God had prepared him for this moment. Listen to what he told the king, he did not tell his brothers,

> *And David said unto Saul, Thy servant kept his father's sheep, and there came a lion, and a bear, and took a lamb out of the flock: And I went out after him, and smote him, and delivered it out of his mouth: and when he arose against me, I caught him by his beard, and smote him, and slew him. Thy servant slew both the lion and the bear: and this uncircumcised Philistine shall be as one of them, seeing he hath defied the armies of the living God. David said moreover, The LORD that delivered me out of the paw of the lion, and out of the paw of the bear, he will deliver me out of the hand of this Philistine. And Saul said unto David, Go, and the LORD be with thee (verses 34-37).*

David did not take credit for his accomplishments. He realized it was the Lord who saved him from the lion and bear and He would deliver this uncircumcised Philistine into his hands. He also connected the slaying of the lion and the bear as preparation for the slaying of Goliath.

Understand that God has prepared you for the issues you are facing or are about to face. Whatever you are going through right now is preparation to deal with issues in the future. Do not be discouraged when you encounter fiery trials they are just preparation to help you deal with life's issues.

Want More Proof

For those who do not have the Spirit, they never feel we are prepared to deal with the issues. Look at what the king did, *"And Saul armed David with his armour, and he put an helmet of brass upon his head; also he armed him with a coat of mail. And David girded his sword upon his armour, and he assayed to go; for he had not proved it. And David said unto Saul, I cannot go with these; for I have not proved them. And David put them off him"* (1 Samuel 17:38-39). They think God's preparation is not adequate enough. You see, they were not there when Jesus touched you and when He wrapped His loving arms around you. They believe they have to help you by providing armor for you to fight the issues. They sincerely think they are helping, they do not understand they are hindering. That is why you have to be patient and not see what they are trying to do as issues. There are just distractions; thus, you will not use up your energy fighting them. You know what God has prepared you to handle.

Be Yourself

God wants us to be ourselves and not someone else. Too often we want to put on other people's clothes and the more popular the person the greater the desire. So we spend a fortune buying designer clothes which is a distraction and we turn it into an issue. David, if he was not focused would have worn the Kings armor. After all, you could not get any more popular than the king. He could brag to his friends that he wore the King's armor. David decided not to make it an issue and took them off, because they were a distraction. It was not him and he would have lost the battle with them. We have to learn to be ourselves if we want to avoid distractions and not make them issues. Look at the difference,

> *And he took his staff in his hand, and chose him five smooth stones out of the brook, and put them in a shepherd's bag which he had, even in a scrip; and his sling was in his hand: and he drew near to the Philistine. And the Philistine came on and drew near unto David; and the man that bare the shield went before him. And when the Philistine looked about, and saw David, he disdained him: for he was but a youth, and ruddy, and of a fair countenance. And the Philistine said unto David, Am I a dog, that thou comest to me with staves? And the Philistine cursed David by his gods. And the Philistine said to David, Come to me, and I will give thy flesh unto the fowls of the air, and to the beasts of the field (verses 38-44).*

Even Goliath tried to distract David with intimidations. He tried to get him to turn those distractions into issues. David refused to be sidetracked. Listen to his response,

> *Then said David to the Philistine, Thou comest to me with a sword, and with a spear, and with a shield: but I come to thee in the name of the LORD of hosts, the God of the armies of Israel, whom thou hast defied. This day will the LORD deliver thee into mine hand; and I will smite thee, and take thine head from thee; and I will give the carcases of the host of the Philistines this day unto the fowls of the air, and to the wild beasts of the earth; that all the earth may know that there is a God in Israel. And all this assembly shall know that the LORD saveth not with sword and spear: for the battle is the LORD's, and he will give you into our hands. And David put his hand in his bag, and took thence a stone, and slang it, and smote the Philistine in his forehead, that*

the stone sunk into his forehead; and he fell upon his face to the earth. So David prevailed over the Philistine with a sling and with a stone, and smote the Philistine, and slew him; but there was no sword in the hand of David. Therefore David ran, and stood upon the Philistine, and took his sword, and drew it out of the sheath thereof, and slew him, and cut off his head therewith. And when the Philistines saw their champion was dead, they fled (verses 45-51).

We must be anointed by God to be ourselves and be comfortable. It does not matter how big the giants get, with God on our side we can topple them. God has equipped us and He will not give us an assignment that He has not prepared us to handle. We do not have to be anyone else or wear their clothes to be victorious.

The major difference is when David had on the King's armor he walked around in it. When he took it off and was himself, he literally ran to the giant. That is when you know you are ready to handle issues, you run to and not away from them.

Know Your Appointment

Know that God has prepared you for this moment—you have all the preparation you need to accomplish this task. Sometimes you have to be ready to iterate to others how God has prepared you for this moment. David could have stormed out after Goliath without anyone's permission. That would have destroyed the very relationships he needed in his life, including that of Saul. You see, David did not know anything about being a king and so he had to learn from Saul what to do and what not to do. Knowing your appointment does not give you the right to be cocky. You still listen to others and be respectful. You will need those same people in the future.

Effects on Relationships

Let us say that you came to church and found it was still locked. It is pass the time for the service to begin. Is that a distraction or an issue? I know in the past I made it an issue and would have ramped and raged about it for days. However, the truth is, this is really a distraction for me, but an issue for them. Whoever was to open the church, even if it is your best friend, made the decision not to be there early and I did not have any control over that. They made the choice and they have to live with that choice, as I have to make my choice and live with it.

If I see, hear, or feel any distraction and turn it into an issue, it will affect how I relate to my friends, the other members and even my God who I came to worship. If on the other hand I see, hear, or feel it as a distraction then I can still relate to my friends, have a pleasant countenance and worship my God with a clear conscious. This is the original intent of my coming to church in the first place. If I made it an issue which it really is not, then my worship would be adversely affected.

I remember being invited home for our church's seventy fifth anniversary celebration. I noticed that I was being treated differently on this trip. It was a week of celebration and I was not asked to do anything, I was not on any of the programs for the week, even though I was the only Anguillan Pastor who worked as a Pastor on the Island. They knew I was coming and I almost turned it into an issue. I remembered the last church service I looked in the bulletin to see if my name was there, it was not. I began turning it into an issue. I told myself, I am not going on the rostrum to do anything even if the Pastor asked me. All of a sudden it was about me, I did not hear what the Superintendent or teacher was saying. When the Spirit asked me the question, "Why did you come here, is it not to celebrate?" and I responded, "Yes Lord" "Who did you come to celebrate yourself or Me." I said, "You Lord." Immediately, I saw this as a distraction and not an issue and began to relax and enjoy the service. It was not five minutes later when the pastor sent me a note saying, please come to his office. I got up and did my part.

If I had not seen this as a distraction my worship experience would have been different. I would have been mad with the brethren and God. I would have had an unpleasant attitude towards the pastor and the church members. My relating to them would have been strained. However, because I saw it as a distraction, it was easy to continue our friendship and was able to continue relating amicably with everyone.

You will notice that distractions are presented by your family, friends and those in authority. Distractions and issues can destroy relationships. Remember it was David whom the Lord used to save King Saul from embarrassment when Goliath was degrading their God. Because Saul did not understand his purposes in life, he went after David. In contrast, Jonathan understood his purpose and was able to accept and develop an amicable relationship with David, even though Jonathan was in line to be Israel's next King.

Choices

It really boils down to choice. Sometimes those choices can be tricky, what might seem to be a distraction can sometimes be an issue. It boils down to that concept that I might seem to over emphasize, and that is balance. Life is always about finding balance, equilibrium. We need the Spirit to reveal to us what is the best choice to make in each decision.

In conclusion, we have to know where we are going, how we are going to get there and what we need for the journey. When we do not know, people will distract us. When we know where we are going they cannot. That is how people get us to do things we do not want to do nor had no desire to do. It is all about knowing who you are and God's plans for your life. When we get a grasp of that, then it will be easier to differentiate between issues and distractions.

When we are anointed by God and become His disciples, the Spirit reveals to us what our gifts, purposes, ministries, vocations and destiny are. Then we will not be easily distracted. Notice I said easily distracted.

Chapter 12

A Forgotten Ingredient

NO RELATIONSHIP ON EARTH CAN EXIST without this vital component that we hear so little of. This is not surprising because relationships and forgiveness are like peas in a pod. Fellowship is impossible without it. If we do not understand friendships, we will not forgive. We cannot have one without the other. Forgiveness is very simple and extremely powerful. But, we becloud it with every possible obstacle, which has nothing to do with forgiveness. A good resource on this subject is, ***"I Should Forgive But..." by Dr. Chuck Lynch.***

Forgiveness

One of the forgotten ingredients in earthly relationships is forgiveness. It is our responsibility to ask for it and to grant it when asked of us. For many reasons: First, we are human, we will hurt those we love and those we love will hurt us, deliberately or not. Second, if we believe that Jesus died for our sins, He also died for the sins of our offenders. Third, since Jesus readily forgives us, we also ought to forgive others. We must learn to forgive and understand that it is not contingent upon the other person. It does not matter what they did, or how hurt we are. We have to learn to forgive just as Christ forgives us. If we do not know how, we will always have difficulty developing lasting relationship. We need an abundance of grace and mercy to maintain fellowship and render it. This is only possible when we allow the Spirit to work through us, to ask for forgiveness when we have done wrong and to grant it, whether it is asked of us or not.

Reasons For

Because we are human beings we will offend and hurt each other whether it is intentional or not. It does not matter, we are still hurt and offended, and the only way to rectify this situation is through forgiveness. It is important that we grant forgiveness to those who ask, at least for three reasons, first, because Jesus commanded us to. If we do not forgive others neither will God forgive us. Second, I will hurt you, you will hurt me, maybe not deliberately, and now it is your turn to ask me for forgiveness. Third, if we do not forgive we end up hurting ourselves. We think we are hurting the person who has wronged us, however, we become angry, bitter, and full of ulcers and we end up suffering from psychosomatic and physical diseases as a result. So, we need to give and receive forgiveness or our lives will be miserable.

Lack of Knowledge

Forgiveness is crucial to maintaining relationships. It is simple, we have complicated it. Sadly, as important as it is, how many sermons have you heard preached? How many Sabbath or Sunday school lessons are prepared? What about courses in school? It has become a subject clouded in mystery. Thus, there are many people in and out of the hospital because we are not practicing this simple principle. Without forgiveness, eternal relationships are impossible. You cannot experience the abundant life Jesus wants to give. We are locked in the prison of bitterness and we are sick.

Control Issues

We turn distractions into major issues which stand in the way of us from granting forgiveness. But the person dealing with the distractions sees them as major issues, and so they cannot be ignored. A lack of knowledge stands in the way of giving forgiveness. So, we have difficulty granting it because we keep being distracted with that which has nothing to do with forgiveness. God is simple and straight forward. We try to complicate all He has given us. This make us feel smart.

There is an even deeper reason; we want to separate ourselves from the common people and control them. Like the Scribes and Pharisees added hundreds of laws to the Ten Commandments just to make it more complicated and control the people. Similarly, the church in the medieval times, they would read the Bible in Latin so that they were in charge. People had to come to them and they could tell them what to do and how to do it. That has not changed. The church is still attempting to control today. Though, we are dealing with a more enlightened liberal group of individuals. Now they want to tell you which version of the Bible and books to read, what you should be doing for the Lord even though you are not gifted in that area. The control is more subtle. You can warn people of the dangers, and let them make their own choices, not you making decisions for them.

Kingdom Oriented

Jesus understood this very clearly so in the middle of the Sermon on the Mount He deals with His reason for coming. He wants us His disciples to be Kingdom minded, *"But seek ye first the kingdom of God, and his righteousness; and all these things shall be added unto you"* (*Matthew 6:33*). He realized that there are some distractions that will consume our focus. He understood, we will see them as major issues. So, He addresses them and we have to do the same. He said,

> *Therefore I say unto you, Take no thought for your life, what ye shall eat, or what ye shall drink; nor yet for your body, what ye shall put on. Is not the life more than meat, and the body than raiment? Behold the fowls of the air: for they sow not, neither do they reap, nor gather into barns; yet your heavenly Father feedeth them. Are ye not much better than they? Which of you by taking thought can add one cubit unto his stature? And why take ye thought for raiment? Consider the lilies of the field, how they grow; they toil not, neither do they spin: And yet I say unto you, That even Solomon in all his glory was not arrayed like one of these. Wherefore, if God so clothe the grass of the field, which today is, and tomorrow is cast into the oven, shall he not much more clothe you, O ye of little faith? Therefore take no thought, saying, What shall we eat? or, What shall we drink? or, Wherewithal shall we be clothed? (For after all these things do the Gentiles seek:) for your heavenly Father knoweth that ye have need of all these things. But seek ye first the kingdom of God, and his righteousness; and all these things shall be added unto you. Take therefore no thought for the morrow: for the morrow shall take thought for the things of itself. Sufficient unto the day is the evil thereof (Matthew 6:25-34).*

Jesus knew before we could focus on His Kingdom there were some things, if they were not taken care of would distract us, like food, clothing and shelter. Thus He said, do not worry about these things I will take care of them for you. Focus on my Kingdom. In the same way, there are some issues that get in our way that needs to be addressed. If they are ignored, we have difficulty granting forgiveness even though they are not related to it. My prayer is that by the time you finish reading this chapter you will have a better understanding of forgiveness and will grant it, regardless to what issues or distractions you are having.

Do Not Know How

Because of these complications and the lack of information on the subject, many do not know how to forgive. There are several reasons. When we do share forgiveness, we have mixed up the results of forgiveness with what it means to forgive. So you will hear some people say I will forgive, if He asks me first. Or I will forgive, if he would only admit how much he hurt me. Forgiveness has nothing to do with the other person forgiving you or admitting they hurt you. These are the results of it. Forgiveness is a command from God.

We are reluctant to relive the pain of the incident. We do not want to go back there. Regrettably, if we do not, we cannot go forward, since our past will keep pulling us back. We cannot bury our emotions, they are alive and will dig themselves through dirt, concrete, gold, silver, iron, no matter what we use to cover them up. They will eventually find themselves in the forefront. That is why, whoever we wronged, no matter how many gifts of gold, myrrh, or frankincense we give them they will never be satisfied, until we ask them for forgiveness.

The person asking for forgiveness does not eliminate the pain, remove the anger, and automatically restore trust; it does not mean immediate restoration or restitution. Forgiveness has nothing to do with these. When Jesus commands us to forgive, there are no preconditions for granting it. Jesus went so far to say if someone has wronged us, we have to go and make peace with them before we come to worship Him (Matthew 5:24).

Excuses for Not Forgiving

We have many of them like,

What do I do with my anger?

What if I cannot forgive and forget?

I cannot forgive myself.

They won't admit that they are wrong,

I have to live with the consequences daily.

I am afraid they will do it again.

Who is going to pay for what they did to me?

The truth is there are absolutely no reasons for not forgiving. The only way we can be forgiven is to forgive our brethren. In Matthew 6 and Luke 11, God forgiving us is dependent upon us forgiving others. It is not that the excuses are not legitimate, these have nothing to do with forgiveness. It is a command from God. It precedes worship (Matthew 5:24).

What Do I Do With My Anger?

Your anger and forgiveness are separate issues. Anger is one of the most experienced; yet, most misunderstood and lied about emotion. It is the number one reason for the destruction of relationships. Still, the good news is that genuine forgiveness is the number one tool in restoring them. We must understand that anger was given to us by God, to point out that something is wrong and needs to be addressed: Not to embarrass us.

Some people cannot handle this, but God Himself experiences anger. *"And they forsook the LORD God of their fathers, which brought them out of the land of Egypt, and followed other gods, of the gods of the people that were round about them, and bowed themselves unto them, and provoked the LORD to anger"* (Judges 2:12). *"They provoked him to jealousy with strange gods, with abominations provoked they him to anger" (Deuteronomy 32:16)*. Jesus also became angry, when He threw the people out of the temple (John 2).

God tells us how to deal with anger. *"Be ye angry, and sin not: let not the sun go down upon your wrath. (Ephesians 4:26)*. Do not sin as a result of your angry. Deal with it within twenty-four hours. One of the best ways is forgiving those who you have wronged and have wronged you.

What if I Cannot Forgive and Forget?

Many mix up these up. One is not contingent upon the other. God has designed us like Himself, not to forget. Forgetting is a biological not a spiritual function. Memory is stored in the brain by chemical transference or electronic impulses.

We make the mistake and quote Scripture to say that God forgets, He cannot if He did He would cease to be God. The Bible does say, *"Their sin will I remember no more"* (Jeremiah 31:34). *"And their sins and lawless deeds I will remember no more"* (Hebrews 10:17). So, is there something wrong with the Bible or me? Sometimes when we use human terms to explain God something gets lost in the middle. Remember in John 3 when Nicodemus came to Jesus and He told him he must be born again. He thought he had to go back into his mother's womb. Jesus was talking of the new birth.

Similarly, when God says He will not remember our sins anymore, He meant He will not hold them against us any longer. Let these passages explain what I mean. *"How blessed is the man to whom the Lord does not impute iniquity"* (Psalm 32:2). *"God was in Christ reconciling the world to Himself, not counting their trespasses against them"* (2 Corinthians 5:19). That is how He deals with our sins they do not count against us anymore. It is not that He forgets, that will mean you are better than God at remembering. Since, we do not forget. You will not forget what the person did to you, but you will no longer hold it against them.

I Cannot Forgive Myself

If you are one of these persons, do not waste anymore of your time. This is one of the most confusing aspects of forgiveness. It makes it harder than it already is. This also hinders us from fully experiencing God's forgiveness.

Only He can forgive sins, no human being has the power or authority to do so. If He forgives you, who is pointing a finger at you? You of course! You are not condemned or judged by God, but, you feel condemned by yourself? Thus you feel, see, or hear the need for additional forgiveness above and beyond what He gives. Paul destroys this argument in Romans 8:31-39.

> *What shall we then say to these things? If God be for us, who can be against us? He that spared not his own Son, but delivered him up for us all, how shall he not with him also freely give us all things? Who shall lay anything to the charge of God's elect? It is God that justifieth. Who is he that condemneth? It is Christ that died, yea rather, that is risen again, who is even at the right hand of God, who also maketh intercession for us. Who shall separate us from the love of Christ? shall tribulation, or distress, or persecution, or famine, or nakedness, or peril, or sword? As it is written, For thy sake we are killed all the daylong; we are accounted as sheep for the slaughter. Nay, in all these things we are more than conquerors through him that loved us. For I am persuaded, that neither death, nor life, nor angels, nor principalities, nor powers, nor things present, nor things to come, Nor height, nor depth, nor any other creature, shall be able to separate us from the love of God, which is in Christ Jesus our Lord.*

If God is for us, then nobody can be against us, including ourselves. Who is the justifier? God is. Who else can point a finger at you? Nobody, not even yourself. Who shall lay the charge to God's elect. Does that include you? If you must forgive yourself, you must also justify yourself judiciously. That is impossible. Only God can justify. In order to forgive ourselves, we must first condemn ourselves, point the finger at ourselves, and this results in false guilt. That's what we are experiencing when we want to forgive ourselves. This makes forgiveness impossible. It muddies our minds and prompts us to feel the need to forgive ourselves in an attempt to get some badly needed relief. It is not that we have not repented—we don't feel forgiven, and see ourselves as the object of condemnation.

What is guilt—I deserve or am worthy of blame. The question is did you ask God to forgive you—did He? Are you still worthy of blame? John the Apostle tells us, *"If we confess our sins, he is faithful and just to forgive us our sins, and to cleanse us from all unrighteousness" (I John 1:9).* Did God forgive all? Are you still worthy of blame? No! We are experiencing false guilt. And what we are saying is God does not have the ability to completely forgive us of our sins, we have to forgive ourselves then it is complete. I believe our biggest dilemma lies in being able to identify the difference between true and false guilt, they feel the same and sometimes are difficult to identify. We have to remind ourselves of God's promises on forgiveness and claim them.

They Won't Admit They Did Me Wrong

This is usually more important for women than men. You do not have to wait for them to acknowledge the wrong in order to forgive. The Word tells us before we could even admit we did God wrong, Jesus came and died for us Romans 5:8. While on the cross Jesus said, *Father, forgive them; for they know not what they do. And they parted his raiment, and cast lots" (Luke 23:24).*

Stephen while he was being stoned looked up to heaven and said to His Father, *"And he kneeled down, and cried with a loud voice, Lord, lay not this sin to their charge. And when he had said this, he fell asleep"* (Acts 7:60).

Jesus command to us in Matthew 5:23-24, *"Therefore if thou bring thy gift to the altar, and there rememberest that thy brother hath ought against thee; Leave there thy gift before the altar, and go thy way; first be reconciled to thy brother, and then come and offer thy gift."* This is interesting because it says if you remember that your brother has wrong you, not you offending him. Go and find him/her first, then come and worship. No one has to admit before you grant forgiveness. It is a command from God.

I Have To Live With The Consequences Daily.

Truth be told, so does Jesus. He has to live with His nail pierced hands and side. The consequences and forgiveness again are two different issues. This does not minimize the pain or agony of you being a victim of rape, or a child dying from a drive by senseless shooting. There are some horrific consequences that you have to live with daily. However, I guarantee you they will not be worst than carrying that person you need to grant forgiveness on your shoulders daily. They will make you sick and will end up in the hospital.

I Am Afraid They Will Do It Again

The Bible says we should be wise as serpents and harmless as doves. There are some situations where you have to remove yourself or your love ones out of harm's way. For example, if there is a family member that is molesting another one, then he or she must be removed. Furthermore, it is your duty to report that individual to the authorities. If you are being physically abused by your spouse you must leave. Still, you must forgive regardless to how gross that sin is for your own health and well being.

Who is Going To Pay?

Another condition we add to granting forgiveness is payment. This makes it difficult to forgive. We believe the person who did wrong should be punished. After all, that is what the Bible says, Without the shedding of blood there is no remission for sin (Hebrews 9:22). Moses told us in Exodus 21:24, an eye for our eye and a tooth for a tooth. We believe if we forgive then the person will go scott free. Human reasoning says my offender deserves punishment, either I must do it or see to it that it is done before I forgive. This presents two problems. One is, we must hand it over to someone else if for no other reason than it takes a righteous judge to exact true justice—none of us is 100% objective or impartial. So, we have to turn it over to the one who is, God. Peter tells us, *"Who, when he was reviled, reviled not again; when he suffered, he threatened not; but committed himself to him that judgeth righteously"* (1 Peter 2:23).

Second, few offenses can be adequately paid for and very seldom does the offended have the power or opportunity to exact the payment—when repayment is not possible revenge becomes the next best thing. Very few of us can repay for the damage done. For example, if you burn down a forest and several homes worth millions of dollars got burnt in the process and you repent—you cannot repay for that damage even if you live several lifetimes. Or if someone killed your child, even if it was accidental, there is nothing the offender can do to repay you.

There is good news. The reason why Jesus died is so that no one has to pay. We cannot separate justice and revenge without the cross, if we did, there would be no moral basis for forgiveness. We think by withholding forgiveness in some small way, we are exacting revenge. Our bitterness would somehow hurt the person and give us relief. There are three problems:

It does not work

It is not right

It punishes the wrong person

One of the reasons it does not work is because sometimes the person is not even aware of what they did to us. It is not right because it goes against Jesus' command to forgive. It punishes the wrong person, you. The writer to the Hebrews indicated, *"See to it that no one misses the grace of God and that no bitter root grows up to cause trouble and defile many" (Hebrews 12:15)*. Unforgiveness makes us bitter. Bitterness is like a stone thrown into a pond; it starts out with us and then begins to spread outwards to people in our sphere.

The Price was Paid

The Bible is replete with confirmation that someone has already paid the price and what a price it was. Listen to what they did to Jesus and see if this was not payment enough for what all the people have done and will do to you:

"Then the high priest tore His clothes" (Matthew 26:65).

"Then they spit in His face and struck Him with their fists" (Matthew 26:67).

"He denied it again, with an oath: "I don't know the man!" (Matthew 26:72).

"What shall I do, then, with Jesus who is called Christ?" Pilate asked. They all answered, "Crucify him!" (Matthew 27:22).

"They stripped him and put a scarlet robe on him. Then twisted together a crown of thorns and set it on his head. They put a staff in his right hand and knelt in front of him and mocked him. "Hail, king of the Jews!"

they said" They spit on him, and took the staff and struck him on the head again and again. (Matthew 27:28-30).

They embarrassed Him in front of His family.

His face smashed and could not be recognized. *"Just as there were many who were appalled at him—his appearance was so disfigured beyond that of any man and his form marred beyond human likeness"* (Isaiah 52:14 NIV).

"But many were amazed when they saw him. His face was so disfigured he seemed hardly human, and from his appearance, one would scarcely know he was a man" (Isaiah 52:14 New Living Translation).

They nailed Him to a cross.

We get so caught up in ourselves that we forget three things:

1. Jesus paid for our pain and offenses.

2. With this admission implies our responsibility to forgive. We believe Jesus died for our sins. We forget He also died for our offender's sins, because we want them to pay.

3. Explains how hard and extremely high a price only God could pay for our shortcomings.

However, we want double payment, Jesus paid and we want our offenders to pay. In our minds we have to turn the person over from our prison to Jesus' prison, the place where they belong and forgiveness is the method we use to release them. If possible, we are now free to pursue reconciliation and establish or re-establish a relationship with our offender, or those we have offended. Forgiveness makes it possible.

Chapter 13

A Must Ingredient

THERE ARE MANY WHO THINK that intimacy takes place in the dark. The Bible says it takes place in the light. Darkness hides our hurts, fears, faults, failures, and flaws. In the light we bring them out and admit who we really are. That is why John admonishes,

> *If we say that we have fellowship with him, and walk in darkness, we lie, and do not the truth: But if we walk in the light, as he is in the light, we have fellowship one with another, and the blood of Jesus Christ his Son cleanseth us from all sin. If we say that we have no sin, we deceive ourselves, and the truth is not in us. If we confess our sins, he is faithful and just to forgive us our sins, and to cleanse us from all unrighteousness. If we say that we have not sinned, we make him a liar, and his word is not in us (1 John 1:6-10).*

I hear you saying this is referring to God, well hear what James has to say, *"Confess your faults one to another, and pray one for another, that ye may be healed. The effectual fervent prayer of a righteous man availeth much"* (James 5:16). We cannot be secret service disciples because God does not give us everything. He shares His wisdom with all and it is as we come alongside each other, we are able to help one another achieve His Destiny for us.

Our Primary Goal

Our primary goal and purpose in life is to become like Jesus—Christ-likeness. This is seen differently by males and females. Most women see Jesus as gentle, meek, and mild relating to everyone. Whereas most men see Him as a go getter, confronting the false systems, doing things for people, it is about action.

Sometimes we tend to forget this is a journey, not a destination and do not enjoy the ride. The journey is long and tedious at times, it seems impossible to accomplish. These are the times when we need all the help we can get. We think we only need people to rejoice with us when things are going well. There will be times of discouragement when we need people to come along side and help us to make it through our trials as well. The Bible is replete with information on how we can help each other on the journey. This can be summarized in one word, accountability. This can have a powerful practical value to achieving our purpose of becoming more like Christ, helping us deal with the problems or issues of life. It is interesting because without being mentioned, we are accountable on our jobs and in our families. These are our responsibilities, areas in which we are expected to be accountable, like showing up on time, fulfilling our job description, or being faithful to our spouse. Where it is most powerful is when it comes from commitments we have made either with ourselves, someone else, or an organization.

Written goals can be a valuable source of personal accountability. That's part of why proper goal setting is so powerful. When we have clearly identified the goal, created a plan and made a commitment for its achievement that puts a sense of responsibility on ourselves and if we do not do the things we have planned then we violate our own integrity. This can cause guilt and depression which hinders us from achieving our goals. That's why we will never meet someone who is in the process of achieving their goals who is depressed. Many do not need Prozac, they need goals and accountability. If we are having difficulty achieving our goals it is often a good idea to seek an accountability partner. Someone you can trust and respect. One you can confide in with your struggles, weaknesses, and insecurities as it relates to the goals and growth you intend to achieve. The Bible gives good advice in this area, *"Do two walk together unless they have agreed to do so?" (Amos 3:3)*. You must respect and choose this person wisely.

Already Accountable

It is true, we are in fact already accountable to many people: Our families, our employers, our friends and so on. But those relationships differ from what I call "essential relationships" we are talking about in this chapter. Typically, accountability is routine, or "part of the job." The difference with "essential relationships" is that accountability would not normally occur, or even be expected to. It is voluntary and intentional; not because we have to, but because we chose to. It is specifically for the purpose of growing as a disciple, dealing with the struggles and deficits in our lives.

Women have a built in mechanism for accountability. It is more difficult for men. We need it because that is the way God designed us. A woman will choose a church based on the programs; men are looking for other men they can follow by working alongside them. We are transformed through encounters with other inspiring men. And the women follow us. Jesus understood this and surrounded Himself with them, and thus attracted women and children also.

Accountability is Not

A support or a Bible study group meeting: Nor people getting together to whine about the pressures of life, to bash the opposite sex, to get in touch with their past or inner child or getting together as a social group. It is not to gossip.

Accountability is

"The quality or state of being accountable; *especially*: an obligation or willingness to accept responsibility or to account for one's actions" Merriam-Webster Online Dictionary. This is a simple but powerful definition. It means being responsible. You want to achieve more success in your work and personal life without having to sacrifice the quality of one for the other. You know you have the ability to, but not sure why you have not or why it is taking so long.

This is not just limited to the Business World; it is also true in the Spiritual, since God has designed it that way. It is two people of the same sex, four the most, getting together, sharing and seeking help from each other to live a Christ-like life. Accountability is getting to know each other beyond the casual and safe conversations of life; being challenged and held to a higher standard than what the world or the church determines; being honest about our pitfalls, prisons, and palace experiences; praying together, and for each other, growing together toward Christ-likeness, reaching our full potential as God's children. This is done in an atmosphere of love and acceptance, without judgment. The Psalmist sums it up superbly, *"Behold, how good and how pleasant it is for brethren to dwell together in unity!" (Psalms 133:1)*.

Further Explained

Accountability can be summarized in the Promise Keepers theme song in '93 or '94.

"Face to face, brother to brother
Face to face, one friend to another
Man to man, shoulder to shoulder
Man to man, serving each other
Brother to brother we'll strengthen each other
Working together, we're building the Kingdom of God."

I would like to change the first two lines for men's sake, instead of face to face which women are comfortable with; to side by side. As men we are uncomfortable face to face, we prefer side by side.

This song has some solid concepts of what accountability really is for men: "Side by side…" It can best be accomplished when as men we work together on a project and honestly, openly discuss what is going on in our lives. For most women it is face to face because they are different, not wrong.

"Shoulder to Shoulder…" We all at certain points in our lives need a shoulder to lean or at times to cry upon. Accountability means standing by your brother's side or holding a sister through the rough and smooth times of life. Not seeing yourself as better, since your day is coming. The tables will turn. We cannot see ourselves as above others; we all are equal and are susceptible to what others experience.

"We'll strengthen each other…" The Bible says, *"Two are better than one, because they have a good return for their work: If one falls down, his friend can help him up. But pity the man who falls and has no one to help him up! Also, if two lie down together, they will keep warm. But how can one keep warm alone? Though one may be overpowered, two can defend themselves. A cord of three strands is not quickly broken."* *(Ecclesiastes 4:9-12 NIV)*. There is no greater argument for accountability.

When we develop "essential relationships," we become stronger, as we help each other through our struggles and shortfalls, rejoicing together as we encourage one another towards God's design for us. The Wise Man puts it this way, *"As iron sharpens iron, so one man sharpens another."* *(Proverbs 27:17)*. Just like swords get sharper during a sword fight. How? Because, as they come into contact, they knock off the small rough spots on the blades, and serve to smooth out each other; thus producing an even more finely sharpened cutting edge. Similarly, we sharpen one another by coming into contact and 'smoothing out our rough edges.'

Our Travel

The moment we are born we are on a journey, whether we want to travel or not. It is to become like Jesus. Some of us know where we are going. It is the ones who do not know that we are to be afraid of. They have a great deal of influence and will try to divert us from our destiny.

If we understand that becoming more like Jesus is a journey, not a destination. Then we will understand that we need help. It does not matter how long our trip. Any human trip involves us calling upon a number of relationships. If by car, we may need help from our mechanic to get it ready for the road, or get our tickets from the airline. Whatever mode of transportation we use, we need the pilot or directions. We have to buy gas. Even if we use a card or the computer, it needed someone to program it, someone to put the gas in the container, program the pump so that we could get the gas. Even if we got our ticket off the internet, there are several people who did their job so that we could be helped.

God has made us to be interdependent. Christ-likeness is a long journey and needs time to let go of anything that messes with our minds and hurts our relationship with God. As 'iron sharpens iron,' we can be changed; shaped, formed, molded by the Master into the person He wants us to be. For this to happen we need people who we are accountable to, as we make this important journey. Like any journey there are many distractions and attractions that can cause us to become sidetracked and not arrive at our destiny safely.

Needed More Today

We need more help today with our relationships because of our fragmented society. Many of us no longer have our extended family around, like grandparents, uncles, and aunts, even cousins to help us to grow up and become emotionally mature. Children today are more intelligent, richer, computer literate and more of everything else than previous generations; but, they are emotionally bankrupt. I believe the main reason is, they do not have the elderly around to teach them what life is all about.

Our children have difficulty talking to us as their parents because they feel that the age gap is too close. They will easier listen to grandparents and older people since they believe these know what life is all about. Instead, they have the television which does not have the interactive ability and the child's best interest at heart. Also, they usually look at shows with people of their age, who have not yet begun to experience life: Thus, lives in a fantasy world. In addition, we have children who are emotionally immature raising the next generation. Many of us make the mistake and put our parents or grandparents in a nursing home too early and do not allow them to spend more time with their grandchildren. At times you do not have a choice since it is beyond your control. But, far too often it is because of our work schedule. At times we are in another state or country to them.

Thus, there is more need for accountability. The church has to stand in the gap and help get the older citizens to spend time with the youth to impart to them their wisdom. Like Paul says, the older women should teach the younger ones, so also the older men. That is a part of what accountability is all about. If we don't, we will lose the next generation.

It's Importance

Because of these and other reasons, we must make a conscious effort to develop and maintain relationships and ask God to lead us to an accountability partner. This is one Biblical concept many churches have failed to develop. God knows that we need help and has made the provision necessary so that we can receive help from each other. Someone has rightly said, "Consider this: It is not ability, but accountability that determines your success."

Even in nature we find this concept. You know why geese fly in a "V" formation? Because the aerodynamics of the "V" enable them to fly over 70% further than if they fly alone. As each bird flaps its wings, it creates an updraft for the bird behind it. When the bird in front gets tired (he's working the hardest), he moves back and another one takes its place. Do you see the analogy here? We can go a lot further in life, if we work together, helping one another. Discipleship on our own is impossible. We need all the help we can get.

An area that we overlook is what the Bible says, we overcome by the word of our testimony—once you testify you are accountable now to whoever listened, to live up to what you said you will do. You do not want to let them down. In a similar manner, if you tell your accountability partner that you will not do something, you are accountable to him/her never to do it again. When you do get the urge, you can call for help. We are quicker to help people we know. So, the deeper the relationship the greater the chances we will help.

It Is Biblical

The Bible is rich with the idea of accountability. Some texts are interpreted in the context of marriage only. For example, "Bear ye one another's burden" (Galatians 6:2). Another is Ecclesiastes

4:9-12 NIV. This is not primarily talking about marriage, but of friendship. That is what it says, "his friend can help him up." If it is marriage, not all of us have a spouse, we all have friends and need help. We are easily overpowered when just one is fighting, our chances of winning increase with the numbers.

Jesus demonstrated this concept very clearly, He sent out His disciples two by two. *"And he called unto him the twelve, and began to send them forth by two and two; and gave them power over unclean spirits;"* (Mark 6:7). One of the reasons for this was for accountability. They were to encourage and spur each other on. Paul chimes in on this accountability and points out, *"If any man speak in an unknown tongue, let it be by two, or at the most by three, and that by course; and let one interpret"* (1 Corinthians 14:27).

Jesus took this concept of accountability to another level in that very often He would go off with three of His disciples Peter, James, and John. We too need a core of individuals around us, especially since He is our example. Remember when they were in Gethsemane He asked them for help. There are and will be times when we will need human help to get through our wilderness experiences. *"Some men came, bringing to him a paralytic, carried by four of them. Since they could not get him to Jesus because of the crowd, they made an opening in the roof above Jesus and, after digging through it, lowered the mat the paralyzed man was lying on"* (Mark 2:3-4). This is a remarkable story because this young man could find four friends to help him in his hour of need. The question we need to ask ourselves and especially us men, do we have four friends who would do something like that for us? How about three? Maybe one? Regrettably, most men do not have one truly close friend.

The Bible tells us how to do this, *"Submit to one another out of reverence for Christ."* (Ephesians 5:21). The reason why we need to submit to one another is because it does not matter how good I am today in overcoming sin in my life. When life throws me a curve ball or a bouncer and my defenses are down, if I do not have help I will be struck out or hurt. I will buckle under the pressure. We are sinners saved by grace who need to support each other.

- Love each other (John 15:17)
- Serve one another in love (Galatians 5:13)
- Be kind and compassionate to one another (Eph 4:32)
- Carry each other's burdens (Galatians 6:2)
- Confess sins and pray for each other (James 5:16)
- Be devoted to one another in brotherly love. Honor one another above yourselves (Romans 12:10)
- Accept one another (Romans 15:7)
- Encourage and build each other up (1 Thess 5:11)
- Spur each on toward love and good deeds (Hebrews 10:24)

All these passages can be summed up in one word, accountability. At its root, accountability involves either the expectation or assumption of account-giving behavior.

Biblical Examples

The Bible is filled with examples of "essential relationships" among the great men of God. Moses had Aaron. David had Jonathan. *"And Jonathan made a covenant with David because he loved him as himself"* (1 Samuel 18:3). David said *"I grieve for you, Jonathan my brother; you were very dear to me. Your love for me was wonderful, more wonderful than that of women."* (2 Samuel 1:26). Paul had Silas, Timothy and Titus, to name a few. In fact, once Paul was led by God to witness at Troas, but he did not, because he would not go there alone: *"I still had no peace of mind, because I did not find my brother Titus there"* (2 Corinthians. 2:12). Jesus had the twelve and an even closer relationship with Peter, James and John. All the men God used to do great things had "essential relationships" with other men? They recognized the need for each other. They did not try to go it alone. Even Jesus, who was fully God and fully man, portrayed the importance of "essential relationships." No one becomes great without help from other people.

Principles Needed

- Sharing our true feelings (authenticity)
- Encouraging each other (mutuality)
- Supporting one another (sympathy)
- Forgiving each other (mercy)
- Speaking the truth in love (honesty)
- Admitting our weaknesses (humility),
- Respecting our differences (courtesy)
- Not gossiping (confidentiality)
- Making the person a priority (frequency)

Necessary Ingredients

In order for accountability to be successful there are some basic ingredients necessary.

Sharing

One of the most widely-recognized characteristics of twelve-step programs is the requirement that members admit that they "have a problem." Attendees at group meetings share their experiences, challenges, successes and failures, and provide peer support for one another. Many who have joined these groups report they found success that previously eluded them. No wonder Jesus said the people of the world are smarter than people in the church.

In the spiritual context it is a few people of the same sex getting together to share their lives, getting to know each other beyond the casual and superficial; beyond "weather and sports." People allowing themselves to be challenged. I believe that is why we fail so often when we try to do things by ourselves. If we share with others what we are going through they can come along side and help coach us through.

Transparency

We must have a desire to share and be honest, to do so one must be willing to be transparent. The truth is our life is an open book, no matter how much we try to close it. There is coming a day when we will have to give an account of our lives to God (Romans 14:12). Why not begin practicing now.

In all twelve step programs accountability is practiced. One must have a sponsor, so that if the person has the craving or the urge for that which he wants to overcome, he could call his sponsor anytime. Even if he ended up at the bar or the place that he hangs out, he could call his sponsor to come and get him. Why, because of accountability. We were designed to help each other. We cannot reach the heights we need to reach without vulnerability. In order to be successful we cannot lie but tell each other the truth even if hurts or is embarrassing. Without transparency, accountability is a waste of time. Many Christians love to hide from the brethren. That is why we are so weak.

Courage

There is the possibility of being rejected and being hurt again. But, it's the only way to grow spiritually and enjoy emotional health. Growth in any area of life only happens when risks are taken. The most difficult is being honest with ourselves and others. This does not mean we are responsible for all God's people; still, we are responsible to them. Courage is needed to speak the truth, rather than gloss over or ignore it. The truth must be spoken in love. It

        You Were Made To Worship God 24/7

is easier to speak it in a condemnatory manner since we are right and it feels better.

It is easier to ignore issues than deal with them, furthermore, we are afraid of conflict. When our issues are never resolved, there is a great deal of frustration. We all know what the problem is, but, it is not discussed openly. Yet, everyone is gossiping about it. Paul advises us, *"Go ahead and be angry. You do well to be angry—but don't use your anger as fuel for revenge. And don't stay angry. Don't go to bed angry. Don't give the Devil that kind of foothold in your life"* (*Ephesians 4:26-27 Msg*). Truth be told, we prefer for people to be honest and open rather than flatter us.

Our Brother's Keeper

It is not that we see the other person as God. It just means we give an account of our abilities or inabilities to others. It is good practice for what is to eventually come. They are teaching personal accountability in the work place. It is improving the moral and productivity of companies. If it is needed in the work place, it is needed everywhere. The Bible implies when Cain asked the question am I my brother's keeper, the answer is yes.

Regrettably, we have become a society unto ourselves: it is like the Israelites in the days of the judges, "everybody did what was pleasing in his sight." We are a law unto ourselves. What we do is our business and nobody else's. Yet, we fail to realize our relatedness and interconnectedness. What we do affect each other. For example, if we do not discipline our children then the State will discipline them. First, they are locked up as juvenile delinquents. They now have a record, and are considered outcasts of society. They join with others, to whom they become accountable, who consider themselves outcasts of society. They create all kinds of havoc in our community, from gangs to murder, and everything else in between. It is our tax dollars that take care of them in prison. We are all affected. If you decide to sleep around even though it is done in private and you get AIDS then you become society's problem. Your life affects your family, friends, relatives, co-workers, boss, and others around you. It is not just about you. We are our brother's keeper.

One Big Family

God is our Father thus, we are one big family, this is a fact whether we believe it or not. He is a God of variety that is why we have different ethnic groups. But, there is only one race, the human race. This means there are certain things we have in common. One of them is burdens and the Bible says, we must bear one another burdens (Ephesians 6:2).

We are first accountable to God. We encounter difficulties since we cannot see Him, and at times we tend to take Him for granted. Other times, since we are not struck down like Ananias and Sappharia, we do what we should not do. Sometimes it is because the flesh is weak. Jesus showed us the need for each other in Gethsemane. He wanted His disciples to help Him go through His agony. That's why He has given us relationships that we can see and experience the need for help from others. When we are unaccountable to anyone, we become like Lucifer. We believe that life revolves around us. We do what is right in our own eyes. Hence, our need for others to keep us grounded.

The Purpose Of

Before we go any further, let me restate the purpose and goal of accountability: To reach our full potential as children of God, to grow more Christ-like, to have a better family life, help with the issues of being a man or woman in this world, getting stronger in resisting temptation and knowing that we do not have all it takes to face our struggles alone; that one or more friends need to stand beside us, support us, encourage us, and pray for us. Striving together *"to be made new in the attitude of your minds; and to put on the new self, created like God in true righteousness and holiness"* (Eph 4:23-24 NIV).

But, if we really want to be all God wants us to be. I believe we eventually have to be held accountable for those lives that are destroying our relationship with God and each other. The 'secret sins' we'd rather not talk about. Some of us struggle with, affairs (sexual or emotional), gossiping, pornography, lying, cheating, stealing. But none of us are without something that diminishes our relationship with God and that affects one another. If we believe otherwise, then pride is one of the things we need to deal with. We need each other to deal with what is tearing us apart. We cannot do it alone! We can comfort others with the comfort we received from God (2 Corinthians 1). *"Therefore confess your sins to each other and pray for each other so that you may be healed. The prayer of a righteous man is powerful and effective."* (James 5:15-16 NIV). James is encouraging us to be accountable and pray for each other. The only way we can become Christ-like.

Difficulties With

Being accountable takes a tremendous amount of character, courage, and candor, especially if we seek an accountability partner for a goal we desire to achieve. It is not an easy thing to do (being accountable) or ask for (accountability). It takes intestinal fortitude and integrity. I personally have some serious difficulty with it because our parents taught us not to let others know what is going on in our lives. Even if we have to drink water and eat dry bread that is no one's business. This interpretation comes from the Bible, going in our closet and not letting our left hand know what our right hand is doing. They misinterpreted this from Matthew 6:3, 6. These have to be balanced with, we are our brother's keeper, bear ye one another's burdens and two is better than one, which are also

Biblical. Many people are not in an accountability relationship because they do not understand what it is, or they do not know how to get started.

It must first be a matter of much prayer. Make a commitment to being accountable. Ask God to send the one(s) you need in your life. Be willing and ready to put in the time and the hard work it is going to take. It will pay great dividends. Do not get discouraged if you feel like you are not progressing quickly. It will take a while to reach the point where you are comfortable revealing anything deeply personal. It does not just happen. It may not come quickly or easily. It takes time, often a long time, to develop 'essential relationship' necessary for meaningful accountability. You may want to phase it in as you build trust, and get comfortable opening up to each other. For instance, you may start by being accountable in "safe" areas, such as prayer and Bible study. Then gradually move to more serious issues as you get to know each other.

Even if you have been friends a long time, remember that accountability is not automatic or even natural. In "essential relationships" accountability comes almost exclusively from deliberate and intentional efforts. We cannot be like Adam and just stand there and do nothing. Most of us men stay to ourselves, a social dilemma that still exists today. We tend to be most comfortable when the conversation is light and we do not have to reveal anything 'deep' about ourselves. We mostly are more task, than relationship oriented. We worry so much about getting from Point A to B, we forget to enjoy the journey. Friends often do not get the priority and attention they deserve as a result.

A common question men ask is why? Being the independent creatures we are, the idea of 'needing' other men does not sit too well with us. Someone jokingly said, "You know the real reason Israel wandered in the desert for forty years? Moses refused to stop and ask

                    You Were Made To Worship God 24/7

for directions!" We do not want to rely on others. Accountability must be a conscious choice. It is not going to just happen. When we do not make this choice we become a law unto ourselves, dictators, like Cain, King Saul, Sadam, Hitler, and others. As difficult as it is, we must become accountable to our fellowmen.

Hindering Factors

A couple of factors that keep especially men from developing close partnerships are pride and fear. Do you ever have trouble admitting when you have made a mistake, or that you are wrong? I do. When we get into 'essential relationships' with others, it will ultimately require us to be vulnerable and transparent, and to admit that we have faults and problems. And that can be quite uncomfortable. "I do not need anybody else!" Sound familiar? I spent most of my life believing that. But, time after time, the Bible shows that *"It is not good for the man to be alone"* (Genesis 2:18). God was not simply referring to a man's need for a wife. I believe He was stating our need for each other. We are prideful when we do not think we have anything more to learn. Or when we know what to do, and refuse to do it, because of how it will make us look in the eyes of others.

We allow fear, because it is unknown territory take a hold of us. The Bible tells us how to deal with it, *"There is no fear in love; but perfect love casteth out fear: because fear hath torment. He that feareth is not made perfect in love"* (1 John 4:18). The antidote for fear then is love. Pride prevents us from loving one another. It comes from believing that the world revolves around us. If it is not about me, it cannot be about anyone else, not even God. It means we do not have room in our heart for others.

Advantages Of

The purpose of these 'essential relationships' is to help us reach our full potential as disciples of Jesus. One of the great benefits of accountability is that we will look at our lives more closely. Raise our awareness of things that, previously we would not give a second thought. Eventually, our actions and behavior will change, as we share our struggles with others, and pray about them. Another is relief to discover we are not the only ones struggling in that area. However, together we can learn to overcome it. This is what Solomon meant 'iron sharpens iron' (Proverbs 27:17). And John tells us, *"They overcame by the word of their testimony"* (*Revelation 12:11*).

As we build relationships, sharing our struggles and make ourselves accountable to each other, we will experience a bonding and friendship like no other. It may not be easy, but it is worth it. It was Andrew Murray who said, "The highest proof of true friendship is the intimacy that holds nothing back and admits to a friend our inmost secrets."

If you ever look at the Nature Channel, you will notice predator's tactics like an alligator attacking a vulnerable doe or a coyote stalking a fawn. They single out the weakest member of a group, like a crippled or injured one. This is not just limited to nature; it is also true in the spiritual. The Bible says we are sent as sheep in the midst of wolves. As God's people we must recognize that the enemy seeks to destroy us through every point of weakness. Wherever weakness is perceived, whether across the oceans, within our homes, or within us, the enemy will attack. The Bible emphasizes that he seeks out the weakness in our personal lives, families, communities, and nations. Like a wild predator, the enemy camouflages his intent, looks for areas of weakness and attacks suddenly. Our vulnerabilities often come from mental, emotional,

 You Were Made To Worship God 24/7

and spiritual injuries. We may, like Jacob, walk with a limp because of our warfare or some bad choices.

We are continually being tested. Are we as strong as tempered steel? Are we a rock-solid wall of protection for those we love? Are we standing on an unshakable foundation? Are we connected to the source that will enable us to make the right decisions and give us the strength to stand firm when the cause is right, as our security depends upon it? We must choose to be connected to and dependent upon power from above and around us. If not, our weaknesses will be attacked and we will fall. Thus the Bible teaches that we are to put on the spiritual armor and consistently resist the schemes and intentions of the Devil. We clearly understand that the enemy is a deceiver and an accuser, seeking to bring division and dissension, tearing down the intended victim's ability to stand strong. Like in the wild, the more the prey depends upon the security of the herd, the safer they are. The same is true in our own homes, churches and communities. In a strong and dependable family unit, the parents and children are less vulnerable to attack. The same is true with accountability partners. If we are divided we cannot withstand the assault and fury of the predatory intentions of the enemy.

How to Get an Accountability Partner(s)

We first must be accountable to God as we seek His help in finding 'essential relationships.' We have to do this by praying for His direction. This cannot be just anybody. We need divine help to choose the right person. We want someone who is not a friend, a mother, a nag and certainly not someone who is going to feel sorry for us and join our pity parties. He or she is not someone we share all our excuses with, why we did not do what we said we were going to do. Not one we dump on or who will give us advice. We are not looking for a counselor. He or she is someone we are serious with.

One who is trustworthy and will not repeat to others the things we discussed or the goals we have. Someone that we have given the right to ask us how we are doing in relation to our goals or struggles we are trying to overcome or achieve. They will even challenge us as to why we are doing what we are doing, thereby causing us to ponder our real motives. They can ask how we are spending our time or our money in relation to the goals we are asking accountability for. We should give them straight and honest answers. If we cannot be straight and honest then we are probably not willing to be accountable yet or perhaps do not quite understand how to best use them.

Questions of Accountability

Questions we can ask and expect straight answers, not excuses or beating around the bush:

- What exactly are your goals? Let me see them.
- What are you doing to achieve them? Show me.
- Can you show me the books you read, classes took, money spent, connections made, commitments and decisions made, etcetera?
- How did you spend your time?
- Show me last week's schedule on exactly how you used your time.
- Why do you have this goal or that goal?
- Why do you think this is valuable to do?
- Why are you doing this or that?
- Who do you model and what you know about them?

You can see this line of questioning asks who, why, what, where, and when. I tend to lean more on the why questions. To quote Wilhelm Nietzsche, "He who has a why to live can bear almost any how." Once the why is clear then it's simply a matter of the plan to achieve the goal and keeping on track making necessary adjustments.

In concluding, whatever your goals make sure they are God's as well. I wish you the confidence and courage to dream big dreams, plan serious plans and be accountable and responsible in your growth and development. Remember, there is no magic formula or technique for developing 'essential friendships.' The best advice is to just get out there and do it. You'll learn what works and what does not. You might find that you do not click with a certain person. Do not worry about it. Try again and do not quit.

THE HOW OF RELATIONSHIPS

Chapter 14

My Responsibility

IT WAS BOOKER T. WASHINGTON who said, "Few things help an individual more than to place responsibility upon him, and to let him know that you trust him." We must take responsibility for our lives. We can make all the excuses now, but, there is coming a day when we cannot use them anymore. Every one of us will give an account of the things we have said and done, the relationships we have formed or failed to form. We have to make developing and maintaining relationships our main concern in life, with the understanding that it requires hard work. It takes the focus off of us and onto others. We have to learn about others, how they view life, their uniqueness, how do I complement them and how they me? How are they different and how can I enhance their lives and they mine?

Relationships Must Be Priority

We have become preoccupied with accumulating things, when God wants us to become obsessed with relationships. Think about it. The only thing we will be able to take into the next life, in addition to our character, are relationships. Everything else will be destroyed. Like I pointed out in my first book, *"You Are Prosperous Believe It Or Not"* this was brought home most forcefully with Hurricanes Katrina and Rita when everything was under water, the rich and poor could not get to the banks or ATMs. All they had to rely on were relationships to get through the ordeal.

Life is hard and when it begins to be cruel to us, all the stuff we have cannot help us. All our money cannot help us bear the unthinkable; it is only people with God's help. That is why Paul admonished us, *"Bear ye one another's burdens and so fulfill the love of Christ"* (Galatians 6:2).

It's Personal

There are many who help to contribute to the problems we encounter in trying to develop relationships—Satan uses our families, schools, teachers, churches, pastors, communities and leaders. But, the Bible makes it clear that we all have to answer to God for ourselves. *"As surely as I live,' says the Lord, 'every knee will bow before me; every tongue will confess to God.' So then, each of us will give an account of himself to God. Therefore let us stop passing judgment on one another. Instead, make up your mind not to put any stumbling block or obstacle in your brother's way"* (Romans 11:11-13 NIV). Anyone who does must answer to God. We cannot focus on them, just make sure that we do not put obstacles in others paths. Why? We have to give an account and cannot pass the buck on judgment day.

It is not my fault is a theme heard very often, he or she made me do it. However, I am responsible for the relationships or non-relationships that exist in my life. I cannot blame anyone or anything. I have to take responsibility. True, this is not politically correct. God does not function according to polls. We have too many frivolous law suits in America. We must be held accountable for our actions and made to bear the consequences of our decisions.

We are responsible for our relationships. We cannot blame others for them not working out. We are answerable for our salvation. The Bible says, *"Work out your own salvation with fear and trembling"*

(*Philippians 2:12*). We cannot be like Adam and Eve and continue to play the "Blaming Game." It is our job to make sure we know what God is saying to us. Once we reach an age of answerability, it is our duty to know God for ourselves. This does not mean we do not need help. Discipleship is not a secret thing between us and God as many believe. This has destroyed many relationships.

Doing What is Right in Our Own Eyes

Like the Israelites during the days of the Judges. We are doing what is right and pleasing in our eyes (Judges 17:6). We do not want to be corrected by anyone. We feel we know what is best. We are so much into ourselves that we have even violated the command found in Hebrews 10:25, *"Let us not give up meeting together, as some are in the habit of doing, but let us encourage one another—and all the more as you see the day approaching"* (NIV). We do not see the need to go to church. All we have to do is turn on our TV and have church. This is a dangerous place to be. We must examine our lives and make sure we are not a part of this group.

Like Micah in Judges 17, we choose our own priests instead of the one God ordained for us. In some cases our television becomes our priest. The same TV has become our god, with the many other gods that we possess. Thus we are totally disconnected from God and our fellowmen. Sure, like Micah's mother, we know the right religious words, *"Blessed be thou of the Lord, my son"* (*Judges 17:3 NIV*). Even though he stole the silver, he was not reprimanded.

I do not understand how we say we love God and come to His house once a week and not involved in any ministry. Yet we feel comfortable. We do not have any physical ailments preventing us. Those ailing, we have to take the church to them. We cannot have a relationship and just come to church for two hours. Do not tell me you have no need for church. Then you are no different to

Micah. It was God who commanded us to come together and more often in the last days. We cannot make it alone. We need and must encourage one another, especially in these last days.

Our Example

Jesus' custom was to go to church every Sabbath (Luke 4:16). He stayed connected to His Father and man. Jesus took time out for building up His relationship with Him (Mark 1:35). He also took time to develop relationships with His disciples and people. Jesus realized He needed their help in accomplishing His purposes. The most important, developing a relationship with them. Then help Him in His ministries for success. For example, going out and making disciples. In the process Jesus was teaching them how to live a successful life as His disciples. Because He needed them to carry on the work He started, when He returned to heaven. Jesus demonstrated most eloquently by the life He lived that "we are our brother's keeper." So it is not just about me, myself, and I.

Acknowledgement

The first thing we have to do is acknowledge we have difficulty with developing and maintaining relationships. Then look within and see where we are encouraging, creating, or fostering problems that are hindering us from meaningful relationships. Are we doing everything in our power to foster good relationships or sabotage them?

We were made for relationships: Living in harmony with God, our fellowmen, nature and ourselves. We encounter difficulties when we do not experience this harmony. It creates conflict in our lives. And the worst conflict is found within. It must come out. Hence, we disconnect with everyone around us. We have to find the areas we are disconnected and with God's help, bring about reconnections with the people He placed in our lives.

Harmony

To develop genuine relationships, we must have harmony within. It must exist between what we believe, say, and practice. We talk a good talk and live differently. Jesus captures this so eloquently, *"So you must obey them and do everything they tell you. But do not do what they do, for they do not practice what they preach"* (Matthew 23:3). Millard J. Erickson in ***"Does It Matter If God Exists?"*** (Grand Rapids: Baker Books, 1996 p 34), puts it this way, "Our official theology is what we believe in theory, what we say we subscribe to…Our unofficial theology is what we actually believe and practice, the belief that underlies what we do and is revealed in our actions." That is, we live our lives by what we believe, not by what we know or say. Herein lies the disharmony. We know God, but we do not believe in Him. So we do not do what He says. If we cannot believe and trust Him, then we sure cannot trust and believe our fellowmen.

Then we become frustrated with ourselves when there is no consistency in our lives. If frustrated, we cannot experience joy. We cannot be happy and frustrated at the same time, when what we believe, say, and do are not in harmony. We believe one thing and do another. Like we believe stealing is wrong, and we actually say to ourselves, "I will not steal today." Not even five minutes pass and you are stealing. While you are doing it you feel guilty. However, your enjoyment is stronger than your guilt and you steal some more. Then you feel guilty, discouraged, and frustrated.

You are trying to figure out, why can't I just stop? You pray and ask God to forgive you and promise you will never do it again. But, you keep stealing. You do not want to seek help because people will talk about you. You cannot overcome addictions by yourself. You need help. You need people to whom you are accountable and who will hold you accountable and show tough love when you mess up.

Hence, we have become very competent in theory and not in practice. So, we will find those who appear to be spiritual giants. They know the Bible from Genesis to Revelation, understand prophecy, and can quote verbatim books of the Bible. Yet, that same person does not know how to treat people or how to act on the job. They are social dwarfs. There are others who can shout and be slain in the Spirit. But, on Monday they are intimidate by a doctor or lawyer. You begin to wonder if they are the same person or if they are suffering from schizophrenia. See the book the Lord gave, ***"The Great Disconnection: Between the Christian in Church and in Life."***

Do Not be Fooled

Many will admonish you to forget your past and move on. They quote Philippians 3:14 to support their theory, *"Forgetting those things which were passed and let us press forward."* This is quoting Paul out of context. When we read the preceding verses, we see that he was not talking about the issues in his life that he dealt with. He was talking about his accomplishments in the flesh: Like circumcised the eighth day, of the tribe of Benjamin, a Hebrew of Hebrews, legalistic, and faultless. There was no one to compare with him. These are the things he forgot. Paul considered these as rubbish in order to know Jesus and the power of His resurrection. He knew who he was and spent three years in the desert dealing with who he was and his issues. He had to re-learn some things. The reasons why he could have said this was because he had come to grips with his past. That's why he was so bold, fearless, and had such a drive to do what God called him to do. He understood his past and lived in the present on his way to accomplishing

God's destiny for him. Our history keeps us anchored to the present and gives us hope for the future.

To know your destiny, you need to know your history. You cannot separate yourself from your past. It is the sum total of who you are. You have to understand and confront your past, use what is beneficial to your present and future and get rid of the rest. For example, I will not use the excuse, "God, I am afraid of injections because of a bad experience while growing up." Instead, I admit I made a mistake by lying to my parents about my physical condition. I know, ask Him to help me not to fear them. This would not be possible if I did not deal with my past and now I use it for my present and future.

Do not try to forget your past. God knows how easily we are prone to that, He reminds us over and over, "Do not forget." You see, when we try to forget who we are or used to be, a disconnection is created. We need to use our past to teach us for now and the future. Let me further illustrate; I am a very messy guy. My mother is a neat freak; so is my wife. My father is the exact opposite. His car, for example, is dirty and unkempt. That is the same way I keep our vehicles. Because I know that, I try with greater effort to keep our vehicles clean to enhance my relationship with Esther. We can only develop solid relationships when we come to grips with our past and deal with it.

God knows the past is important and easy to forget and disconnect. Hence, He has given us certain memorials to remember the past so that we can stay connected. Like our birthday, conversion day, baptismal day (the latter two are normally forgotten by many as important as they are), the Sabbath day, a memorial of Creation, and the communion service that reminds us of His death, burial, and resurrection. God is constantly connecting us with the past so that we do not forget Him. If we forget our past we will forget God and each other.

Sharing

God designed us to share everything that He has given us. We are made in the image of God and it is part of His nature to share, and He wants us to do the same. And we want to, the problem is we end up sharing what we have and who we are with the wrong people and get hurt in the process. This adversely affects how we develop eternal relationships. It makes us afraid. Still, it is in our nature to give and we are not sure why we are giving. True, sometimes the motives are selfish. That does not matter, we will give. We must understand why we give or we will deny who we are and continue forming destructive relationships and give to the wrong persons and for the wrong reasons.

We not only want to give things, but ourselves to someone else physically. So we get married, shack up, or have one night stands. Why? We want to share our bodies. Not only do we want to share what we have, we want to share who we are. At times there is a trade off by giving sex and hoping the other person would get to know the real you. Many times we are dissatisfied since that is putting the cart before the horse. Before sleeping with someone, they should have already known the real you, gotten married and then made love.

We are searching for a connection with God and each other. We long to share who we really are, flaws and all, with others and be accepted just as and for who we are. That is, we want to be loved unconditionally. We all are on a quest for that and we are willing to sell our souls in the process if needs be. We long for a place to belong where we can be ourselves. That is why homes or churches that create this type of atmosphere, the children and members want to be there. When they leave, they cannot wait to come back. When this is not found, they join gangs or go places like the club where they are accepted or feel accepted for who they are. It does not matter how wrong or bad it is. The desire to have relationships where you are accepted at times is greater than what is right or wrong.

The church can learn some things from gangs. Some of you cringe when you read that line. Are the gangs successful in recruiting and keeping their members? They have members who would rather die than give up their association with what is illegal, immoral or anti-social. There are some principles they use that the home, school, and church should be following. Many young people are making the choice not go to church. One of the main reasons is because they do not feel as though they belong or a part of church. The older folks have difficulty relating to them. Some of you are saying they are the problem; however, we are the adults and we have difficulty relating to them and each other.

Provision needs to be made for people to share who they are without criticism. Be free to make mistakes and know they are still loved and accepted. It is important to have friends and relationships where we can be ourselves or else we become prisoners of our emotions and we will find ways to break free. God made us with emotions to be expressed and they will find a way to be expressed, negatively or positively. Since we have not been taught how to express them positively, we will naturally express them negatively.

The truth is we will share who we are with somebody. Sometimes because no one who cares is listening, we will find a stranger, prostitute or anyone who will give us the time of day and pour out who we are. The responsibility still rests with us; we have to be aware of the disharmony in our lives. If our church is not teaching the Word, if we are not being discipled and taught to disciple others, find a church that is and attend. You will have to give God an account for your life and not that of any other, not even your children.

Not knowing who we are, we do not know our potential, abilities, gifts, resources, heritage or inheritance. We cannot share them with others. Also, we do not have the capability to know any other person. When we do not know who we are, we are not aware of God's plans, purposes, ministries, vocations and destiny for us. We cannot help people to know what He has deposited in them. We have no idea of the greatness He wants us to accomplish. It is a sad thing when we do not know what we possess. We cannot pass them on to others so we can all benefit. For more see the book, **God Created You for Greatness! Are you Experiencing It?"**

Our Concern is Bread

We are so caught up in laboring for the bread that fills us temporally. We have isolated ourselves, even from our children. Jesus warned us in John 6:27, *"Labour not for the meat which perisheth, but for that meat which endureth unto everlasting life, which the Son of man shall give unto you: for him hath God the Father sealed."* This is not new. In the days of the prophet, Haggai, the temple of the Lord was lying in ruins, even though God had brought His people back to Jerusalem to rebuild it eighteen years earlier. Ignoring Him, the people got caught up in building their own houses, enjoying their new freedom, and partaking of the bounties of the land. In short, they were living by bread alone. They became so busy with themselves and the blessings of God, they forget about the temple lying in ruins. He had to remind them, get their priorities straight in Haggai 1:3-14.

Today, God is speaking to us individually. We have lost sight of our Divine destiny. We too have gotten caught up with living by bread alone. How? By building our own houses, making a living, enjoying the riches of the land, we have neglected God and His people. It is true we've built grand edifices in the last fifty years, with wall to wall carpet, stained glass windows, antique furniture, and the latest electronics and instruments. However, they are just white-washed

                    You Were Made To Worship God 24/7

sepulchers filled with dry bones. We have neglected the real house of God, the temple made without hands, our bodies.

It is time for us to consider our ways. It seems as if we have a great deal to boast about—our great meetings in the most expensive hotels and stadiums, healings, revivals, miracles, signs and wonders. When these are tested they crumble under pressure. There is no lasting transformation. We have spent billions of dollars with very little to show for it. We work hard and have so much yet, we never seem to have enough. That's why there is so much begging for money (bread). There is really no real church growth, but dissatisfied, discontented and disgruntled members moving from one church to another. They have difficulty relating one to another. There is no real conversion. You ask how I know. Why is there so much fighting, backbiting, division, and gossiping among church members and minister? Why are we spending billions every year with so little to show? We must consider our focus. Is it on bread alone or every word that proceeds out of God's mouth?

God has blown upon what we have. We lack the power and His anointing. We are busy building our kingdoms, making a name for ourselves, seeking our own bread. We go to church, but as money changers, robbers and thieves. We have made God's house of prayer one of business transactions instead. It is time to get up out of our places of comfort and entertainment and, like Moses, Abraham, Peter, James, John and Jesus, go up the mountain to worship and develop a relationship with God. It is not an easy road. We have to climb; and will encounter snakes, scorpions, lions, bears and other creatures. Make a path up the mountain to get to the top. It calls for blood, sweat, tears, and blisters to get there. We have been made to believe Discipleship is smooth sailing into the Kingdom. So, when we encounter any difficulties we run back down the mountain. We do not have any deep abiding relationships with people to come along side us and see us through. The climb is a difficult one; that is why the Bible says that two is better than one, when we fall we have someone to pick us up (Ecclesiastes 4).

Worry

In spite of all I just wrote, there is no need to worry because the God we serve is loving and forgiving. He is willing to forgive us right now if we ask Him, even though our motives were impure in the beginning. Even if we were more concerned about physical bread and not seeking Jesus, the bread of life, accept Him now (Please turn to the back page).

Jesus says not to worry about what we should eat, drink or wear. He promised to take care of these things for us just like He clothes the lilies and the grass which are here today and gone tomorrow. He reminds us we are more important than these. Why would He not take care of us, His children? (Matthew 6). The main reason why I believe Jesus helps us in this area is that we can find the time to develop relationships, like He did while He walked this earth. He found the time to help people because He knew His Father was looking out for Him. The reason why we can believe this is because of His past record. He demonstrated this when He created Adam and Eve, He provided all they needed first, then, created them. When the children of Israel left Egypt they did not have to worry about money. God told them to go and ask for all the gold and silver they needed from the Egyptians, even though they worked for it and it was now pay day. However, they would not have gotten it if God did not tell them to ask for it. They did not have to worry about food. It was provided every day without fail. Water was not a problem because at times it came from a rock. If it were bitter, all Moses had to do was throw some bush in it and miraculously it became sweet. Their clothes did not wear out for forty years. Could you imagine them wearing the same clothes for forty years? They had the cloud to cool them off and it was used as a means of direction. At nights when the desert became cold, there was the pillar of fire to keep them warm. In the day it shielded the sun. All these were miraculously provided daily.

We need to be reminded that this same God is alive and is doing what He has to do to take care of us, His children; just like we do everything to take care of our families. However, all this is merely bread, the physical. God has never had a problem providing the physical bread for His children. After all, *"For he spake, and it was done; he commanded, and it stood fast"* (Psalms 33:9 KJV). All Jesus has to do is speak and it happens, or he can command a bird to feed us and our family and not just any bird, a vulture if you please, just like He did for Elijah (1 King 17). He can multiply the little oil or flour that we have to last for three and a half years (1 King 17). Or, like the widow of the prophet whose little oil multiplied until it paid off all her debt (2 Kings 4). It is easy for God to miraculously provide all the bread we need. Let us concentrate on developing and maintaining relationships for now and eternity as we build up His Kingdom.

In Conclusion, what God cannot do is, get us to seek first His Kingdom or live by every word that proceeds out of His mouth. We have to want it earnestly and make that choice. That's why He does not want us to worry about the physical. He already has it covered and promised to give us our daily bread. So, we are without excuse, every person has a chance to make it into the Kingdom. There is no need to be distracted with bread. What we need to be focusing on is His Kingdom which is based on relationships. God made sure we would not have any excuses and so He has made sure we do not have to worry about our daily needs. We can focus on developing our partnership with Him and each other. He knows worrying about these things disconnect us from Him and each other.

Chapter 15

A Biblical Example

IN ORDER TO DEVELOP LONG LASTING relationships, we need to have a solid relationship with One who will never leave, forsake, or let us down. One who will always love us unconditionally, and who assures us of a glorious future. You must accept Jesus as your personal Lord and Savior. He has to be so close to you, it is personal. He will fill every void in your life. If you want a husband, father, wife, mother, doctor, lawyer, judge, He can be to you whatever you need (Exodus 3:14). He will change your approach to relationships.

We had friendships and people let us down, intentionally and unintentionally. We need a solid Rock to fall on. Jesus is that Rock, when others let us down He will always be there. He promised and the good news is He cannot lie (Titus 1:2). I recommend to you this Friend who sticks closer than a brother. If you do not know Him personally, please turn to the back of the book. You need this most important relationship, with the One who defines all other relationships.

A Solid Foundation

Jesus gave us a solid foundation on which to develop or restore friendships. It is found in the story of the Good Samaritan. Here was a man who knew who he was, why he was here and where he was going. He knew that one of the best ways of developing a relationship is by meeting people's needs: Ministering to those who need our help regardless of color, creed, or class. The needs are not always that obvious as in this story, sometimes they might be mental, social, financial, or psychological. The Spirit who has provided us with all that we need to minister, will reveal the needs of people He places in our lives. He will give us the ability to love, help, and accept help from those who hate us. Jesus Himself implemented these principles, when we hated Him, He died for us (Romans 5:8).

Our Greatest Quest

The first step in developing or restoring any relationship is to believe in God with all our mind, body, and soul. When we do, here is Peter's admonition to us, *"But grow in grace, and in the knowledge of our Lord and Saviour Jesus Christ. To him be glory both now and forever. Amen" (2 Peter 3:18).*

In Luke 10, Jesus lays down a good foundation as to how we should go about relationships. A lawyer came up to Him with a trick question, trying to trap Him. What must I do to inherit eternal life? Jesus answered with a question, *'He said unto him, What is written in the law? How readest thou? "And he answering said, Thou shalt love the Lord thy God with all thy heart, and with all thy soul, and with all thy strength, and with all thy mind; and thy neighbour as thyself. And he said unto him, Thou hast answered right: this do, and thou shalt live. But he, willing to justify himself, said unto Jesus, "And who is my neighbour?" (Luke 10:26-29).* It is only after we have found God that we can love our neighbor as ourselves. There are some neighbors who are hard to love. That's because we focus on what they are doing to us, rather than what are we doing for them?

If the truth be told this lawyer really was on a quest to find and know God. He did not know he was searching for Him. Jesus' desire was to reveal to him who God is, this is one reason why He came. We do not understand that our greatest quest in life is to know our Heavenly Father. We try to substitute Him with everything else in life, money, sex, drugs, education, food, etcetera. I believe this lawyer substituted God with his education and money. He thought he was smarter than Jesus, who was God.

When we come to realize that all our addictions are an attempt to find God, it is liberating. He wants us to be His disciples, if you are not, turn to the back and become one now. Make Jesus your most important relationship.

Find Yourself

When we believe in God with everything we have and are, in the process, we discover who we are and why He created us. He is our source and sustenance. We cannot know who we are or others until we know who God is. There was no way that the Good Samaritan could have effectively helped this man if he did not know who he was. He accepted that he was not defined by his ethnicity, religion, or geography. He realized that he was bigger than all these. Thus, he saw his fellowman in a similar light. He was a brother in need of help. And since he was secure in who he was, he was able to render the help to his brother.

The Priest and Levite did not know who they were that's why they passed on the other side. They were defined by the office they held. They did not want to become ceremonially unclean, that meant they could not participate in the upcoming service, and it might have been the big one, the Day of Atonement. They did not want to dirty their clothes, because if people saw them what would they think. People defined and controlled them. When we are defined by our office, people are not important to us, our office or title is. It might appear as if we are about people because we listen to them, we only listen because we want it to appear as though we are about people. Or we are afraid, and do not know who we are and they will tell us who we are. I remember I used to be upset when people called me Kennedy and not Pastor Vanterpool. I know the reason now is because my identity was wrapped up in my title. I had a hard time after I resigned from the last church I pastored because I was no longer recognized as a Pastor. After investing so much in the title, it was my identity.

When our title, based on our job or education, is more important than people we are more concerned about carrying out our functions, rather than caring for people. In other words, if there was a choice in helping someone, then the function took precedence over the person. We are not concerned about people and their needs. Let someone else take care of them, like the folks we consider them dogs of society. I do not have time to waste on them, I have more important things to do, my office demands it.

We fail to realize that it does not matter what our vocation, it is always about people. Whatever we do involves people. It is either we are doing something for them or to them. When we know who we are, we will be seeking occasions to be always doing what we are doing, for people, and they take priority. What we do is not what is important, it is people. But, when we do not know who we are, we are always doing things to people. What we are doing takes precedence over what we are doing for them, like the Priest and Levite.

Find Your Neighbor

According to Jesus our neighbor is anyone who is in need of our help. Here we see Jesus doing to this man what He is asking us to do, being the lawyer's neighbor. Jesus knew his heart. He could have shut him up. Sometimes, even when we know people's evil intent, it does not mean we have to be rude and obnoxious to them. Jesus tried to establish rapport with him. He gives him a way out as He allowed him to ask the question, who is my neighbor? He tells the story of the Good Samaritan. This was not just for the lawyer but all mankind (Luke 10:30-37).

Love is important to all relationships. The Good Samaritan demonstrates that he loved God by showing his love for his brother. The Priest and the Levite really did not love God or the wounded man. John reminds us we cannot love God whom we have not seen, if we cannot love our brother we can see. If we love God we will love our brother (1 John 4:20-21). The true test then of our love for God is how much we love our fellowmen.

Find Time

All three of these men I believe were busy like us today. They had places to go, things to do, and people to see. Still, our busy schedules should take a back seat to our fellowmen when facing trouble. When people need our help, we cannot be making excuses about what we have to do. The Samaritan was a busy man, however, not too busy to help his brother. He stayed and took care of him all night. He was in a hurry and maybe did not plan to stay the entire night. But, he chose to help his brother who needed him.

There are times when we have to put our agenda and schedules on hold and take time to care for each other. I have to be aware of this myself, because by the Grace of God I am on track to finish ten books by 2010 and if I am not careful, the books can become my agenda and not people. Like when my children or wife come and want to talk or ask a question and I am in the middle of a thought. I used to see my writing as being more important. I am learning to accept they are and I need to find time for them.

Sometimes if we are not careful our health suffers because we are so wrapped up in what we are doing. That is why I have to go to sleep now because I am not sleeping enough, it is now 3:15 a.m. Sabbath morning and I did not sleep on Friday during the day because I worked in the Texas hot sun for many hours.

Find Time to Listen

The Priest and the Levite heard the man's groaning and did not understand the pain he was in. They did not see and understand his condition. They actually fulfilled the prophecy of Isaiah, *"And in them is fulfilled the prophecy of Esaias, which saith, by hearing ye shall hear, and shall not understand; and seeing ye shall see, and shall not perceive:"* (Matthew 13:14). The Good Samaritan on the other hand heard the man's groaning and saw his anguished condition, felt his agonizing pain. What was the difference? He took the time to listen. His concern was not the dangerous environment and fearing for his life. The thieves could come back and he could become a victim. His concern was not what region or religion the stranger was from. He took the time to listen and heard his groans, cries, and helped him.

We cannot help people until we find time to listen. Relationships are built on time. We must stop what we are doing, physically, mentally, emotionally and hear what the other person is saying. That is, our world has to stop as we enter the other person's world and begin to hear what they are saying, see what they are seeing, and feel what they are feeling. This takes a great deal of time. Because after entering their world and understanding what the issues are, it is

     You Were Made To Worship God 24/7

time to take action. The work has just begun and we have already invested a great deal of time. Like the Samaritan, he bound up his wounds and still had to take him to the inn, spend the night with him, and spend his money which also represented his time. He had to return to pay the innkeeper.

We may have to bandage up our neighbors wounds. People may have hurt them physically and so we have to sit there and listen to the many years of abuse, like Jesus and the Woman with the issue of blood (Mark 5). He stood there and listened to her twelve years of history. Like the Samaritan we may have to spend all night, when we did not plan too, because we had other plans. We may have to return to refund their cost.

The wounds may be psychological, which are just as painful. We might not be able to help them any further than we have already. We might have to take them to a counselor for further help. They might not be able to pay the counselor so we have to pay the bill and we are willing to, until the person is made whole. God will provide the resources.

Find Respect

How do we show respect? By hanging on to every word people say. Sometimes like the Good Samaritan those words may not be audible, they might just be groans. However, he showed respect to the wounded man by demonstrating that what he was experiencing was worthy of his full attention.

The Levite and Priest had no respect for their wounded brother. Lack of respect is our number one problem in our society and one of the greatest barriers to relationships. We listen to people we respect and even more so to people who respect us. Could you imagine what would happen if we would only show respect to others, they would listen to us. It is impossible to truly listen to someone if we do not respect them. The children of Israel were able to leave Egypt with what they needed for over forty years because the Lord put respect for the Israelites in the hearts of the Egyptians, *"And I will give this people favor and respect in the sight of the Egyptians; and it shall be that when you go, you shall not go empty-handed"* (Exodus 3:21 AMP). They listened to their needs and fulfilled them. We must respect people regardless to who they are or where they came from. We are one family.

Find No Embarrassment

Jesus could have easily embarrassed the lawyer. If He did, then He would not have treated him as His neighbor. Instead He showed respect. The truth is the lawyer had a spiritual need and Jesus met it, plus the need of the others present. This also reminds me of Joseph in reestablishing his relationship with his brothers. He did not treat them the way they treated him. He did not give them what they deserved. He forgave them. After revealing himself to them listen to what he said, this is remarkable,

> *Now therefore be not grieved, nor angry with yourselves, that ye sold me hither: for God did send me before you to preserve life. For these two years hath the famine been in the land: and yet there are five years, in the which there shall neither be earing nor harvest. And God sent me before you to preserve you a posterity in the earth, and to save your lives by a great deliverance. So now it was not you that sent me hither, but God: and he hath made me a father to Pharaoh, and lord of all his house, and a ruler throughout all the land of Egypt. Haste ye, and go up to my father, and say unto him, Thus saith thy son Joseph, God hath made me lord of all Egypt: come down unto me, tarry not: And thou shalt dwell in the land of Goshen, and thou shalt be near unto me, thou, and thy children, and thy children's children, and thy flocks, and thy herds, and all that thou hast: And there will*

I nourish thee…lest thou, and thy household, and all that thou hast, come to poverty. And, behold, your eyes see, and the eyes of my brother Benjamin, that it is my mouth that speaketh unto you. And ye shall tell my father of all my glory in Egypt, and of all that ye have seen; and ye shall haste and bring down my father hither (Genesis 45:5-13).

This is respect, notice he took them off the hook and let them know it was God who sent him ahead of them to preserve their lives. He did not tell them to tell their father about what they did to him; instead, just give him the good news. He even told them what to say to him, knowing he would ask many questions. It was not that Joseph was ignoring what happened, he had dealt with it and with his brothers, and forgave them. To avoid embarrassment he told them what to say to his father. That is when we know we have truly forgiven. You can put people in jail or you can release them.

Just like the Good Samaritan could have argued with himself, this man might have been one of those who called me a dog. You know how we like to generalize. He hates our people, he got what he deserved and walked away like the Priest and Levite. He forgave the man and treated him the way he would have liked someone to treat him.

Find Common Ground

I believe that this was a Jew. Here we have a Priest and a Levite who were fellow Jews and they passed by on the other side. The Jews did not want to have any dealing with the Samaritans. Yet, it was a Samaritan who helped the man who hated his guts. We have to see culture as a means of distractions. Most cultures are manmade distractions. It does not matter what culture we come from, like the wounded man, we bleed, groan, feel pain, hurt, grieve, laugh, have joy in similar ways. People are people regardless to what part of the world they come from. Needs are not confined to culture, nor restricted to certain professions. These do not determine if we should help or not.

The Priest and the Levite even though their job was to help people, who are in need, did not. Part of their responsibility was ministering to the needs of others. But, they passed on the other side. Belonging to a certain denomination or group of people does not mean you will help when there is a need.

Jesus made friends with everyone He met, in spite of their culture or status in society. We should not put restrictions on who will be our friends. We normally do, they must be from our culture, church, club, neighborhood, make a certain amount of money. Jesus says none of that matters. Anyone of us could have been the one beaten up, and none of these things would matter to us then. Our concern would be anyone please help me. Let us not wait until this happens to us to realize that the external things do not really amount to a hill of beans. It is about relationships and all people have needs. Let us use what God has given us to help meet those needs. We have a lot more in common than differences. However, we focus on the differences and cannot see the commonality we share as human beings.

Find the Distractions

The Enemy's job is to distract us from accomplishing our purposes in life. One of the ways he does this is getting us to turn distractions into issues. Jesus did not allow the lawyer to hinder Him from accomplishing one of His purposes and that is to teach. Jesus saw him as a distraction and not an issue.

The Good Samaritan saw the area the victim was from, the hatred of his people, the danger of the environment, his life being at risk,

 You Were Made To Worship God 24/7

the money he had to pay, and the time he had to spend, as mere distractions. None of these were the issue. He did not know the man therefore he did not prejudge him (that is what prejudice is, judging people before we even know them). The issue was this man needed help and as a human being he had a moral responsibility to help him because he is his brother's keeper.

Of course, any one of these distractions, the Good Samaritan could have turned into a major issue. He could have argued I do not know this man, he might have thought the victim was faking it to trick him into coming over and then rob him. I do not have the time, I have too many appointments today. He could have come up with many more distractions and turn them into issues, like the Priest and the Levite did. They saw this man as a major distraction and not an issue. That is why they walked away and left him who was almost dead.

Find Your Ministry

What if the tables were turned? Would not we have wanted the first person, the Priest to help? The reason why the God's Kingdom is not having a more forceful impact on our society is because we do not understand ministry. To me it is simply meeting the needs of others by utilizing the gifts that God has endowed us with. What is ironic is that neither the Priest nor the Levite understood ministry even though they were ministers. Today we all are ministers and we need to know how to minister meeting people's needs using what God has given us, our gifts.

Ministry is not complex; it is learning to put ourselves in other people's shoes and responding to them as if we were in the same situation. Jesus realizing that in order for us to understand that He understands, He put Himself in our shoes by becoming a man. That is why the Bible says we have a High Priest who was in all points tempted as we are yet without sin, and He is touched with the feelings of our infirmities (Hebrew 4).

We have to be able to enter into people's feelings and feel what they are feeling, see through their eyes or hear with their ears. Then we respond according to our comfort and giftedness. *"Blessed be God, even the Father of our Lord Jesus Christ, the Father of mercies, and the God of all comfort; Who comforteth us in all our tribulation, that we may be able to comfort them which are in any trouble, by the comfort wherewith we ourselves are comforted of God"* (2 Corinthians 1:3-4). God comforts us in our suffering so we can bring comfort to those who are experiencing similar problems. Thus, God prepares us for ministry.

Notice how the Samaritan ministered, he got down off his donkey, got down to where the man was, cleaned his wounds, getting his clothes soiled in the process. Then he puts him on his donkey. He gave up his place of comfort and ease and gave it to someone else who needed it more than he did. The Bible said the reason why he stopped and helped was because he had compassion, felt sorry for him. And I am sure He thought if I was in this predicament I would want someone to help me. The Priest and Levite did not have any compassion for their brother.

Find Humility

Being humble means stooping down and lifting up our brethren, being of service. Sometimes it means getting our hands and clothes dirty. There was no way he could have helped this wounded man without getting bloody. I picture him as a business man, well dressed; however, he was not defined by his dress because he was not concerned about them getting dirty.

Find Forgiveness

The Samaritan knew how this man viewed him and forgave him. We cannot be effective in developing relationships if we are not genuine in forgiving those who have wronged us. We will only pretend. We might go the first mile, by calling 911, and we think we have done our duty. This is only when it is for show or we want to score points with God, the church and be able to brag to our friends what a good person we are. When we are genuine, then we will go the second and third mile or any amount of miles we have to go, and be like the Good Samaritan. He paid for future expenses and promised to take care of any extra charges.

Like the Prodigal, the father had fully forgiven him. Notice the extra miles he went, he covered him with his robe, gave him a ring, and threw a party on his behalf. He wanted to reestablish a relationship, in spite of what the son did. He was totally forgiven. We have to do the same and help each other.

Find an Accountability Partner

The Good Samaritan had a problem that he could not fix on his own, he needed someone to help him. So, he had to partner with the innkeeper. He asked him to help take care of the man for him. He did not have all the resources or he would have asked how much it would cost. He had to rely on the innkeeper to continue taking care of the man until he returned. He had to place his faith in the innkeeper to help him deal with his problem. He made the man his problem and he needed help and was not afraid to ask for it.

In rendering help, he needed someone to come along side of him and finish what he started. Today we need to do the same like the Samaritan. There are some problems we cannot handle ourselves and we need relationships (same gender) to come along side of us and help us bear our burdens. Just like the Spirit led him to the right innkeeper, He will do the same for us. Directing us to the best person to assist us in dealing with our problems or those we are helping.

Find the Wisdom of God

There will be people out there who will want to take advantage of our friendship. Here is where we need God's wisdom to know when people are trying to use us and abuse us. This will harden our hearts like the Priest and the Levites and we do not want to help people any more. The Bible says, *"Happy is the man that findeth **wisdom**, and the man that getteth understanding"* (Proverbs 3:13). How do we find wisdom? We must begin by respecting God, *"The fear of the LORD is the beginning of **wisdom**: and the knowledge of the holy is understanding"* (Proverbs 9:10). Then just ask, *"If any of you lack **wisdom**, let him ask of God, that giveth to all men liberally, and upbraideth not; and it shall be given him"* (James 1:5). It is that simple.

Go Thou and Do Likewise

In concluding, we are all like that beaten man and Jesus came down and rescued us, paid our bill in full, all future expenses are taken care of. We have to go and do the same to and for our fellowmen. This involves knowing who we are, finding time, forgiveness, respect, wisdom, an accountability partner and finding common ground. We have to take time to listen and hear when and where others are hurting. We cannot allow ourselves to become distracted and turn those distractions into issues. At times we are not going to feel like doing it, that is why we need the Holy Spirit in our lives and an accountability partner. Only God can sustain our relationships because we will continually fall off the wagon and resort back to our old ways. Thus, we need to have a solid relationship or partnership with God. When other relationships fail, as they will, we can always lean on Jesus.

        You Were Made To Worship God 24/7

Chapter 16

How Do We Relate to Ourselves?

OUR RELATIONSHIPS FALL into three categories. How we relate to ourselves, others and God? These are interrelated. We try to separate them, but we cannot. They are inextricably bound together, like the Godhead. They are separate beings yet they are One and they relate very well to each other. They do not upset each other or have to carry-out the other person's responsibility; never jealous, envious, or see the other as being more important. They love and get along great. They want the same for us, with each other and with God. This is what we will be looking at in these three chapters.

Dangerous Ground

I know that this is a dangerous chapter. First, I began with us rather than with God. Second, we are so much into ourselves, we seldom have time for anybody else. Third, many books are written with emphasis on bettering ourselves, the truth is we cannot. The Bible says, we were born in sin and shaped in iniquity, we do not even know our own hearts (Psalm 51:5; Jeremiah 17:9).

For most people the "in thing" nowadays is to be all that I can be. Instead, we are like the Laodiceans who claimed, *"I am rich, and increased with goods, and have need of nothing; and knowest not that thou art wretched, miserable, poor, blind, and naked:"* (Revelation 3:17). We are no different, we have our three car garage homes, fancy cars, prestigious jobs, and attend a multimillion dollar church. We are content. We do not have need of anything or anybody. That is until tragedy strikes and then we understand how much we really have. We do not understand our true condition. Therefore, we need the Holy Spirit to show us.

There is a problem with being all you can be. Are we willing to let everyone else be all that they can be? Where does my being who I can be end and the other person being all they could be begins. Also, this concept presupposes we created ourselves and we know what our destiny is. It is not about us, but God. We cannot be all we can be without Him. God has to reveal it to us.

Also, this theory continues to break down since we believe the world revolves around us. The sun rises and sets at our command. The biggest problem with earthly relationships, including the one with ourselves, is that they stem from selfishness. We are more concerned with what we can get out of them rather than how much we can contribute. The paradox is we cannot be of help to anyone unless we have a healthy concept of who we are. We cannot have a healthy or true concept of who we are, until we know who God is.

God Gives

The buck stops with us. We can no longer go around blaming anybody for our lack of friendships. We have to take responsibility for our lives by relying on God to do what He promised to do for us to be successful. He is committed to a successful relationship with Him and each other and He has deposited within us all that we need to accomplish them.

According as His divine power hath given unto us all things that pertain unto life and godliness, through the knowledge of Him that hath called us to glory and virtue: Whereby are given unto us exceeding great and precious promises: that by these ye might be partakers of the divine nature, having escaped the corruption that is in the world through lust. For if these things be in you, and abound, they make you that ye shall neither be barren nor unfruitful in the knowledge of our Lord Jesus Christ (2 Peter 1:3-4, 8).

The only problem is all things that pertain unto life are given in seed form. We must work along with God to provide the right environment for growth into trees and bring forth fruits in our lives. See the book He gave me, *"There Are Some Things We Don't Have To Ask God For! Because He Is Our Father,"* for more details on the seed concept. I believe we are given all we need at conception. It is in our genes. The Psalmist tells us, *"For you created my inmost being; you knit me together in my mother's womb....your eyes saw my unformed body. All the days ordained for me were written in your book before one of them came to be. How precious to me are your thoughts, O God! How vast is the sum of them!"* (Psalms 139:13-17). God had a plan for us before we were born. At birth, we came with His blessings, thus guaranteeing our success, if we cooperate with Him.

When we understand that God deposited within us everything we need to be successful, prosperous, and victorious, we would not be going after bread, stuff, people and our own success. Instead, we would be going after God, getting to know Him, who is life eternal and will supply our desires, needs, and wants. His desires for us are more than we want to do for the person we love the most in this world. The method He chooses to do this is through relationships.

Steps Needed

The first step in any solution is to acknowledge that the problem exists. Second, admit that we contributed to this dilemma. Remember the woman caught in adultery. *"Let him without sin cast the first stone"* (*John 8:7*). None of us can say we are innocent. Third, repent. Ask God for His forgiveness for our contributions and anyone we have hurt in the process. It would even be more effective if we could name the areas and persons. If you do not know, ask the Spirit to reveal them to you and He will.

This helps in many ways. First, we no longer want to continue contributing in those areas and thus hinder the growth of God's Kingdom. Second, we will help others who are struggling in similar areas. Third, the Spirit is now ready to begin to do some rebuilding in our lives and others. We become a part of the solution, repairers of the breach.

> *If you take away the yoke from your midst, the pointing of the finger, and speaking wickedness, if you extend your soul to the hungry and satisfy the afflicted soul, then your light shall dawn in the darkness, and your darkness shall be as the noonday. The Lord will guide you continually, and satisfy your soul in drought, and strengthen your bones; you shall be like a watered garden, and like a spring of water, whose waters do not fail. Those from among you shall build the old waste places; you shall raise up the foundations of many generations; and you shall be called the repairer of the breach, the restorer of streets to dwell in (Isaiah 58:9-12 ESV).*

The Lord now becomes our guide, not people, politics, or policies. It is the Spirit working in us both to do His will and good pleasure.

You Were Made To Worship God 24/7

Triune Beings

This is further complicated because in addition to the three areas of relationships, we have three components. Being made in the image of God and like the Godhead, there is Father, Son, and Spirit, we also are comprised of three; spirit, soul, and body, but we are one being. Paul confirms this fact when he wrote, *"May God himself, the God of peace, sanctify you through and through. May your whole spirit, soul and body be kept blameless at the coming of our Lord Jesus Christ. The one who calls you is faithful and he will do it"* (1 Thessalonians 5:23-24).

What's more we live in trinities. In Biblical Numerology three is the number for divine perfection, resurrection, and completeness. The universe has three qualities: Time, which comprises of Past, Present, and Future: Space, which comprises of Height, Width, and Depth, and Matter which is made up of Solid, Liquid, and Gas. Human Ability is Thoughts, Words, and Deeds. In our Relationships there are God, others, and ourselves.

God has asked us to love Him with these three aspects of our lives, *"And thou shalt love the LORD thy God with all thine heart, and with all thy soul, and with all thy might"* (Deuteronomy 6:5; Matthew 22:37). We are triune beings just like God. We are not three different persons, we are holistic beings. In order for us to enjoy life there has to be agreement and balance in all areas. All must be fed and nourished or we will have difficulty relating to ourselves, others and God. Each part is important and has to be balanced because it serves a different function that is crucial to our survival and well being as humans.

Our greatest challenge is to be like God having all three components working together harmoniously. We tend to compartmentalize everything and decide which is more important. We do the same with God, there are those who think the Father is the most important member, some say Jesus. Very few say the Spirit, they see and treat Him like a step child. The truth is none is more important. They have different and equally important functions. So is everyone else on the face of the earth. We cannot accept this until we accept ourselves as three in one and work to bring harmony with the aid of the Spirit.

We do the same with our spirit, soul and body. Many say the spirit is the most important. And they will overwork the spiritual part of their lives at the expense of the body and soul. Here is what happens; the body and the soul negate or cancel out the spirit. Since none is more important, they have different functions. They are to work together so that we can be who God created us to be. As triune beings, when we develop one more than the other or one gets more attention, then the other two cancel it out. Hence, the reason why we feel so miserable even after a great spiritual encounter or accomplishment.

Consequently, one of the main reasons Jesus came, is to bring about reconciliation, to restore the harmony that existed, not merely in the universe, but also within us. Once sin entered our world these three entities were at war with each other. Like everything else they became disconnected, disjointed and disorderly. We then have difficulties in our relationships because we project on to others what is happening inside of us.

The Greatest War

The greatest war being fought is not the one in Iraq, it is within us. If we can conquer ourselves by surrendering to the Spirit there would be harmony. Solomon puts it this way, *"He that is slow to anger is better than the mighty; and he that ruleth his spirit than he that taketh a city"* (Proverbs 16:32). Thus, there is a war, disconnection going on between our body, soul, and spirit. Each is fighting for dominion over the other. *"For the flesh (body) lusts against the Spirit, and the Spirit against the flesh; and these are contrary to one another, so that you do not do the things that you wish"* (Galatians 5:17 NKJV). Even though our minds tell us to do something like develop relationships, the spirit and the flesh are at war and are interfering with what we know we ought to be doing. That is why Paul tells us we have to renew our minds (Romans 12:2). Have the mind of Jesus (Philippians 2:5).

Paul, who wrote about half the New Testament, talks about this struggle he had in Romans 7. What's interesting is, this was many years after He was saved. When we are in such a strait, all we need to do is cry out for help. There is Someone who can deliver us from this dilemma, this predicament and His name is Jesus. All we have to do is call and He will answer, that is His promise to us, *"He will call upon me, and I will answer him; I will be with him in trouble, I will deliver him and honor him"* (Psalm 91:15). God is so anxious to help us resolve our dilemmas He made this promise, *"Before they call I will answer; while they are still speaking I will hear"* (Isaiah 65:24). He wants to help us so much that He will not even let us finish our prayer before He is by our side to render whatever help is needed. When He is through helping us, then He will honor us.

Why does this predicament exist? God made us like Himself with all three components, He uses the spiritual component to communicate with us and we with Him. However, because of sin and separation the body wants to take over. This is further complicated since we live in a physical world and we rely on our senses. In the spiritual realm, we have to exercise faith in God.

Conflict Within and Without

God is the only one who can bring about this peace, harmony and sanctification in our spirit, soul, and body. These were in unity before sin, now they fight against each other. Once there are internal conflicts, automatically there will be external. When we are having difficulty relating, the first place we need to look is on the inside. Ask yourself, what am I having difficulty with? What am I struggling with? Who am I allowing to control my life? There cannot be genuine and long lasting relationships among us if we do not first have harmony within ourselves. I dare say the main reason why we have external conflicts and disconnections is because of the internal ones. What is happening on the outside is an indication of what is happening inside. Jesus puts it this way, *"What goes into a man's mouth does not make him 'unclean,' but what comes out of his mouth, that is what makes him 'unclean.' "* *(Matthew 15:11 NIV).*

Jesus, because He had harmony within, did not have to prove anything to anyone. He did not have to hurt people's feelings so that He could feel good about Himself. Neither pulled them down to lift Himself up nor step on others to reach to the top. He was already there because there was harmony within, He knew who and whose He was.

It is God's desire that we have harmony within and without. As Jesus said, it's not what goes in that defiles, but what comes out. Like the saying, "Insults are taken not given." It is not what people say, but how we react to it. Our reaction is based upon how we feel, see, hear, and what we are experiencing internally.

We Need Harmony

The key to life is that all three must be in harmony. Today, great emphasis is on our body. There are more people exercising and eating healthy. Many are going to great extremes to take care of their body and have become obsessed with it: Spending enormous sums of money to get our bodies looking just right. For example, cosmetic surgeries have escalated dramatically in the last few years. Even with a healthy body, many are not finding much joy and satisfaction in life. That's because they are not taking time to develop and challenge their soul and the spirit.

For example, we are only using less than ten percent of our brain. We do not spend time thinking and questioning. We allow others to do our thinking for us, the church, politicians, television, and school. They tell us how to live, where to live, what to buy, where to go, how to dress etcetera. Those who do not follow the crowd feel like a fish out of the water and worry ourselves to an early grave.

The spirit for most people gets the least attention, even as disciples. It is fed for about an hour on the weekend, when we go to church to hear a sermon, sing a few songs, and say or hear something about God. There is the misconception that this is the most important aspect of man. I disagree, it has a different function. What we need to do is understand their functions and allow the Spirit to help us bring about balance in all three areas. Then we need to teach others to do the same. We are most miserable when one is out of balance and it does not matter which one, because all will be affected. When we have internal disconnections, then they are manifested on the outside, in our relationships. What we have within must come out and we cannot stop it. God made us to share who we are and what we have and it does not matter if it is bad or good. We will share whether we intend to or not.

Let me show you how connected these three components are, if you stump your toe not only is the body affected. You scream because your mind told you that is excruciating pain, your emotions become involved, you may even cry. You call upon the Lord to help you bear the pain.

Misconception

There are those who subscribe to the fact that the spirit is the most important and hence spend a lot of time doing church work and religious things. They have become so heavenly minded that they are of no earthly use. Their heads are in the clouds so they cannot see what is happening around them and be of any help to their fellowmen or themselves. You talk about disconnection. They can quote scriptures, but they lack social skills, they cannot carry on a sensible conversation. Their world view is warped. They are social misfits. They cannot keep a spouse, because they are not well rounded. They have disengaged from the rest of who they are and thus with the rest of the world. They are out of balance.

If the spirit is the most important what happens when our bodies are injured? Or we have to take an examination can we just rely on our spirit only (not the Holy Spirit). You see all have their different functions. As with nature, when there is an imbalance, it will not rest until there is a balance. When there is an imbalance in our bodies we experience illness. What's happening is a cry for balance in all three areas. The majority of people in the hospital, says former Surgeon General Everett Koop are for psychosomatic illness. That is to say there are more psychological than physical.

We Need Reconciliation

God who knows the end from the beginning, knew that man would have messed up. So before the world was created, they had a plan to get rid of sin and bring about reconciliation. Originally, when God created the universe, it was perfect, including relationships. There were differences and differences are not bad, contrary to what we have learned. In God's realm, in order for anything to work there must be differences for functional purposes; however, harmony and unity existed. It was perfect. Even though He was God, He would literally come down in the Garden walk and talk with Adam and Eve, nothing separated them. The moment Adam sinned, a disconnection immediately took place. Man who was created to be holy and live forever began to die. And God had a plan to maintain an eternal relationship with mankind.

It is because of our vile human nature He cannot come down literally like He did in the Garden, because He is holy and His holiness will kill us. To God, sin is a consuming fire (Deuteronomy 4:24, Hebrews 12:29). Jesus had to come down in human form to reveal to us who God really is. We do not know and the longer the world lasts the farther removed we become from God. After Jesus left; the Spirit came. This is a challenge for us because we want to see, feel, and hear Him; we want the Spirit in the form of flesh and blood. We have to switch from the physical to the spiritual and the Spirit is here to help us. We have to make that choice.

It is now our responsibility to get to know God who created us. The best way to know who this fantabulous God is, we must know and experience Him for ourselves. He is so incredible, that we cannot find Him by searching, yet, we can find Him if we search for Him with all our hearts. This can only happen when we accept Jesus as the Lord and Savior (2 Corinthians 5:16-21). Once we do, we see Him in a new light, as our Savior and the Savior of the world. This is because when we come to Jesus we are made over. There is a reconstruction, recreation in our minds since we need to be reconciled to God and thus remove the disconnection that sin has caused. We have the same body, but we are no longer ruled by the flesh; instead, by the Spirit. In addition, we no longer see God as our enemy. We become just like Jesus and join Him in reconciling the world to Himself, through relationships.

Now What?

Once I understand who I am, how do I now relate, perceive and treat myself? The truth is we see people the way we see ourselves, so if we have a problem in the area of stealing then we believe every one we come in contact with is a thief. Or we will forgive others if we believe that God has truly forgiven us. When others ask for forgiveness we freely grant it. We need to know who we are and be comfortable with ourselves. Only God can do that for us, so ask Him.

In conclusion, how we perceive life will determine our destiny. This will decide how we live and the decisions we make with our money, time, relationships, purposes, etcetera. If we see life as a game, then winning will be our focus, if as a party, then it is about having fun. If as a race, we are in speed mode, this produces stress. The danger about our view of life is everyone else should have our view which is right. Relationships cannot survive in this type of environment. We must understand and accept how we view life, see and understand how others view life and accept them.

Chapter 17

How We Relate to Each Other?

NOW THAT WE HAVE UNDERSTOOD who we are and what God wants from us. We are now ready to relate to each other and accomplish His destiny for us and His Kingdom. He designed us to have a personal relationship with Him, never intended to be private. There is evidence in the Bible where we are admonished to: be members together, build together, join together, heirs together, fitted together, held together, bear together, and caught up together. The test of our friendship with God is determined by our relation to each other (1 John 4:20). Jesus said, *"By this shall all men know that ye are my disciples, if ye have love one to another (John 13:35).*

Ministry of Relationships

The greatest desire that God has placed within us is for relationships and the strongest one is with Him. There is a void in us when we do not have meaningful relationships. When there are none, we are ready to commit suicide.

Jesus came to show us how to be ministers of relationships. Paul tells us, *"All this is from God, who reconciled us to himself through Christ and gave us the ministry of reconciliation: that God was reconciling the world to himself in Christ, not counting men's sins against them. And he has committed to us the message of reconciliation"* (2

Corinthians 5:18-19 NIV). God is so serious about relationships that He has given to us the ministry of restoring them.

We should not decide to destroy a relationship because of a conflict, rift, or been hurt. The Bible is about how we should relate. He wants us to love one another, when we do not, it is a disgraceful testimony. This does not mean that Jesus wants us to be peace lovers, He wants us to be peacemakers. The Bible says, *"If it be possible, as much as lieth in you, live peaceably with all men"* (Romans 12:18). It means that we will not be able to live with everyone. Some will be impossible to live with. Peter tells us to be hospitable to one another without grumbling. Use our gifts to minister to each other, as good stewards of the manifold grace of God (1 Peter 4:9-10). We have to do as much as lies in our power with the aid of the Spirit. If not we have to move on.

Relationships are symbiotic in nature, that is, we all benefit. We take turns serving or ministering to each other. There must be balance, and it is not a logical one. By this I mean, no one will decide when there is balance; the relationship determines that not the individual. If we do it will be biased. For example, too many of us know how and what to give in a relationship. But, we have difficulty receiving, because of obligation. We do not want to be obligated to anybody, not even our friends. So, balance is important, there are times we will give and times when we should receive. Jesus demonstrated this in Garden of Gethsemane when He was ready to receive help from His disciples. He gave and now He was ready to receive from them. If you have difficulty with receiving, one reason is, you are not comfortable with who you are. There is disharmony within. Examine yourself.

The Importance of Others

As important as prayer and Bible study are they are not enough for our growth, we need people. God works through them and more than miracles. This helps us to grow together. It is not about isolation. Isolation is used for domination. We cannot become like Christ without love and we need each other to demonstrate this love, people will know we are disciples of Jesus if we have love one for another.

We try to become like Jesus by reading through the Bible every year, learning your Church's doctrines and how to pray better. These are good and are very important. The Word was not given to increase our knowledge, it was given to change our lives. I am not minimizing the Bible because Jesus said, Man shall not live by bread alone but by every word that proceeds out of the mouth of God (Matthew 4). Job saw it as more necessary than his food. The Word is our authority. Many of us read our newspapers, other books and magazines, watch more religious TV than we spend reading the Bible. The more we read the Word the clearer we hear the Spirit telling us how important relationships are and how to develop and maintain them. The Word is about relationships.

I am not trying to minimize prayer. But, Jesus warns us about praying and worshipping Him, *"Therefore if thou bring thy gift to the altar, and there rememberest that thy brother hath ought against thee; Leave there thy gift before the altar, and go thy way; first be reconciled to thy brother, and then come and offer thy gift"* (Matthew 5:23-24). We cannot worship if we are not relating to our fellowmen. It is about how we apply these principles. This is seen in how we relate to God and our fellowmen. Do we see others as better than ourselves?

One thing that always hits me is how we are nicer and talk to one another in times of crisis. We slow down enough to talk, people who would not give a second look, but we will be having friendly animated discussions, analyzing what happened and showing compassion about other people's troubles. Why is it we need a trauma or crisis in our lives to connect to one another, to help, or even just talk?

How Many?

Let me ask you, "How many genuine, solid, reliable, and fantastic relationships do you have?" I submit to you, if you do not have friends it is because you do not have solid relationships with your spouse, children or your relatives. It is the same principles we use for any relationship. If we cannot develop relationships, life becomes very unattractive, stressful and harder to live.

How many people in your life can you count on to help you if you find yourself helpless? We have an example of this in Mark 2, the man sick with the palsy. He needed a miracle to be healed, Jesus was in town. However, he could not take himself. Four of his friends decided to get him there, when they got there, the crowd was too big and they could not get through. They were so intent on getting their friend to Jesus that they decided to take the roof off and let him down.

They went through much expense just to get their friend the help he needed. If you find yourself in a crisis like this man, do you have four friends you can count on? Friends who are willing to go through any expense to get you help. Examine your life and see if you have such friends because if you have not been in a major crisis, as yet, you will soon be. And will need them to see you through. It does not matter how rich or poor you are. In like manner, can four people count on you to see them through their crises in life? Just like we need others, others need us.

Stop Comparing

Someone will always be prettier, smarter, richer, more educated than you. Their house will be bigger, drive a better car, children will do better in school and their husband will fix more things around the house. So let it go, Be Happy! Love yourself and your circumstances. Think about it. The prettiest woman in the world can have hell in her heart. And the most highly favored woman on your job may be unable to have children. The richest man you know might be lonely. The most handsome guy you know might have AIDS. And as Paul says, if "*I have not Love, I have nothing.*" So, again, love you. Love who you are. Look in the mirror in the morning and smile and say "I am too blessed to be stressed and too anointed to be disappointed!" "Winners make things happen. Losers let things happen." Know that to the world you might be one person, but to one person you just might be the world.

Stop Judging

Here are some conditions that affect our relating. Anytime we see anyone or anything happening we begin to prejudge. This is what prejudice means. Jesus had something to say about it,

> *Do not judge, or you too will be judged. For in the same way you judge others, you will be judged, and with the measure you use, it will be measured to you. "Why do you look at the speck of sawdust in your brother's eye and pay no attention to the plank in your own eye? How can you say to your brother, 'Let me take the speck out of your eye,' when all the time there is a plank in your own eye? You hypocrite, first take the plank out of your own eye, and then you will see clearly to remove the speck from your brother's eye (Matthew 7:1-5 NIV).*

Another method of judging is stereotyping or racial profiling. This is a great hindrance to developing relationships. It is when we see people of the same ethnicity as capable of doing what a few in the group are guilty of. For example, all black people love watermelons. I am black and hate them. We judge people based on their ethnicity and we believe that they are all alike. They love and do the same things. With such an attitude, it is impossible to learn about the other person as an individual, when we have already formed our conclusion.

We also judge base on culture and cultural differences. We do not take time to listen to other cultures and understand that we all feel the same pains, bleed the same red blood, laugh, sing, play, and have fun like any human being.

- When I judge another there are things that instantly happen,
- I lose fellowship with the Lord.
- I expose my own pride and insecurity.
- I set myself up to be judged by God.
- I harm the fellowship with my fellowmen.
- It is the devil's job to blame, complain, and criticize. Let us encourage rather than criticize or judge one another.

How Should We Relate

The Golden Rule

It is very simple and can be summed up in the *Golden Rule, "Do unto others as you would have them do unto you"* (Matthew 7:12). Observe that this is a command and instruction at the same time. If as disciples we could live by this rule, we would have great relationships. Regrettably, this rule is only considered golden when it is how people are treating us. It is not golden how or when we are treating others. We do to others based on what they do to us, even though the command contains no conditions. Yet, we add them on. Jesus did not say sometimes we are to do to others. We want to complicate what God says by adding or taking away from it. Since He is God, He knows what is best. And Jesus demonstrated this in His own life. He did not discriminate even with lepers. It means that everybody is important; they were created by and for God's pleasure.

I have failed terribly in this area towards my family. So you know I do not have many great relationships. There are only a few people I can really count on. I have to develop more solid and intimate relationships. I have started by developing a closer walk with God, myself, my family and with others.

Unconditional Love

We have to learn to love others the same way that God loves us. Here is another command given by Jesus Himself, *"This is my commandment, that ye love one another, as I have loved you"* (John 15:12). Again, there are no conditions or options. We have to love others like Jesus loves us and them. The only way we can do this is to be born again. (If you are not, please turn to the back of the book and experience how simple, but powerful it is). The impulsive Peter tells us, *"Now that you have purified yourselves by obeying the truth so that you have sincere love for your brothers, love one another deeply, from the heart. For you have been born again, not of perishable seed, but of imperishable, through the living and enduring word of God"* (1 Peter 1:22-23 NIV).

We spend a great deal of our time hating, as Solomon puts it, *"And I saw that all labor and all achievement spring from man's envy of his neighbor. This too is meaningless, a chasing after the wind. The fool folds his hands and ruins himself. Better one handful with tranquility than two handfuls with toil and chasing after the wind"* (Ecclesiastes 4:4-6). We try to outdo our neighbors. If they get a new car, we get one bigger and more expensive. We have to learn to be content where we are in life and not make our decisions based on where others are and their accomplishments. One of my mother's favorite sayings is, "Do not envy what you see other people have because you do not know what they had to do to get it."

Unconditional love draws people to Jesus. It drew us to Him. That is how they are attracted to Jesus, how we relate to them, treating them the way we want to be treated.

Genuine love can only be based on the love of God that is shed in our hearts. God has already put His unconditional love within us. It cannot be our love. It must spring from our love for Him so that we can love the unlovely and those who hate us. Like Samuel who mourned for Saul when God said he was no longer going to be king. Samuel cried and prayed for Saul all night even though Saul was wicked and not worth it (1 Samuel 15). In the next chapter we see God had to come to Samuel and ask, *'How much longer are you going to mourn for Saul? Come and go anoint the new king of Israel'* (1 Samuel 16). Samuel loved Saul and wanted what was best for him, in spite of His awful behavior.

David was hunted like a dog and almost killed by Saul on several occasions. Look at his response to the death of Saul, *"Then David and all the men with him took hold of their clothes and tore them. They mourned and wept and fasted till evening for Saul and his son, Jonathan, and for the army of the Lord and the house of Israel, because they had fallen by the sword"* (2 Samuel 1:11-12). He mourned, fasted and prayed for his worst enemy. That was the love of God shed abroad in his heart. That is what we call a relationship with God and our fellowmen. You might be tempted to say it is for Jonathan, but wait a minute, look at verse 15. David killed the man who said he acted as a Jack Kevorkian, even though Saul was wounded and he asked to be killed, and he killed himself.

Another one of David's enemies was Abner, Saul's army commander. When Saul died, Abner took Saul's son, Ishosheth, and made him king of Israel, while David was king of Judah. Abner, like Saul, wanted David dead, but the house of Judah loved him. David was content to wait on the Lord to direct him and so he ruled over Judah for seven and a half years. There were fights between the followers of Saul and David. David's side grew stronger. Abner left because of the confrontation he had with King Ishosheth for sleeping with one of his father's concubines. He decided to join forces with David to help make him king over all of Israel. David agreed; however, his commander, Joab, was upset with David for joining forces with his archenemy. When you love people, many will not understand it is God working in you. Behind David's back, Joab went after Abner and murdered him in cold blood. David was disappointed in Joab and he pronounced a curse upon his family (2 Samuel 3).

Jonathan and David, you cannot talk about human relationships without talking about them. They both knew the Lord and His will for their lives. That is the only way Jonathan could have accepted he was not going to King of Israel. We have to understand God's gifts, purposes, ministries, vocations and destiny for our lives. Then we would not be jealous of what He has given to others. We see what we have and they have as coming from Him. It eliminates our disconnections and brings with it an authority, security, a solid foundation and we cannot be blown by every wind of doctrine or conflict.

Service

Relationships really boil down to service. We are not willing to be anybody's servant; but, we want as many servants as possible. We want them cheap, free would be even more enticing. We are not willing to serve our fellowmen. We cannot be of service to anyone unless we know who we are. Our identity does not come from us. We did not create ourselves thus we cannot tell ourselves who we are or the reason why we were created. The creator or inventor is the only one who tells the true purpose of anything. That is why they produce manuals for their products. God did the same in providing the Bible. We are who we are because of Him. We need to know Him in order to know who we are. *"It's in Christ that we find out who we are and what we are living for. Long before we first heard of Christ and got our hopes up, He had his eye on us, had designs on us for glorious living, part of the overall purpose he is working out in everything for everyone."* (Ephesians 1:11 Msg)

We were made by God for God. We were made to serve Him and we do that by serving our fellowmen. Jesus said if you have done it unto the least of these my brethren you have done it unto me (Matthew 25:40).

Honesty

The truth is all of us have problems and issues in our lives. When we allow the Spirit to answer or reveal to us the answers to our problems and honestly accept those answers: Then we will be comfortable with ourselves. We can then be honest and truthful with others and our God. If we cannot be honest with ourselves, we cannot be with anyone else.

We can acknowledge our struggles because we all have them. Even Jesus had struggles, being led in the wilderness by the Spirit to be tempted by the Devil. The one in the Garden of Gethsemane was the greatest, because our salvation hung in the balance. Jesus had to contend with the Scribes and Pharisees on a daily basis. The Apostle Paul admits, the things he wanted to do he found myself not doing (Romans 7). We are afraid to admit we have struggles, because some of us think it will cause others to struggle, not realizing we are helping those who are struggling. Paul tells us, *"Blessed be God, even the Father of our Lord Jesus Christ, the Father of mercies, and the God of all comfort; Who comforteth us in all our tribulation, that we may be able to comfort them which are in any trouble, by the comfort wherewith we ourselves are comforted of God"* (2 Corinthians 1:3-4).

If we are honest about our failures we can also be about our victories. People cannot point fingers at you knowing they have their own struggles. We cannot have victories without struggles. Our testimonies would be more powerful if we can admit our failures and shortcomings. That is why Jesus could have accepted what Mary said and saw that Simon was just putting on a show. Mary acted from the heart, Simon's was just to show off. He felt as if he was better than Mary because she was a prostitute; it is believed that Simon was one of her customers (Luke 7).

Humility

Humility is thinking of others, focusing on serving them more than serving ourselves. Pride builds walls around us and keeps people out; humility builds bridges which allow people to come in and out of our lives. One way this is accomplished is by admitting our weaknesses, being patient with others weaknesses, accepting corrections, honoring others (Romans 12:16 NLT).

When we are humble, we will always be the one to take the initiative, it does not matter who is at fault. We are obedient to Jesus' command to leave our offering, go and be reconciled with people who have wronged us before worshipping God (Matthew 5:24). We will use our ears twice as much as we use our mouth. We will choose to attack the problem not the person—we will be careful how we say, since it is just as important as what we say. We will heed Paul's admonition and not be condemning, belittling, comparing, labeling, condescending, or being sarcastic (Ephesians 4:29 TEV).

We will focus on the relationship and not on the problem. We see reconciliation as more important than resolution. The former is about the relationship, the latter is about the problem. Even if we cannot come to a solution, we can still have a relationship, because we esteem the other person better than ourselves (Philippians 2).

Contentment

Our lives will be miserable if we are not content. Paul the Apostle said, I have learned to be content in whatever state I am in (Philippians 4:11). He was not talking about settling, because Peter told us to grow in grace and in a knowledge of our Lord (2 Peter 3:18). They believed in growing in Jesus. We cannot move to the next level unless we are contented with where we are. In other words, find acceptance and fulfillment where God has brought us at this moment. Then we are ready to move on. It is like a promotion in class or on the job. You are only promoted after you have learned to do well at your previous level, you did not settle. You accepted where you were and did your job well. You rejoice, happy you are promoted. Now more is expected of you so you cannot settle. You have to work harder to go higher.

Without contentment we cannot enjoy life or be happy for others who are experiencing progress. We will have difficulty with people who are happy for their accomplishments. They are content but we are not. This will affect the way we relate to them. The problem is not the people, it is with us. This reminds me of Joseph in Potiphar's house. He was prospering as a result of Joseph and Joseph appeared to be getting nothing in return. Actually, he ended up in jail. He had learned to be content, no matter what his situation. That is why he was able to continue relating to Potiphar and the Warden. When we are not content it affects our relationships.

View of Ourselves

God was not surprised when we were born. He had us in mind before we were even conceived (Ephesians 1:4). He put together two people with the right genetic and DNA makeup to create us. God took sin and human failure into consideration. It does not matter if our mother was raped or we were conceived out of wedlock. God wanted us here on His earth. Actually, He custom made us just the way He wanted, with our uniqueness, gifts, talents, personalities, abilities, idiosyncrasies, shortcomings, and inclinations to certain sins that easily beset us. God was so detailed in us being here, He knows the number of hairs we have on our head (Matthew 10:30), the exact place we should live (Act 17:26). The reason is He has a destiny He wants each of us to accomplish specifically.

Many of us do not like the person we see in the mirror, because we are fake. We have tried to hide and cover up so much that we do not know what is false and what is true anymore. Unless we can definitely answer this question why are we here? We will have difficulty in all our relationships because we will be seeking the answer to this question in every relationship we enter.

If we have unanswered questions within, these will be projected outward and we will believe everybody else has the same problem. And those who know why they are here will be resented by us who do not know. If we do not know who we are and love who God made us, then we cannot love and appreciate our neighbors and how He created them.

Then there are those of us who think more highly of ourselves than we should. When we do, we start putting people down. The objective is really to stand on them so that the world can see us and like us how we see ourselves.

We are hardest on people who are committing the same sin as we are. Since we have not overcome that shortcoming in our lives and we want to hide it so no one else can see it. We believe the more adamant we are the less likely people will suspect we have the same problem. After all, the attention is on the other person. However, your secret is out, more and more people are now beginning to understand that the person who is most vocal is normally suffering from the same or similar sin. May the Lord help us to see ourselves as we truly are, accept who we are, and help others to do the same.

Motives

We have to be careful with unrealistic expectations. Most of our conflicts are rooted in unmet needs. There are some needs that can only be met by God. When we expect others to fulfill those needs we become bitter and resentful. We need God's wisdom to know the difference.

Most commonly men get into relationships looking for sex, women go looking for love and most times there is a trade off. Women give sex to get love and men give love to get sex. Both motives are impure. Our motive should always be in the best interest of the other person not what can I get out of it.

All of our lives are motivated and propelled. What is the driving force in your life? Is it guilt, fear, bitterness, riches or approval by others? The best motivation is by knowing God's destiny for your life. When we do, life becomes simple, passionate, and Kingdom oriented. We will love people and will use our God given gifts, purposes, vocations, and destiny to minister to their needs.

Do I know my gifts? This is crucial to our belief in who we are. It is the way God has wired us to function in life. Life cannot be fulfilling without this knowledge. Once we know what these are, then God will reveal to us our purposes. Without these we will be men most miserable. We will be like a ship tossed to and fro by the angry and boisterous waves of life. Without these we cannot minister effectively to ourselves, our fellowmen, or our God.

Chapter 18

How We Relate to God

THIS IS NOT ABOUT FINGER POINTING, but mending the relationship that exists between us and God. We have seen how we relate to ourselves and each other. When this is positive, we are relating to God (Matthew 25:40). This is an outward manifestation of His love in us.

How Do We See God?

We will relate and interact with God depending upon our view or perception of Him. If we see Him as a God of Justice, we are afraid of Him. He has a great big stick ready to use, the moment we mess up. I do not know where we got this concept from. Even in the Old Testament He is a God of mercy and grace. Yes, there were times when He seemed harsh and severe. Yet, if you read the context carefully you will notice that He gave many warnings before He destroyed them or allowed their enemies to. Even with the flood, before He destroyed them, Noah warned them for many years. When God took the Israelites into the Canaan, He told them often to drive out the inhabitants or they will worship their gods and carry out their customs and they did.

If we see Him as a God of grace we do not believe He will destroy anybody because He is Love. As humans, we go to extremes.

However, He is a God of balance. He has to administer justice. Yet, He always tempers it with Mercy.

Do you see yourself as being made for God's pleasure? You are (Revelation 4:11). He was delighted at our birth. We are alive for God's purposes, delight, glory, and pleasure. He wants us to bring enjoyment to Him, living for His pleasure is the first purpose of life. Thus, there is no need to feel insignificant, this reveals our worth.

Relating To God

We have been led to believe that God is only pleased with us when we are doing religious stuff, like praying, reading the Bible, going to church or witnessing to others. He is concerned about all areas of our lives, even the smallest details. The Psalmist reminds us, *"The Lord directs the steps of the godly. He delights in every detail of their lives"* (Psalm 37:23 NLT). He is so concerned, He knows the number of hairs we have on our heads. I like the context in which Luke puts it, we are more valuable than sparrows (Luke 12:7). The Psalmist says, He was present in our mother's womb putting us together (Psalm 139).

Everything we do, except sin can be done for God's pleasure, if we do it with an attitude of praise. Sweeping the yard, typing, reading, watching TV, at work. We bring the greatest enjoyment to Him when we use the gifts, purposes, ministries, vocations, and destiny for which He created us. That is, when we are being ourselves. Not accepting any part of ourselves is rejecting God.

We believe that we have to be perfect or mature for God to enjoy us. Our parents enjoyed us while we were growing up and we were not perfect. God delights in us while we are maturing in Him. Even if our parents did not enjoy us that does not mean He does not. God remembers we are made of dust and looks at our hearts. Is it our greatest desire to please Him? When we have the Kingdom as our agenda, it is no longer how much fun I am getting out of life. Instead, it is how much pleasure is God getting out of my life. How much are others getting out me?

Surrender

A relationship with God calls for surrender or submission. Surrender is not politically correct, it implies losing the fight, being defeated in battle. It is criminals who surrender to the police. We are admonished today never to give up, stand our ground. Surrender is not taught even though it is Biblical, *"Submitting yourselves one to another in the fear of God" (Ephesians 5:21)*. We often hear of wives submitting to their husbands we seldom hear about us surrendering to one another. We hear much about winning, overcoming, succeeding. Surrender to God is not only necessary, it is the heart of worship. We are actually offering ourselves to God which is what worship is all about. Fear keeps us from surrendering, still, love cast out fear. Life is a struggle and we fail to realize like Jacob we are in a fight with God. We want to be God; we will never win that fight. It was A. W. Tozer who said, "The reason why many are still troubled, still seeking, still making little forward progress is because they have not come to the end of themselves. We're still trying to give orders, and interfering with God's work in us."

Surrender is the best indication of obedience. We are obedient to the Word even when we do not understand it. That's because we trust God, like Abraham we will follow Him even though we do not know WHERE we are going. Like Joseph not knowing WHEN our dream would become a reality, like Hosea not understanding WHY he had to marry and buy back his prostitute wife, and Mary not knowing HOW we would become pregnant. The reason they could do this was they submitted self to God. We must surrender daily as Paul tells us (1 Corinthians 15:31). When we do, we no longer want to work things out our way by manipulating others, and trying to control circumstances. Instead, we wait on the Lord, who knows best, we will not be asking for what we want, but for what He wants. Not asking for healing or relief from suffering: but, for Him to show us the purpose for what we are going through, and complete it.

We are victorious when we surrender to God. It is our innate desire to surrender to someone or something. If not God, then to the opinions, other's expectations, money, food, power, prestige, popularity or even ourselves. We must remember we will have to live with our choices.

God's Glory

Our ultimate goal in life is to display the glory of God. Everything was made for God's glory. What is it? It is who He is and can be seen everywhere. The Psalmist tells us *"the heavens declare the glory of God"* (Psalm 19:1). It is best seen in Jesus, *"And the Word was made flesh, and dwelt among us, (and we beheld his glory, the glory as of the only begotten of the Father,) full of grace and truth"* (John 1:14). We cannot add or improve on it; still, we are admonished to reflect, recognize, declare, honor, praise and live for His glory. Why must we do this? God deserves it, *"Thou art worthy, O Lord, to receive glory and honour and power: for thou hast created all things, and for thy pleasure they are and were created"* (Revelations 4:11).

Sin hinders us from giving and reflecting God's glory, *"We all have sinned and come short of the glory of God"* (Romans 3:23). We can only truly give and reflect His glory when we ask for forgiveness from our sins and God will cleanse us from all unrighteousness (turn to the back to know how).

How Do I Glorify God?

Jesus told us how, *"I have glorified thee on the earth: I have finished the work which thou gavest me to do"* (John 17:4). He did it by doing what God commanded Him to do. Jesus fulfilled God's purposes for Him on earth. In like manner, we honor God when we fulfill our purposes. The dog honors God by barking, running, playing and anything else a dog is designed to do. A duck honors God by quacking, swimming, flying and anything else it was made to do. These bring glory to God.

Through worship, that is to say, how we live our lives, not merely going to church. It is how we enjoy God, loving and giving ourselves to be used for His purposes. When we use our life in this manner, to glorify God, everything we do becomes worship. Whatever you do, Paul says do all to the glory of God (1 Corinthians 10:31).

Our View of Worship

Anything we do that brings pleasure to God is worship. It is innate and is as natural as breathing or eating. When we serve others we are worshipping Him. When we are utilizing our gifts to serve God and others, we are worshipping. He designed us this way, to accomplish His purposes for us. It is no accident we are the way we are, to help others (1 Peter 4:10-11). We are saved not by service, but for service to God and our fellowmen. Anything we do that is Christ-like is worship. That is to say we are becoming more like Jesus in what we think, feel, and act. This brings glory to God. It is by beholding we are changed from glory to glory.

We are without excuse if we are not involved in ministry. Abraham could have made the excuse that he was old, but did not. Jacob's excuse could have been I am insecure. Leah could have said she was unattractive. Joseph could have used the abuse card. Moses tried using the stuttering tongue. Gideon the poor card. Samson was the classic case of codependent. Rahab could have said she was immoral, a prostitute. David's excuse could have been I had an affair, and some serious family problems. Elijah's excuse might have been I am suicidal, Jeremiah was suffering from depression. Jonah wanted to have his own way. Naomi was a widow and motherless. John the Baptist was strange and weird, to put it mildly, Peter was always putting his foot in his mouth and bad-tempered, Martha was a workaholic, the Samaritan woman had multiple affairs, Zacchaeus was ostracized, Thomas was a doubter, Paul had poor health, Timothy was young. That is a bunch of oddballs, but God used each of them to minister for Him and others. He will use us too, if we stop making excuses (**The Purpose Driven Life, Rick Warren, p 233).** How? By introducing others to Him. This means we have to change our priorities, schedules, relationships, work habits, and view of stuff. It is no longer about us, but worshipping God by doing His will. At times we will have to make difficult choices, like Jesus. While in Gethsemane His decision was Father if it be possible can I get out of this, nevertheless, not my will but yours be done.

Christ-likeness

It is God's desire that we become like Jesus. This has always been His goal for man once sin entered our world (Romans 8:29). Some of us want a quick fix to be like Jesus, just give me three principles, so that I could be Christ-like. Maturity takes time. God is never in a hurry like we are.

He does not want to take away our personalities, uniqueness, distinctiveness or else we would become robotic. He created our individuality, then it is about character development. We become like Jesus when we live the fruit of the Spirit, love the way Paul described in 1 Corinthians 13 or live like the Sermon on the Mount as taught by Jesus. He demonstrated these in His life. When we forget this, then we are frustrated by people and our circumstances. We will begin to question God, why me? Why are you allowing this to happen to me? Why are my friends and family members treating me so?

Paul tells us in Romans 8:17, life is supposed to be difficult. Difficulties are one of the tools that God uses for our growth. When we do not understand this, it produces a life of frustration, because the Bible says it is God's purpose that prevails not ours (Proverbs 19:21).

Many try to be Christ-like in their lives through New Year's resolutions, will power, or their own strength. We cannot because the Bible says, "*Work out your own salvation with fear and trembling. For it is God which worketh in you both to will and to do of his good pleasure*" (Philippians 2:12-13). How does He do it? By dwelling in us. He helps us make the choices according to His will through His indwelling Spirit. We have gone to the extreme of grace, yes, it is what saves us. Once we are saved we do not just sit around. We need to work so that we can grow, not to be saved because we already are. We are told often to "make every effort." This is a collaborative venture, we are co-workers with God. The Spirit works with and in us. The Bible admonishes

- Work out—our responsibility
- Work in—the Holy Spirit's responsibility

It is not about working for our salvation. We already have it. It is like if I want a six pack (rippling abdomen of muscles) I go to the gym and work out, not to get muscles, I already have them.

Will power does not work since it is about using our thoughts. You say to yourself, I will not be like my father, this becomes your focus and this is all you know. You find yourself acting and behaving just like him. Eventually you give in and become just like your father. The best way is to change your thought pattern. Our thoughts determine our behavior. We have to see ourselves becoming like Jesus. Let this mind be in you which was also in Jesus. Christ-likeness is impossible without people, the Bible and our daily situations. The truth of the Word makes us free to be who God wants us to be. Our situations help mold us into the new creature. People are necessary to support us as we do.

Our View of Suffering

God uses suffering to help us become like Jesus. We tend to get more intimate with Him through suffering. We have to be real, our energy is sapped so we do not have the strength to fake our prayers, we must be honest. We have no choice but to lean on Him rather than ourselves. This can only be a reality when we are at the end of our rope dangling from a steep cliff and our strength is gone. God is the one who designed it this way or else we would see no need for Him.

This is the same road that Jesus traveled and so must we. His Father hid His face from Him, the pressure was so intense at one time, He sweats drops of blood. The Bible says Jesus learned obedience through suffering (Hebrews 5:8-9). We have to do the same (Romans 8:17). When we try to avoid or escape from suffering we short circuit the process of growth. God will take us through the same process until we learn the lessons we need to learn. Before we pray for relief we need to ask Him what is His purpose in our suffering.

Satan uses temptation to harm us, God uses it to grow us (1 Corinthians 10:13). We have many Biblical examples of suffering: Job, Joseph, Jeremiah, John the Baptist, and Jesus. Joseph, whose character is closer to Jesus than any other person in the Bible, did what was right, telling on his brothers when they did wrong, and not sleeping with Mrs. Potiphar. Yet, he ended up in a pit, a slave and a prisoner for doing the right thing. He had to patiently wait for thirteen years before the dream that God had given him was fulfilled. In fact, other people's dreams were fulfilled before his, Pharaoh's butler and baker.

Another is David. The Bible describes him as a man after God's own heart. After being promised to be Israel's second king: He had to be running, hiding, and sleeping in caves. He spared King Saul's life when he could have killed him twice. He had to wait twenty years before he became King of Israel.

It is not just about doing right. It is about being in a right relationship with God. We cannot understand how He works, He is not our puppet. It is not just about the rewards. It is our relationship and a journey of faith we take with the Lord. It is walking with Jesus and finding out what He is up to next. It is like a roller coaster ride, a thrilling adventure.

To identify with Jesus, the apostle Peter tells us, *"Dear friends, do not be surprised at the painful trial you are suffering, as though something strange were happening to you. But rejoice that you participate in the sufferings of Christ, so that you may be overjoyed when His glory is revealed"* (1 Peter 4:12-13). Paul reminds us, *"And if children, then heirs; heirs of God, and joint-heirs with Christ; if so be that we suffer with Him, that we may be also glorified together"* (Romans 8:17). As a disciple we are not surprised when we encounter trials and suffering. We know we are suffering with Jesus. These are designed to develop character and to keep us humble. A relationship with God carries with it power and a boldness that makes us feel invincible. If that is not curbed, it can cause us to sin. Take for example Joseph and his brothers. Because of his special relationship with his father and his dreams, Joseph thought he was better than his brothers. That is why he wore his pretty coat in the pasture. Actually it was a kingly robe. Why? Because he was backed by the power and authority of his father. If God did not rescue Joseph, they would have killed him, because he was arrogant, proud and boastful. He knew his brothers had to bow down to him.

When we connect with the resurrection power of God, He has to keep us humble to remind us that we are not God, just sons and daughters of His. We still have within us, like Adam and Eve, the desire to become God. We are not satisfied with being like Him; we want to be Him. God does not want us to forget. He knows how easy we forget, so He has to provide reminders along the way through our pain and suffering.

Our View of the Devil

Do not have a relationship with him. The Bible says to resist him. Do not try to argue with him. We will lose every time. He has had thousands of years to practice, we only have a few. Even Jesus who was from eternity did not argue with him. In tempting Jesus to turn the stones into bread, Jesus did not say to him, "I'm not hungry" He quoted Scripture. One of the ways to avoid a relationship with the devil is to know and live the Bible. Be careful though, he knows the Bible very well, you have to know the Author personally. If not, you are no different to the devil.

Relationship with God

The first step in establishing a relationship with God is to believe He loves us and wants an everlasting relationship with us. This is demonstrated in Jesus coming down from heaven to die on a cruel cross so that we can live and reign with Him eternally. God put Himself out of the way to mend the disconnection that exists between us and Him. The best way to start dealing with our broken relationship is by accepting Jesus as our personal Savior and Lord. Do it again, even if you did it before. It is the best decision you will ever make. How? Turn to the last page in this book. It is very simple; but, powerful. This is crucial in understanding and developing other friendships. Then, read the Word and it will tell you how to maintain your relationship with God and others. Next, find a church that will teach you how to become Jesus' disciple and make disciples.

We need to know how to develop solid and intimate partnerships with God, our fellowmen and ourselves. If we read the Bible carefully we will understand that it is a book about relationships, how to begin and maintain them. You must become a student of the Word. Someone rightly said, "The Bible is about loving the Lord our God with all our heart, mind, and soul and loving our neighbor as ourselves the rest of the book tells us how to do that."

Life is About God

I am convinced after living for over half a century, life is about God—period, end of discussion. It took me a while, but, I got it. Life is about pursuing Him. It takes on new meanings, new dimensions, and there is a peace and joy that is found in the Spirit. We begin to see life differently; even our problems and sufferings are seen in a whole new light. Life is really worth living. The quality of life is fantabulous.

The thing that God wants the most from us is to pursue Him and search for Him with all our hearts. How do we find God? We cannot find Him; He has to reveal Himself to us. Like Jesus told Peter when he said Jesus was the Messiah, it was not flesh and blood that told him, it was revealed to him by the Spirit (Matthew 16:16-17). We need the Spirit to reveal to us who God really is. There are many who are trying through research, reading the Bible, going to church, keeping the commandments, like the Rich Young Ruler. We still have to ask, "What must I do to be saved?" It is only as we allow the Spirit to reveal to us who God is and who we are that we can truly know Him (Romans 8:16).

Once God finds us, He performs a heart transplant. He takes out our stony heart and gives us a heart of flesh, a heart that is bent on obeying Him. He makes it easy because He writes His law upon our new hearts (Jeremiah 31:31-33). This is accomplished through the blood of Jesus (Hebrews 9:13-15).

Knowing God must be our number one priority. It is through the knowledge of Jesus that we know who God really is and who we are. Like Jesus said, we shall know the truth and the truth will make us free (John 8:32). This knowledge cannot be gained through second-hand, but through a personal and experiential basis. It is the Spirit connecting with our spirit and revealing to us who God really is. It is in this context that faith is developed and nurtured. Then we have to admit, like Solomon, 'I do not know what to do, give me wisdom.' It is not always as obvious as we think. The Lord is pleased with such an admission. Like him, our focus should be on wisdom rather than riches (1 Kings 3:5-12). With pure motives God gives us what we need even if we do not ask.

Relationships Involves Time and Hard Work

Everybody in relationships understands that they require investments. So much so, that we often give up on relationships rather than put forth the time and effort that is needed. Look at the prisons and divorce records.

We are into working and sometimes we do not know when to stop and spend time with God and our loved ones. We can get so caught up in being like Martha and not spending time with Jesus, like Mary. We live in a society where everything is fast-paced and instant. We want to include relationships in that mix. But that is impossible. Not willing to invest the time and effort has produced the many divorces, overcrowded prisons, delinquent children and disconnection from God.

It still baffles me how I was trying to develop a relationship with God and only visit with Him and His people once or twice a week. I would pray and read a devotional book in the morning and maybe at night. That is all the time God got from me. We cannot develop a relationship with Him like that. When we are in love and developing a relationship with someone we love, we cannot see one person without the other. When we see them, they are joined together at the hip and not even wind can pass between. The person is constantly on our mind. We are texting, emailing, calling, visiting, or dreaming about them. That must be the same kind of relationship we develop with God, otherwise we will fall in love with someone or something else.

Since we do not have the time, we want others to go to God on our behalf and then come and tell us what He said. Like the Children of Israel. Moses climbed the mountain and went into the cloud with God and was changed. He experienced Him in a personal way. The Israelites refused to come near, choosing to let Moses go and then tell them what God said. Hence, they never knew God personally and continually rebelled. Today we want the same, others to tell us about God and who He is. We are not willing to invest and get to know Him. Instead, we are too busy doing our own thing. We do not want to climb the mountain; too much hard work. Even if we do, like the disciples, when we get on the mountain, we do not want to come down to help others get up there. Too much time and work is involved.

We have become a bunch of lazy, wannabe disciples. So we love to run after signs and wonders from meeting to meeting. Never taking time to go up to the mountain of God, nor waiting on Him for His transforming work. We want to see His acts, but we'll readily pay someone else to wait upon the Lord, then tell us what He has to say. Is there any wonder we have so many golden calves in the churches today?

First-Hand Knowledge of God

We do not know who God is, because we are still seeing Him as our parents, pastors, neighbors, or evangelist God. When we do not know Him personally, we do not know what He is capable of, what our potential and abilities are. We are living a substandard life and not up to our God given greatness.

He wants to constantly reveal to us who He really is. He chooses not to do this based on hearsay. When we want to know about someone, in the beginning we may ask someone else. However, to truly know the person we have to meet with them, spend time, communicate, laugh, play, sing, eat, and do many things together. Like when I met my wife, I asked folks who knew her, they gave me a good report. However, two of them said she would not make a good preacher's wife. I could have taken their word, but it was second-hand information. I chose to find out who the young lady was for myself: I found, contrary to their beliefs, she made an excellent pastor's wife and we have been married and ministering for almost thirty years.

The truth is, not even her family members could have told me who my wife really is. Notice I said **is**, because we are constantly changing. I had to get it directly from her, both consciously and subconsciously. I had to observe her in different settings, under different circumstances, her interaction with people, her behavior at home, her attitude toward her parents, how she carried herself, how much she loved the Lord, not merely by her words, but more so with her actions. That took time and effort.

It is the exact same thing when it comes to God. You must want to know Him, not just about Him. Know who He is and what He is capable of. The greatest thing we can know about Jesus, other than He loves us and gave His life for us, is He rose from the dead. That is one of the reasons Paul says,

> But what things were gain to me, these I have counted loss for Christ. Yet indeed I also count all things loss for the excellence of the knowledge of Christ Jesus my Lord, for whom I have suffered the loss of all things, and count them as rubbish, that I may gain Christ…that I may know Him and the **power of His resurrection**, and the fellowship of His sufferings, being conformed to His death, if, by any means, I may attain to the resurrection from the dead (Philippians 3:7-11, My Emphasis).

Knowing Jesus and the power of the resurrection was foremost on Paul's mind, "*For I determined not to know anything among you, save Jesus Christ, and him* **crucified**" (1 Corinthians 2:2). That is why it became Paul's quest, he was not interested in flowery speeches, or for people to see how smart he was. He had one goal and this too should be ours.

We have neglected the cross of Jesus and thus deny the efficacy (effectiveness) of his blood to deliver us from the power of sin and self. We have a boldness by the blood (Hebrews 10:19-22). We have regulated His resurrection to the realm of the Spirit and settled for a positional relationship with Jesus rather than a personal and intimate one. We have frustrated His grace in the guise of freedom from legalism. To cover our nakedness, we have woven a form of godliness that denies His power.

It is so Simple

We are evangelicals and we know it all. We do not leave room for questioning. We are always evangelizing, spewing out of our mouths what we have been taught. There is not much time for meditating, thinking and questioning. We are so busy doing that we do not have the time to be a disciple. We become irritated with people who ask questions. The more they ask the more irritated we become, especially when we cannot answer; because it is someone else's information not ours, or when we think those questions are too simple.

Unfortunately, we have complicated Discipleship. We are deluded into believing the more complicated we make the information, the smarter we are. That is exactly what the Jews did with Judaism. They made it a burden for the people. That is why Jesus' call is still relevant today, *"Come to me, all you who are weary and burdened, and I will give you rest. Take my yoke upon you and learn from me, for I am gentle and humble in heart, and you will find rest for your souls. For my yoke is easy and my burden is light"* (Matthew 11:28-30 NIV). Jesus came and simplified it by introducing discipleship His way.

Stop listening to people only and get to know Jesus for yourself. Spend time in His Word, fasting, praying (listening before and after praying), praising, and start telling others of His love. If you follow the life and teachings of Jesus, you will see how simple He made it. Do not settle just for second-hand information. When you get to know Jesus, people will know that you have been with Him. Samuel saw that David had a relationship with God (1 Samuel 16:12). That is the greatest compliment we can receive.

Understanding Our Relationship with God

We were designed by God to have fellowship and communion with Him as His own special people. He wants to be our Daddy, *"I will be a Father to you, and you will be my sons and daughters, says the Lord Almighty"* (2 Corinthians 6:18). There is no greater relationship on the earth. That is why God has given us the capacity for love, so that He can love us and we in return love Him, ourselves and our fellow man, in that order. Jesus told us to love the Lord with all our hearts and our neighbors as ourselves, this presupposes we have learned to love God first, ourselves and then others. We are incapable of loving ourselves purely if we have not learned to love God first. In like manner, we are unable to love others purely until we have learned to love ourselves.

God's greatest desire has always been a relationship with us. That is why we were created. Thus, we must make the pursuit of God the primary purpose of our lives. Jesus said it this way, *"But seek first his Kingdom and his righteousness, and all these things will be given to you as well"* (Matthew 6:33 NIV). That is the kind of God He is. Since He made us, He knows we like rewards. Hence, He lavishes them upon us, not only in this life, but also in the life to come.

The writer to the Hebrews sums it up this way, *"And without faith it is impossible to please God, because anyone who comes to Him must believe that He exists and that He rewards those who earnestly seek Him"* (Hebrews 11:6). God gives incentives to those who faithfully seek Him. Moses had a long list of the rewards for our relationship with God in Deuteronomy 28. They are based on the condition we are obedient to Him. But, here is where many preachers stop and this creates a disconnection since this is only half the story. There are times when He chooses not to give us these things in this life. He is unpredictable. At times, He allows us to suffer even when we are being obedient and doing what's right. Still, He promised He will always be with us.

Bribes

We try to bribe God to get Him to do what we want. Sometimes we think we can buy Him by returning our tithes and offering, coming to church and doing good deeds. We try to rack up brownie points. That is no different to penance. True, we may say we do not believe in penance. If we believe that our money or good deeds can buy us God's favor, we believe in it. Even though the truth is we cannot bribe Him because it is not ours in the first place. We, and all we have, already belong to Him. The difference between our rewards and God's is He gives them to us after we are obedient. We try to use our rewards to manipulate God by getting Him to do what we want.

For example, I was making a presentation at one church on a Sabbath morning and I asked them to show, by the raising of hands, who believed if Jesus came now they would be saved. Almost every hand was raised. Then I said, imagine it is Monday morning and your boss got upset with you for something you did not do. It was so bad he decided to reduce your pay. You became angry and you told him a few curse words. Then you died. Would you be saved? Only one lady put her hand up. Our being saved is not based on what we do. It is based on what Jesus did. It is getting to know who He is and wanting to be like Him. It is about being and not doing. It is simple. If you are like Him, you will do His will.

We give God the greatest joy when it is our desire to be His friend. When we want the same things that He wants, a relationship, it makes Him so happy He endows us with quality life. Here is His promise, *"This is what the Lord says to the house of Israel: 'Seek me and live'"* (Amos 5:4). Whenever we do something for God, He always has something in it for us. We have not yet begun to live and enjoy life until we make God our number one pursuit in life. We have been pursuing everything and everyone else except the One we should be searching for in the first place.

Works

Because of sin we are heavily into works. We want to work for our salvation. God's grace is too simple: hence, difficult to accept. Yet, our works are dead. Hebrew 9:14 tells us. *"How much more shall the blood of Christ, who through the eternal Spirit offered himself without spot to God, purge your conscience from dead works to serve the living God?"* How do we know they are dead? When our works are done out of selfish motives and ambitions, it does not matter how religious they are. The works pleasing to God are works of righteousness, done in the will of God.

We do not have to look far to see our dead works, works of the flesh, and the stronghold it has on the Church. We see it in our desire for power, the love of money, our emphasis on materialism and covetousness, the division and strife in our midst, racism, immorality—the list is endless. We have not learned to walk in the Spirit. We are still operating in the flesh. Thus, we are emphasizing works or grace and not a friendship. It is not about doing; it is about being. It is about knowing a person as opposed to a body of doctrines.

An Exclusive Relationship

Remember the Lord our God is a jealous God and He wants us to have Him as our primary relationship. He must be above everyone or everything else. We cannot love anyone or anything more than God (Matthew 10:37). That is why we cannot be friends of the world and develop a relationship with God. John tells us, *"Do not love the world or anything in the world. If anyone loves the world, the love of the Father is not in him"* (1 John 2:15). Many want to enjoy the best of both worlds. During the week we have a relationship with the world, listening to their songs, dancing to their music, watching their movies, rapping to their beat. Then on weekends we want to switch to the spiritual. We have a hard time because we have fed our minds with the food of the world and the spiritual food is not palatable. We feel like we want to vomit, we are critical, judgmental and uncomfortable.

Always Consult God

We have to stay connected to Him always because God is not predictable. He is not always obvious. David knew this very well. When God sent Samuel to find a king among his father's sons, it seemed obvious to him who the choice was—the oldest, tallest, most handsome and most stately of the brothers. Here is how the Bible describes it, *"When they arrived, Samuel saw Eliab and thought, 'Surely the Lord's anointed stands here before the Lord.' But the Lord said to Samuel, 'Do not consider his appearance or his height, for I have rejected him. The Lord does not look at the things man looks at. Man looks at the outward appearance, but the Lord looks at the heart'"* (1 Samuel 16:6-7). God said no, it will be the youngest and lowliest, a shepherd boy.

So when David was told, *"'Look, the Philistines are fighting against Keilah and are looting the threshing floors.' He inquired of the Lord, saying, 'Shall I go and attack these Philistines?' The Lord answered him, 'Go, attack the Philistines and save Keilah'"* (1 Samuel 23:1-2). He wanted to make sure that is what God wanted. This is not the only time David did this. One day when he and his men returned home from war they found it destroyed by fire and their wives and children were taken captives. David and his men wept aloud until they were tired. They were talking of stoning David. He turned to God who strengthened him. David asked Abiathar the priest, to inquire of the Lord if they should pursue the raiding party. The Lord said yes and David and four hundred of his six hundred men went and recovered their loot and families (1 Samuel 30:3-10). To me it seemed pretty obvious what David should have done. He and his men were soldiers and that is what they did, fought, and they were fighting for their families. David did not like to assume what the will of God was. He asked. To stay connected with God we cannot assume we know what His will is, we must ask.

Here is why it was so important for David to consult God about his decisions. He realized he was living in a house made of cedar and the ark of God was in a tent and he was uncomfortable with that. There was a need to build a temple for the Lord and he called the prophet Nathan and told him his dilemma. It was obvious that since David was a man after God's own heart and there was a definite need for a temple, he should begin building immediately. It was clear to David, Nathan, and Israel; but, it was not apparent to God. His plan was not for David to build the temple, but Solomon.

Do not take anything for granted; ask God even when it seems obvious. We need to stop making our decisions based on our senses, traditions or the church. We have to rely on the Spirit because with God it is not as obvious as it seems.

Designed to Grow

Once we get to know God, our relationship must be one of growth and excitement. Peter admonished us, *"But grow in grace, and in the knowledge of our Lord and Savior Jesus Christ. To Him be glory both now and forever. Amen"* (2 Peter 3:18). This means sometimes we have to struggle, fall down, and get up. As the Psalmist points out, a righteous man falls down seven times and gets back up again. Peter puts it this way, *"Add to your faith, goodness, knowledge, self-control, perseverance, godliness, brotherly kindness, and love. If we possess these qualities in increasing measure, they will keep us from being ineffective and unproductive in our knowledge of Jesus Christ. If anyone does not have these he is nearsighted and blind, and has forgotten that he has been cleansed from his past sins"* (2 Peter 1:5-9).

In concluding, when our relationships stop growing we forget who God is. We become narrow-minded and self-centered. We begin to back slide into the flesh and do not hear the Spirit. In developing our relationship with God, He helps us to focus on others and not ourselves. Thus we grow in the process because in friendships it is not about us; it is about the other person. Most times, if we focus on the other person long enough, they normally respond by loving us back. That is what God had to do; the Bible says that while we were yet sinning, Jesus died for us (Romans 5:8). While we were alienated from God, He sent His Son down on our behalf. We have to do the same for others. Even if they hate us we have to continue loving them.

—•◆•—

Chapter 19

Our Greatest Example

JESUS IS OUR GREATEST EXAMPLE for all relationships. He knows how to develop and maintain them since He created them. He even went a step further and showed us how to do so by coming as a human being and demonstrated it daily.

We have become a self-centered society, God wants us to focus on others. Jesus verified this in every area of His life. He was God and became man. He became sin for us who knew no sin. He was tempted in all points, so that we could know that He knows when we are tempted, what we are going through. He was rich and for our sake He became poor. He died so that we may live. He was resurrected so that we can experience resurrection every time we awake out of sleep and eventually on that great day.

How Jesus Relates

The Apostle Paul captures it eloquently and has given us the best example on relationships, Philippians 2:3-10,

> *Let nothing be done through strife or vainglory; but in lowliness of mind let each esteem other better than themselves. Look not every man on his own things, but every man also on the things of others. Let this mind be in you, which was also in Christ Jesus: Who, being in the form of God, thought it not robbery to*

be equal with God: But made himself of no reputation, and took upon him the form of a servant, and was made in the likeness of men: And being found in fashion as a man, he humbled himself, and became obedient unto death, even the death of the cross. Wherefore God also hath highly exalted him, and given him a name which is above every name: That at the name of Jesus every knee should bow, of things in heaven, and things in earth, and things under the earth.

Humble

This is considered the greatest piece of poetry in the Bible. It helps us to understand how Jesus went about establishing and sustaining His friendship with us. There was a problem with the brethren in Philippi, they were having difficulty relating to one another. Paul was pointing out to them that they needed to be humble and see the other person as better than themselves. Then he told them to look out for each other, not only for themselves. That is what Jesus actually did.

This is interesting because Paul is here telling us that humility begins in the mind. So, our thought process has to change. We have to learn to think on the positive things. *"Finally, brethren, whatsoever things are true, whatsoever things are honest, whatsoever things are just, whatsoever things are pure, whatsoever things are lovely, whatsoever things are of good report; if there be any virtue, and if there be any praise, think on these things. Those things, which ye have both learned, and received, and heard, and seen in me, do: and the God of peace shall be with you"* (Philippians 4:8-9). Notice these cannot just remain in our thoughts, they will be demonstrated in how we treat each other. It is not what we say, it is how we relate that is the measuring rod of humility.

Paul's thesis is, this is exactly what Jesus did. That is why we need His mind. He was God, and He did not hold on to being God and all that goes along with it. He gave up that status and became a slave and die like one: a cruel and embarrassing death, one of a common criminal. That is humility at its highest level. All this was done not for Himself. He did it so that He could continue an eternal relationship with us. This is what Paul was trying to get the Philippians to understand and relate. This is how we are to relate to each other. We go to whatever lengths necessary to maintain or develop relationships with people, even if it means dying.

Are you willing to go that far in a relationship not just for your spouse, but to lay down your life for your friends. In developing relationships we have to reach the point where we are willing to die for the other person. *"Hereby perceive we the love of God, because he laid down his life for us: and we ought to lay down our lives for the brethren"* (1 John 3:16).

Slave

Jesus was willing to become a slave so that He could continue relating to us forever. Can you imagine being God of this universe and sinking to the lowest rung of the social ladder? This was demonstrated where He was born in a barn or stable among the animals, not even among human beings. The only way we can be successful in any relationship is to become a slave to those we are relating to. This is very difficult depending upon how prestigious or high we think we are. If we see ourselves as better than people because of our position, then we will have difficulty seeing, feeling, or hearing ourselves as a slave. There was, nor is there any higher position than what Jesus has. Yet, He became a slave and was born in a manger. What is paradoxical about all of this is that, He who is God, saw us as better than Himself. He did not see Himself as better or superior to us. If He did, then He would not have become a man and die for us.

He further demonstrated servant hood with his disciples, *"He riseth from supper, and laid aside his garments; and took a towel, and girded himself. After that he poureth water into a bason, and began to wash the disciples' feet, and to wipe them with the towel wherewith he was girded"* (John 13:3-4). This was the job of a servant. This is what they did when people came to their master's house. Jesus did it for His disciples, instead of them doing it to Him.

If like Jesus, we approach relationships from a slave stand point, it will help us in developing better relationships. We will respect the other person since we esteem them as better than ourselves. It's because we can serve them, we have a contribution to make to their lives and that responsibility is of such that it makes us humble. Like Jesus who has and is making the greatest contribution to our lives, He humbled Himself. Thus, the greater our contribution to anyone's life the more humble we must be, not proud, boastful and arrogant. The more knowledgeable we become, the humbler we must be: Since there is still more to learn and we have a responsibility to impart this knowledge to whom the Spirit tells us to. Not just knowledge, whatever we have more of, as Jesus said "to whom much is given, much is expected." He had much to offer and much was expected of Him.

Service

As we just saw Jesus came into this world to serve, that is what a slave does. Here is what we prefer. In Matthew 20, the mother of James and John came and made the request for her sons to sit on the left and right of Jesus in the Kingdom. When the other ten disciples heard it they were mad, because she beat them to it. Listen to His response, *"Jesus called them together and said, "You know that the rulers of the Gentiles lord it over them, and their high*

          You Were Made To Worship God 24/7

officials exercise authority over them. Not so with you. Instead, whoever wants to become great among you must be your servant, and whoever wants to be first must be your slave—just as the Son of Man did not come to be served, but to serve, and to give his life as a ransom for many." (Matthew 20:25-28 NIV).

This is why we were created. Service is the highest and best form of developing and maintaining relationships. It is the backbone of re-lationships. We serve God by serving others. The world's measure of greatness is diametrically opposed to God's. The world measures greatness based on power, prestige, position and possessions. It is about how many people are serving us. If you can make people do what you want, you are great. It is not about serving others. You would be ridiculed like Jesus if you decide to serve others. God measures greatness by how many people we are serving. The dis-ciples wanted to be in line, wanting the most prominent position. Look at what we do, *"But when thou art bidden, go and sit down in the lowest room; that when he that bade thee cometh, he may say unto thee, Friend, go up higher: then shalt thou have worship in the presence of them that sit at meat with thee"* (Luke 14:10). **We want to be noticed so we run to the seat of prominence. Jesus says no.**

We are more concerned about leadership than discipleship, power rather than service. Do not agree? Look at how many books are written on leadership and how many are written on service. We all want to lead and no one wants to serve: Even those who empha-size service speak of servant leaders rather than just servants. Jesus called Himself a servant not a servant leader.

Problems with Slavery

We have a negative concept of slavery based on how slaves are treated or how we would treat them. Thus, nobody wants to be a slave. We can pretend that we do, but when we are called upon to do the work of one, we back down. Like get up at two in the morning and serve me breakfast, or if someone keeps deliberately messing up the floor just to see you get down on your knees to clean it. Slavery to us means giving up our status in life or a change in our status diminishes who we are in the eyes of our fellowmen. And sometimes that does occur. Yet, God comes along and highly exalts us and changes our name.

Furthermore, we were all designed by God as leaders. We have to learn from Him, who is the best on how to lead and treat others. He did not do it according to the customs of the day, like touching the lepers—it is how we want others to treat us. Your see being a slave means that we are no longer in charge. We cannot call the shots, our Master does. He decides when and where we serve. Thus, He can interrupt our plans anytime and we cannot get angry. It reminds me of Joseph who knew his brothers would bow down to him and God needed to humble him first by understanding that leadership is about becoming a slave. Moses had to learn to serve sheep first.

Jesus has shown us that in order to develop or maintain relationships we cannot emphasize our superiority or our equality. We have to see others as better than ourselves. We cannot think of ourselves more highly than we should. The more we know ourselves the humbler we should be, that is contrary to human nature so we need help outside of ourselves. Jesus verified this perfectly when He came to do for us what we could not do for ourselves, while we were yet sinners. It had nothing to do with deserving or not deserving.

Without a slave's heart we'll misuse and abuse people. Using whatever God has given us for ourselves rather than using it to serve others. Being a servant means we have to be concerned about the little things of life. The menial tasks; hence, we will be considered sub-human. Notice though how it will all end, Jesus saying to us well done thou good and faithful servant, enter into the joy of the Lord (Matthew 25:21, 23). Being a servant shows how much we care.

Ministering to Needs

Jesus came to this earth and became a man because we had a need that only God could fulfill. It is not about being superior because Jesus sure could have claimed superiority. Instead, He chose to be a slave. We have to learn to do the same as we met one another's needs. God has equipped us to fulfill them. As a servant, Jesus was aware of people's needs and met them, so should we. God has endowed and equipped us to carry out His purposes and you will notice His purposes involve meeting the needs of people. And He gets the glory.

We cannot be selfish when meeting people's needs. That is why Jesus said and demonstrated in His life in **Luke 14:12:** *"Then said he also to him that bade him, When thou makest a dinner or a supper, call not thy friends, nor thy brethren, neither thy kinsmen, nor thy rich neighbours; lest they also bid thee again, and a recompence be-made thee."* Friendship is about servant-hood, or to put it another way, it is about ministry: Meeting the needs of our fellowmen, that's ministry. How can we help our fellowmen? We have to find out what God has gifted us with. How unique am I? What special gifts and abilities has God given to help those people He puts in my life daily to carry out His purposes? Paul admonishes us, *"Now we exhort you, brethren, warn them that are unruly, comfort the feebleminded, comfort the weak, be patient toward all men. See that none render evil for evil unto any man; but ever follow that which is good both among ourselves, and to all men"* (1 Thessalonians 5:14-15).

One of our greatest needs is learning to forgive. Forgive us our debts we forgive those who hurt us (Matthew 6). The truth is they hurt me today, but, we forgot we hurt them just yesterday. We want them to forgive us but we had a hard time forgiving them. We will have serious difficulty with relationships if we do not forgive. If we look at Jesus we see how easy it was for Him to forgive. His response to the woman caught in adultery was, *"Neither do I condemn thee: go, and sin no more"* (John 8:11).

Lead by Example

The greatest example of all is Jesus coming to earth to show us how to live and love. He did not just tell us how to relate to each other. He actually entered a human body and lived how He wants us to. This was not based on any conditions. In others words, the Father, like His Son, Jesus, does not treat us the way we treat Them. Their attitude towards us is not dependent on our attitude towards Them. They did not react to our negative behavior. We believe in an eye for an eye and a tooth for a tooth. Jesus did not believe this and did not treat those around Him that way.

He said we ought to love our enemies and do good to them that hate us and spitefully use us (Matthew 5:44; Luke 6:27). He did not just say it. When the mob came to take Him to be tried and crucified, Peter took out his sword and cut off Malchus' ear. Jesus miraculously healed the ear and told him, if you lived by the sword, you will die by the sword (Matthew 26:52). By extension, it also means that if we live by the golden rule, we will die by it.

While on earth Jesus established relationships with His parents, His neighbors, and then as He was ready for ministry. He called disciples and worked with them and left them to carry on the work He started. In the Garden of Eden the Bible says that God would come down in the cool of the day and hang out with Adam. Since sin separates us from Him, He is not here with us now physically. In the earth made new however, God Himself will be with us and be our God, thus fulfilling His intention to be with us.

Attitude

Our attitude determines our altitude. Because of Jesus humility, God has exalted Him and given Him a name above every name that at the name of Jesus every knee will bow and every tongue must confess that Jesus is Lord. Even though Jesus knew that we cannot make it without Him, He did not rub it in our faces. He became one of us, He who knew no sin became sin for us. He did not have to, yet, He chose to. Jesus restricted Himself. That is why He needed the help of the disciples to feed the multitudes with the loaves and fishes.

Jesus' motives were always pure. He had nothing to prove to anyone. He was never selfish or arrogant. Our motives must be pure. We normally do things from selfish motives. We are arrogant and proud and want things to be done our way. This brings about strife and vain glory. Jesus was concerned about doing things His Father's way. We must have the same attitude and make the choices that will demonstrate to people that we care. Not with an attitude of you cannot get through life without me. But more like how can I help you? Have you noticed in relationships, it is not about you it is about the other person? When we deal with it in this manner then we will not come across as arrogant, but with an attitude of humility. The Wise Man puts it this way, '*Do this now, my son, and deliver thyself, when thou art come into the hand of thy friend; go, humble thyself, and make sure thy friend*" (Proverbs 6:3).

We all have a superior attitude built within us. God has made us with a desire to want to lead because we are born in His image. We want to be in charge, rule, and dominate. Even though this was given so that we dominate the birds of the air, the fishes of sea and every creature that moves upon the earth. Instead, we want to use that rulership ability to dominate people. That is why we have to humble ourselves as the Apostle Paul points out in Romans 12:3, "*For I say, through the grace given unto me, to every man that is among you, not to think of himself more highly than he ought to think; but to think soberly, according as God hath dealt to every man the measure of faith."*

Sacrifice

This was something Jesus verified throughout His life on earth. Paul reminds us even though He was equal with God, He did not hold on to His equality. He saw that the only way we will be saved and live with God eternally is to give up His exalted position and become just like man. That is sacrifice. It might be a bit easier if you have never been exalted to humble yourself. But, if you have never been a servant to become one is hard. All Jesus knew was rulership and yet He decided to humble Himself to the point where He agreed to die in the process. This was not just a mere act. This was the real deal.

The greatest sacrifice to me was living daily. Imagine you have the ability to miraculously do anything, and you had to do it like everyone else. Most of us use the power we have. Jesus had to refrain daily from using His power to His advantage, to live an exemplary life. That's sacrifice.

Choice

Relationships actually boil down to making choices. These cannot be based on how we feel, what time of the day it is. We need to make choices based on the leading of the Spirit. That's how we were chosen, *"Ye have not chosen me, but I have chosen you, and ordained you, that ye should go and bring forth fruit, and that your fruit should remain: that whatsoever ye shall ask of the Father in my name, he may give it you"* (John 15:16).

Like Jesus, we have to make the choice to love. He did not just say He loves us. He demonstrated it and commands us,

"This is my commandment, that ye love one another, as I have loved you. Greater love hath no man than this, that a man lay down his life for his friends. Ye are my friends, if ye do whatsoever I command you. Henceforth I call you not servants; for the servant knoweth not what his lord doeth: but I have called you friends; for all things that I have heard of my Father I have made known unto you" (John 15:12-14).

King Solomon puts it this way, "A *friend loveth at all times, and a brother is born for adversity*" (Proverbs 17:17).

In order for us to be a friend or make a friend we have to make the choice to be friendly. "*A man that hath friends must shew himself friendly: and there is a friend that sticketh closer than a brother*" (*Proverbs 18:24*). It has always been **Jesus' desire to make us His friends,** "*And the scripture was fulfilled which saith, Abraham believed God, and it was imputed unto him for righteousness: and he was called the Friend of God*" (*James 2:23*). **It is easy to become a friend of God,** "*Ye are my friends, if ye do whatsoever I command you*" (John 15:14).

Related to Himself

Jesus denied Himself and did the will of His Father because He loves Him with an everlasting love. He took the time to grow in wisdom and statue in favor with God and man. He saw Himself as coming to do the will of His Father in Heaven. He knew His purposes for coming so He was not distracted. For example, one time they wanted to make Him King. Jesus was already King and that did not distract Him because He knew when it was His time to be reinstated. People did not determine what and when to do what He did. He took His instructions from His Father.

When He encountered issues, He dealt with them right away. In Matthew 21 Jesus literally overthrew the tables of the money changers. Yet, he refused to be distracted and there were many who tried: The Jewish leaders, the Scribes and Pharisees, the disciples, the Romans and the devil. Because He was so focused on His mission He did not even allow death to distract Him. Some reasons for His success:

- Jesus knew who He was, *"Before Abraham was I am"* (John 8:58).
- He knew who loved Him, *"Therefore doth my Father love me"* (John 10:17).
- He knew who sent Him, *"as my Father hath sent me"* (John 20:21).
- Was not afraid of work, *"My Father worketh hitherto, and I work* (John 5:17).
- He knew His mission, *"I must be about my Father's business"* (Luke 2:49).
- Wanted others to succeed, *"greater works [than me] shall he do"* (John 14:12).
- These attributes:
- Gave Jesus a peace of mind, *"my peace I give unto you"* (John 14:27).
- Gave Him authority, *"taught them as one having authority"* (Matthew 7:29).
- Gave Him a confidence, *"Never man spake like this man"* (John 7:46).
- Gave Him a humble spirit, *"became obedient unto death"* (Philippians 2:8).
- Gave Him ability to relate to all, *"in favour with God and man"* (Luke 2:52).
- To deal with those different, *"a friend of publicans and sinners!"* (Luke 7:34).

Related to God

This could be summed up in six words uttered by Jesus Himself in John 10:30 *"I and my Father are one."* That is how He lived His life, total reliance on His Father because He was human. He did nothing other than the will of God, *"Jesus saith unto them, my meat is to do the will of him that sent me, and to finish his work"* (John 4:34).

Relate To Others

Jesus demonstrated in His earthly life the need to relate to others. He chose seventy disciples at one point. He needed them to help Him accomplish His purposes and to carry on His mission of building up the Kingdom.

The Individual

The Bible tells us that Jesus became a slave. Interestingly, most times a servant has to serve one person at a time. The key to Jesus success in relationships was the ability to reach the individual. Jesus was always about the individual. It did not matter where they were. He had the gift to minister to the individual in a crowd. For example, at the Pool of Bethesda in John 5:3, *"In these lay a great multitude of impotent folk, of blind, halt, withered, waiting for the moving of the water."* The Bible tells us in verse 5, *"And a certain man was there, which had an infirmity thirty and eight years."* Jesus zeroed in on this man out of an entire crowd of people, to meet his need. He was not so much into the multitude; He spoke and ministered to the individual even in a crowd. In ministry we want the big crowd; however, we are not ready for it, until we are ready to minister to the individual.

In Matthew 9 this is brought home clearly and often, a crowd was always following Jesus. First, He focused on a man with palsy and healed him. Then He saw Matthew a tax collector and called him to be His disciple and went to his home to eat. That was unheard of in Jesus' day, tax collectors were sinners and religious people did not hang out with them. Then, there was Jairus the ruler whose daughter was sick and Jesus was on His way to heal her, when He turned his attention to the woman who had the issue of blood. It was not that He forgot Jarius, here was a daughter that needed His immediate attention. When He was through healing her he went to Jarius' house and brought his daughter back to life.

There are some people who have mastered this skill: The ability to make you feel as if you are the most important person in the room. One of my college professors, Dr. K. S. Wiggins, has that ability. Jesus had that skill. It would be in our best interest in developing relationships to learn to do the same to be successful. It had nothing to do with the status of the individual either. This is not what motivated Jesus to help, it was the need of the person and their faith in God. Look how they referred to Him, *"The Son of man is come eating and drinking; and ye say, Behold a gluttonous man, and a winebibber, a friend of publicans and sinners!"* (Luke 7:34).

Commend People

Few things in life feel better than genuine commendations from others. God loves it as well. He smiles when we express heartfelt praise and appreciation. When we commend people it does something to our hearts as well, it gives us joy. Jesus knowing this showered it upon people.

The centurion whose servant was sick of the palsy. *"Verily I say unto you, I have not found so great faith, no, not in Israel"* (Matthew 8:10b).

The woman with the issue of blood, *"he said, Daughter, be of good comfort; thy faith hath made thee whole. And the woman was made whole from that hour"* (Matt 9:22).

The woman of Canaan whose daughter was demon possessed, "*O woman, great is thy faith: be it unto thee even as thou wilt. And her daughter was made whole from that very hour*" (Matthew 15:28).

Peter, "*Blessed art thou, Simon: for flesh and blood hath not revealed it unto thee*" (Matthew 16:17).

The woman with the alabaster box, "*Why trouble ye the woman? For she hath wrought a good work upon me. For ye have the poor always with you; but me ye have not always. For in that she hath poured this ointment on my body, she did it for my burial. Verily I say unto you, Wheresoever this gospel shall be preached in the whole world, there shall also this, that this woman hath done, be told for a memorial of her*" (Matthew 26:10-13).

The poor widow, "*Verily I say unto you, That this poor widow hath cast more in, than all they which have cast into the treasury*" (Mark 12:43).

Like Jesus we have to learn to commend people. It is more beneficial to others and us. But it is easier to condemn.

Stayed Connected

Jesus went everywhere the people were, it is true that the Bible tells us it was Jesus' custom to go to church every Sabbath (Luke 4:16). However, He spent more time meeting people in their daily activities. He stayed connected to God and man. He did not wait for them to come to Him even though He had what they needed.

Jesus took time out for building His relationship with His Father (Mark 1:35) and His disciples. He realized He needed them to help Him carry out His purposes; first and foremost He wanted to develop a friendship with them. Then He needed them to help Him in His ministry for it to be successful. In addition, He taught them how to live a successful life as one of His disciples. Since He could not be everywhere, He sent His disciples out two by two to stay connected to the people also. Jesus needed His disciples to carry on the work that He started when He returned to heaven. He showed most eloquently by the life He lived that "We are our brother's keeper." So it is not just about me, myself, and I.

How Can the Church Help?

THERE MUST BE A PARADIGM SHIFT in how we think, what we do, and how we view church. We must change our emphasis from doing church to being disciples. Jesus said we shall be witnesses. The church says do witnessing. That is why people have difficulty with church, they do not feel the church really cares about them. They just want them for their money and to make up numbers. Jesus was about caring for people. That's why there were so many baptized at Pentecost and after. It was because of what Jesus had done and the disciples began to get and live the message. Meet the needs of the people, show them you care.

Teach and Demonstrate

It is About God

Sometimes we forget the true church of God is not a building, a social, activist group, nor is it the group of people who gather on Saturday or Sunday mornings. Instead, it is people gathered to the Lord for the Lord's purposes. The Bible says, *"Gather My saints together to Me"* (Psalms 50:5). The Lord told Israel, *"You have seen what I did to the Egyptians, and how I bore you on eagles' wings, and brought you to Myself"* (Exodus 19:4). God delivered the Israelites out of Egypt for the express purpose of bringing them to Himself. He delivered us for the same reason.

It is His desire, before the creation of this world, to have us fellowship with Him. He is not impressed with buildings or crowds. He is interested in us personally. The true church of God is the "called out ones," His saints, gathered together to Him in a covenant relationship based on a sacrifice of surrender. *"The sacrifices of God are a broken spirit and a contrite heart; these, O God you will not despise"* (Psalms 51:17). We must totally surrender and deny ourselves. We are not our own; we were bought with a price. It is not about us, all about Him. When we understand this, we will enjoy our fellowship with Him and each other and help people feel a part of His church.

Importance of Relationships

The Church must teach that life is about relationships and they are the number one solution to our problems. If we know how to develop and maintain eternal, deep, and intimate relationships many of our problems will be solved. They are the most important facet of life, barring none. This characteristic of life in God's economy is supreme on His list. Everything in life is inter-related. The greatest inter-relationship is between God and man, then between man and man, followed by man and his environment. Relationships are so important to God that He sent His Son to die, so that His relationship with us which was severed by Adam can be reconnected. That is how important relationships are. Now we can live and reign with Him forever. Therefore, if we reconnect with God and each other the way He designed it, we will have minimum disconnections.

Life is so much about relationships that we cannot survive long on this earth without them. Thus, it is important to understand and learn how to develop them. They are so important to God that He chooses to bless or whop us through them. I know God has the ability and capability to use anything He wants. However, He chooses people to bless or curse us most times.

God's Greatest Desire

He created in us an innate desire for relationships. Because we are like Him, we want and long for deep, awesome and unending relationships. Many of us do not know how because we have not been taught and we do not have too many role models to emulate. Furthermore, we are very selfish and operate in the flesh and not the Spirit. We behave like two-year-olds and think that the world revolves around us. We do not want to allow anyone into our world who we think will take from us, or who can do some things better than us. We fail to see our inter-relatedness. It is impossible to succeed in anything without people's help. They are the most important in God's creation. That is why He created the earth—for man. However, we have made materialism God's crowning act of creation and hence, we are suffering the repercussions of such a philosophy.

It is God's greatest desire to have a relationship with us and share all that He is and has. He wants to bring about a connection and He has done and is doing everything in His power to bridge the gap that exists between us. This is very difficult to fathom. Why would a holy, righteous, perfect God want a relationship with us? When we look at Him and how powerful He is, when we consider the vastness of this universe. Man is discovering more and more its enormity. I am sure, like the Psalmist, this question has crossed your mind: *"What is man that you are mindful of Him, the Son of man that you care for Him?"* (Psalms 8:4). This is what we tell ourselves. And that is why we are still disconnected from God and our fellowmen. We have to change our self-talk. Examine what we are saying to ourselves and who we are listening to: ourselves, our friends, teachers, bosses, parents, or the Spirit of God? This will determine if our disconnections continue or if there will be reconnections with God and others. When we do not accept the fact that God is concerned about us personally, then we cannot develop an intimate and loving relationship with Him. Neither can we develop meaningful relationships with each other.

Emphasize Being

The church has focused too long on **doing** rather than **being** disciples. This is seen in our focus on flashy programs and hyped-up services. We put the majority of our resources and efforts into the 11 O clock service which do very little to bring about any real transformation in people's lives. We are driven by numbers, money, and reputation. We have created a system of church that ultimately succumbs to self-preservation, using and abusing its people and resources to sustain its own insatiable appetite. We build bigger and better buildings to house newer and more enticing programs to draw more and more people to get more and more money to build bigger and better buildings. It is not about the Kingdom, but the church.

We spend untold hours in conferences and seminars learning how to do church, how to imitate anyone who is doing anything that looks successful. We promote professional worship, superstar Christians, the latest revelation, any kind of manifestation, and anything to draw crowds that bring in more offerings. The point is, we have been striving to please God by what we do and in the process we have lost sight of Him we strive to please. When we take our eyes off Christ, it is not long before we deceive ourselves and become self-centered. In God's Kingdom, doing only comes out of being. You shall be witnesses, so He calls us to be before we can do. If not, Jesus will say to us in the last day, depart from me I never knew you.

Independent Thinking

The church has to stop thinking for the individual. When we learn something from another church, even though it is Biblical, it creates a disconnection because we were taught and believe God will not use people from other churches to teach us. Instead, He will teach us to teach them. But, God is no respecter of persons, He spoke to King Josiah through Necho, King of Egypt and he would not listen and died as a result (2 Chronicles 35). We have to know God personally to know when He is speaking.

Some members, instead of asking God ask their pastor or persons higher up the organization structure to find out if they should accept it or not. I found when I conducted crusades and a member from another church heard something from the Bible. If they did not hear it from their church, they said they would have to talk to their pastor. This is not usually someone who has just become a Christian. That is because we are taught according to the doctrines of a specific church. Anytime anything is not familiar, we run to our pastor and not God. However, if we teach our members to be disciples, they would be independent thinkers, like Jesus, it would help. I remember, some ten years ago, the first time I heard the twenty-three-hundred-day prophecy being explained by Pastor Chuck Swindol, similar to how we teach it. I was sick to my stomach. I was taught this message was unique to my church. Just this week a sister asked me, "I thought the health message was unique to our church. How come I hear others preaching it like we do?"

We are no different to the Jews when Jesus came upon the scene. The official church was about Judaism. Because the Jews felt they were children of Abraham, they were automatically in the Kingdom. Today there are so many who believe that membership in church means membership in the Kingdom. Being a member and being a disciple do not mean the same thing.

The church encourages disconnections. When individuals convert from one denomination to another, their previous walk with God is discredited. They are encouraged to be re-baptized to show they have been fully converted to the fact that this church is the only true church God has here. They are encouraged to be cut off from their families, if they are not converts of the same church. We forget that these are the best people to win their family, if we teach them to be disciples instead of members.

This superior attitude by churches breeds bigotry, a holier-than-thou attitude, exclusivism, and self-sufficiency; we are just like the Pharisees. This in turn affects our ministry in reaching out to others. We become judgmental and we think we know what is from God and what is not. We must remember God does not limit Himself to any group of people or nations. He never has and never will; He is no respecter of persons or nations. He is God. Listen to what John told the children of Israel.

> *John said to the crowds coming out to be baptized by him, 'You brood of vipers! Who warned you to flee from the coming wrath? Produce fruit in keeping with repentance. And do not begin to say to ourselves, 'We have Abraham as our father.' For I tell you that out of these stones God can raise up children for Abraham. The axe is already at the root of the trees, and every tree that does not produce good fruit will be cut down and thrown into the fire' (Luke 3:7-8).*

God's objective is service and He is willing to work with anyone who repents, is humble and obedient. It does not matter your color, creed or class. It is okay to feel secure in your religion; we should never feel superior.

   You Were Made To Worship God 24/7

Integration

In Church we are disconnected individually, congregationally and denominationally. Those of us who move around to other denominations know that they all have the same claim we have—the truth. Jack Nicholson made one of the most profound statements that is applicable to us today, "You cannot handle the truth." As I have propounded, Jesus is the Truth. Nobody can handle Him. He cannot be contained or boxed into our church's body of doctrines. Not even the tomb could contain Him.

The disciples displayed they could not handle the truth, they told Jesus, *"There is someone casting out demons in your name and we tried to stop him, but he was not following us." But Jesus said, "Do not stop him; for no one who does a deed of power in my name will be able soon afterward to speak evil of me. Whoever is not against us is for us"* (*Luke 9:49-50*). That is a truth that too many denominations cannot handle. Like the disciples, we believe that everything the Lord wants done, has to come through our church. So, we cannot listen to what other churches teach. Jesus said, "Whoever is not against us is for us." They were not following Jesus like the twelve disciples. However, these were also Jesus' disciples because they were doing the will and works of God. The disciples felt that they had the prestigious privilege of being with the Master and if the others wanted the true power they had to come through them. They could not see God bypassing them to give others healing power without consulting them. Similarly, we refuse then to listen to what others have to say. If it is not sanctioned by our religion, we want nothing to do with it. Thus, we do not receive all that God has for us. He speaks to us through whom He chooses; we have to be Spirit-led. Remember Moses' father-in-law. If He did not receive the truth that God had for him through Jethro (a non-Jew) about decentralization Moses would have died before his time, like King Josiah.

Look for a moment at Jesus' lineage in Matthew. He was not into aristocracy or nobility. There is a prostitute, Gentiles, former worshippers of foreign gods, and the worst king in Judah, Manasseh. This is true integration. We need to learn from Jesus.

Be Different

One of the things that bothered me when I became a disciple was how Christians could act the same way as the people of the world. Doing the same things, like drinking, smoking, adultry, play the lottery, say the same dirty jokes, watch the same movies, sing and dance to the same songs. Do not talk about that—there are many Christians who can dance better than people who do it for a living. In the Seventh-day Adventist Church, every social function now is turning into a dance fest at the end. There is no difference in the homes of the saved and the unsaved. We are so concerned about being normal and accepted, not remembering that God does not want us to be normal. This is not new. God gave this message to one of His prophets: *"For from the least of them even unto the greatest of them everyone is given to covetousness; and from the prophet even unto the priest every one dealeth falsely"* (Jeremiah 6:13). The love of self and money is the driving force of much of the competition we see in the church today. We are constantly trying to create bigger and better programs than the church next door, to attract more members.

Most of the growth today comes from disgruntled, carnal, offended members moving from one church to another. We have developed a herd mentality, charging after the latest Christian fad. There are many mega-churches, but most members are babes filled with selfishness and carnality who are ever hearing and never coming to a knowledge of the truth. A small percentage is actually involved in the Kingdom. The majority show up for their ritual morning service. Do you think we might be spending all that money building all these buildings for nothing, if this is all we are producing? Maybe we need to start examining our motives for doing what we do and get our priorities back in order.

When God calls us, like He did His disciples, we are not merely called to make converts but disciples. The disciple does not love the world or the things of the world because the love of the Father is in him. And it is his desire to work with God to get others out of the world into His Kingdom.

Provide

Discipleship Classes

Provide discipleship classes so that the members can know what it is to be a disciple and make others disciples. It is not a buddy program that is a substitute for what God says—that has not, nor ever will be as successful as discipleship.

Insist that each member utilize the gifts that God has given and get rid of elections. I believe this is what causes the greatest disconnection in the church after someone is saved. It is so important that God has already put in my spirit a book to help us understand His Divine Order, *"Why Are So Many Christians Are Miserable."*

Provide a balance for the disciples by providing ministries that can meet their needs and those of community. We are holistic beings and our spirit, soul, and body, need to be fed. Insist on pastors presenting a balanced meal for the disciples, not just in his pet area where he is at his best. Better yet, get others gifted in different areas to teach on certain subjects. If it is not taught at your church, insist that suffering be taught as part and parcel of the gospel. The Bible is replete with material on every subject under the sun. The church has to stop regurgitating information. *"Truth is like a shining light that shineth more and more unto a perfect day"* (Proverbs 4:18).

Hence, Churches must get rid of the concept we have the truth, that creates a superiority complex. And teach who is Truth according to the Bible. It is not a body of doctrines; it is a person. Jesus says, "*I am the way, the truth and the life.*" (John 14: 6).

Emphasize that the entire day of worship is holy and not just the 11 o'clock service. The old system of holy and most holy no longer exists. Yet, we still practice it in church. We have to learn to tie what happens during the week with what happens on the weekend. We cannot divorce who we are from what we do during the week. If we are being taught to do so, then, maybe that is not where God wants us to be. Ask Him.

Learn to stop depending on the program and learn to depend on the Spirit. Sometimes it should be just about seeking the face of God. Sadly, we order our lives the same way we do the service of God. They are planned down to the minutest detail and do not leave any room for the Spirit to work. I remember with some of my planning a fixed time was given for each item on the program. I became angry when anyone went over the allotted time. We cannot worship freely when we are restricted by time.

Be a church for all people and do not discriminate against any group. God has endowed the church with every gift that is needed to minister to all who need help.

Individual Power

We fail to realize church is made up of individuals and it is up to them to stop the disconnection. Regrettably, the church's political system has taken the power from the individual and given it to the pastor or the organization. In this system, there are a few benefiting and it will be a dogfight to take it back. Yet, thank God we do not have to fight, the battle is not ours, it's the Lord's. All we have to do is be the best disciple He wants us to be and He will give us back the power.

We have been chosen individually by God not as a group. It is our individuality that makes up the group. Here is how Paul puts it, *"But one and the same Spirit works all these things, distributing to each one individually as He wills"* (1 Corinthians 12:11). Peter said it this way, *"As every man hath received the gift, even so minister the same one to another, as good stewards of the manifold grace of God"* (1 Peter 4:10). This does not mean we can and will do our own thing, it means our lives are governed by the Spirit and we will operate as one. Just like the Godhead or as Paul sees it, we are a body with individual functions working together as one.

That is why when Jesus said, *"My kingdom is not of this world"* (John18:36). There are implications that stretched far beyond His immediate setting. For instance, in this world human beings make choices on the basis of personal preference as long as those choices break no laws. But in the Kingdom, man does not make ultimate choices—He submits to the choices of God. Take spiritual gifts, for example. Based on our desires, talents and abilities, we might like to choose our own spiritual gifts, and thereby our role in the body of Christ. But God does not pass out a "Spiritual Gifts Request Form" when we become His followers. He makes the choice and assignment of the spiritual gifts for us, the Spirit *"distributing to each one individually as He wills."* Acceptance of our gifts is another of many opportunities to be submissive and obedient to God, trusting that He knows what is best for us and His church.

Are you enjoying ministries in the church based on your spiritual gifts? If not, you may be missing out on blessings God designed for you. Henry P. Liddon rightly said, "Nothing is really lost by a life of sacrifice; everything is lost by failure to obey God's call."

Fellowship

The church has to understand and teach this very important concept. When it is rightly understood, will do a great deal to help develop and enhance relationships. God created us for fellowship with the Godhead and each other.

God's Desire

Fellowship is one of those subjects least understood and taught. We yearn for good fellowship with God and people. That's because it is placed in us by Him who also desires to have close fellowship with us. *"God, who has called you into fellowship with his Son, Jesus Christ our Lord, is faithful"* (1 Corinthians 1:9). This was demonstrated in Eden when God came down and hung out with Adam and Eve.

When sin entered our world, God made a covenant with His people. A covenant is the closest fellowship between God and man. He has always promised He will never leave nor forsake us, if we are obedient to Him. He wants us close to Him always. That has been His plan all along. Hence the Bible says we are co-laborers with God. We are never working for Him; we are always working with Him. He does not see us as His employees; we are His sons and daughters. There is a big difference between being an employee and being a child of the employer. As a child, you have access to the business records and privileges that an employee does not have. The relationship and fellowship are totally different.

Definition

Fellowship comes from the Greek work **koinonia.** This word was used in three ways in the first century. First, it was the personal interaction between people. Second, it was used for the intimacy enjoyed in marriage when the couple was deeply committed to each other. Third, it was used for the wrapping of a scroll around the central shaft, like how we would describe the closeness of the pages of a bound book.

The Encarta Dictionary describes it this way: "A sharing of common interests, goals, experiences, views, companionship or friendly association." This is not limited to God, but a close union with man, a brotherly bond between men. Fellowship involves spending time together and sharing who we are with God and man.

Limit the Concept of Fellowship

Unfortunately, we have limited it to the fellowship hall where we eat together or when we sing, "What a fellowship, what a joy divine." We do not see fellowship in its broader sense. The synonyms give it a broader meaning: companionship, friendship, camaraderie, partnership, and association. Hence, fellowship cannot be limited to church. It must extend beyond the four walls. Our fellowship is not dependent upon buildings or programs. It is Christ in us, the hope of glory. It is out of Him flows all ministries for building up the Kingdom. We do not measure ourselves with ourselves. Jesus is our yardstick. It is the fellowship of the saints, one with Jesus and each other, having things in common, and willing to lay down our lives for one another. It is people with a passion for Jesus, wanting to know love, trust, obey, serve, and ultimately, be like Him. The early church understood this very clearly,

*They devoted themselves to the apostles' teaching and to the **fellowship**, to the breaking of bread and to prayer. Everyone was filled with awe, and many wonders and miraculous signs were done by the apostles. All the believers were together and had everything in common. Selling their possessions and goods, they gave to anyone as he had need. Every day they continued to meet together in the temple…They broke bread in their homes and ate together with glad and sincere hearts, praising God and enjoying the favor of all the people. And the Lord added to* *their number daily those who were being saved (Acts 2:42-47, Emphasis supplied).*

Notice their fellowship did not end at church. It extended in each other's homes. They would visit, eat and spend time together on a consistent basis. The apostle Paul tells us, *"For the Kingdom of God is not a matter of eating and drinking, but of righteousness, peace and joy in the Holy Spirit"* (Romans 14:17). You will notice that the disciples gave to anyone who had a need. The way the church knew they had a need was because they spent time together. They were not suspicious and not sure if the person was trying to rip off the church or not. They met in church and in homes, so they knew each other. I believe they did not even have to ask. They saw because they had the gift of discernment. Our fellowship must be beyond the fellowship hall. We do not have time for that today. We are too busy living by bread alone. We are alone and lonely to the point it continues when we go to church. That is why we feel like the odd person because we only know each other superficially.

One of the missing ingredients in church today is our doors are closed during the week. A disciple's life never becomes too busy to minister for God. If needs be, he can meet in church every day; of course, there are exceptions. There are some Christians who cannot even come on the weekend; surely they cannot come one night during the week. The church's doors should be opened twenty-four seven. People should have access to church when they need to. This can be accomplished through ministry.

As members, we are so caught up in the hectic pace of life, we do not have time for anybody else, not even our own families, moreover others. Going to church once a week, cannot build a sense of community and be able to enjoy fellowshipping together. The early church had things in common and shared everything. This automatically created accountability. Sometimes we do not see each other for a week. There is no contact by phone or email. Fellowship cannot be enjoyed in such an atmosphere. You cannot visit people today without calling first.

How is Fellowship Spelled?

Fellowship is fellows getting in and spending time in the same ship. God made us with the desire to want to get on board the old ship of Zion. Just like God got into Adam and Eve's ship by coming down to earth and spending time with them. Fellowship then means sometimes putting ourselves out of the way to get in someone else's ship, making and spending time together.

One of the biggest problems is finding time. We are so caught up in this fast-paced world we do not have time for anyone, including ourselves. I remembered when I used to be so stressed out. Time was my enemy. One of the ways I decided to handle it was to get rid of all my watches, prioritize and leave what I could not accomplish. Time is a precious commodity and we have to learn to use it wisely, asking God to teach us what is important. High on God's list is fellowship. It should be on ours also.

The key ingredient to fellowship is time. It is only a disciple who is disciplined that will find the time necessary to minister to the needs of people. It takes time to know what people's needs are, to enter into their feelings and be touched by their infirmities. That is fellowship in its highest form. When we gain their confidence then we can get them to come aboard the old ship of Zion.

Sometimes, like Jesus, we have to learn to get on other people's ships, spending time with them and getting to know them. Unless we can first fellowship with people, we cannot get them to come and follow us. Jesus demonstrated this in His life with His disciples even after His resurrection. He went to find them and fellowshipped with them. In those forty days before going to heaven,

He spent time with His disciples. He ate and drank with them. He went where they were. He got onto their ship as it were. Many people are not willing to get onto our ship. They prefer to stay where they are in their pain and misery before wanting to sail with us and receive what we have to offer. They want to know that we care, can we sympathize, empathize, or listen to them?

There are other problems. They do not know us. Some are afraid of the sea, others are not sure of our abilities in handling our ships (our lives). Hence, they are afraid our ship may sink when the storm comes. Time again is of the essence. It takes time to convince people to get on the ship of Zion. One of the ways to get people on our ship is to do as God did with Adam, get on their ship, spend time with them and then they will get on our ship and enjoy what we have to offer—the Love of God. It is being concerned about our fellow brothers and sisters, doing everything in our power to help them.

IN CONCLUSION: Even though we are wired before birth for relationships, many are unaware that they do not just happen. We must know who God is, who we are and who others are. This requires a great deal of time, work and sacrifice on our part to be successful at them. We have to be like the Good Samaritan and see all people regardless of color, creed, or class, as God's children and when anyone is in need, we help. It will not always be physical, sometimes it will be mental, financial, or psychological.

Following our example Jesus, we must find time and accountability partners, learn to listen, forgive, bond, know the difference between distractions and issues so that we can develop solid relationships. And as our friendship with the Spirit deepens then He will reveal to us those who need help and how to help them. We will gladly help and accept the help from others as we develop long lasting relationships with them that will last through out eternity, just like the relationship we have with God.

HOW TO BECOME A DISCIPLE?

Becoming a disciple is one of the easiest things in the world. As easy as **ABC**, however, it is difficult to maintain. The biggest obstacle is its simplicity. It's a three step process:

A—*"All have sinned and fallen short of the glory of God" (Romans 3:23); and "the wages of sin is death" (Romans 6:23).*

B—*"Behold the Lamb of God who takes away the sins of the world" (John 1:29).*

C—*"Come unto me all who are weary and heavy-burdened and I will give you rest" (Matthew 11:28).*

There are no exceptions. We all have sinned, the Greek actually says, "All have sinned and are coming short of the glory of God." It does not just happen once, but over and over again. **A**ccept this truth, **B**elieve there is only One sinless being that can save you, and His name is Jesus. Then **C**onfess by praying the prayer of forgiveness and acknowledge who Jesus is to you. Or you can repeat this prayer or one similar:

"Lord Jesus I have sinned against heaven and against you and I am sorry. Please forgive me of all my sins and come into my heart and live as Lord and Savior of my life, Amen."

CONGRATULATIONS
YOU ARE A DISCIPLE OF JESUS

I do not feel any different.

You do not have to; *"For it is by grace you have been saved, through faith and this not from yourselves, it is the gift of God not by works, so that no one can boast"* (Ephesians 2:8-9).

How do I live now?

"For in the gospel a righteousness from God is revealed, a righteousness that is by faith from first to last, just as it is written: "The righteous will live by faith" (Romans 1:17).

What happens if I sin again?

"If we confess our sins, he is faithful and just and will forgive us our sins, and purify us from all unrighteousness" (1 John 1:9).

Why can I believe this promise God made?

"God is not a man, that he should lie, nor a son of man, that he should change his mind. Does He speak and then not act? Does he promise and not fulfill?" (Numbers 23:19).

What do I do next?

Pray and ask God to lead you to a church that will disciple you and then teach you how to make disciples. Ask the Holy Spirit to reveal to you your God-given gifts, purposes, ministries, vocations and destiny. Use these to meet the needs of the people He places in your life with the objective of making disciples and building up His Kingdom. This will produce congruency within and eliminate most of your misery.

CPSIA information can be obtained at www.ICGtesting.com
Printed in the USA
LVOW040404260412

279190LV00001B/1/P